Policy Experiments, Failures and Innovations

NEW HORIZONS IN PUBLIC POLICY

Series Editor: Wayne Parsons, *Professor of Public Policy, Wales Governance Centre, Cardiff University, UK*

This series aims to explore the major issues facing academics and practitioners working in the field of public policy at the dawn of a new millennium. It seeks to reflect on where public policy has been, in both theoretical and practical terms, and to prompt debate on where it is going. The series emphasizes the need to understand public policy in the context of international developments and global change. New Horizons in Public Policy publishes the latest research on the study of the policymaking process and public management, and presents original and critical thinking on the policy issues and problems facing modern and post-modern societies.

Titles in the series include:

Public Policy in Knowledge-Based Economies
Foundations and Frameworks
David Rooney, Greg Hearn, Thomas Mandeville and Richard Joseph

Modernizing Civil Services
Edited by Tony Butcher and Andrew Massey

Public Policy and the New European Agendas
Edited by Fergus Carr and Andrew Massey

The Dynamics of Public Policy
Theory and Evidence
Adrian Kay

Ethics and Integrity of Governance
Perspectives Across Frontiers
Edited by Leo W.J.C. Huberts, Jeroen Maesschalck and Carole L. Jurkiewicz

Public Management in the Postmodern Era
Challenges and Prospects
Edited by John Fenwick and Janice McMillan

The Tools of Policy Formulation
Actors, Capacities, Venues and Effects
Edited by Andrew J. Jordan and John R. Turnpenny

Analysis and Public Policy
Successes, Failures and Directions for Reform
Stuart Shapiro

Public Policy Transfer
Micro-Dynamics and Macro-Effects
Edited by Magdaléna Hadjiisky, Leslie A. Pal and Christopher Walker

Policy Experiments, Failures and Innovations
Beyond Accession in Central and Eastern Europe
Edited by Agnes Batory, Andrew Cartwright and Diane Stone

Policy Experiments, Failures and Innovations

Beyond Accession in Central and Eastern Europe

Edited by

Agnes Batory

Central European University, Hungary

Andrew Cartwright

Center for Policy Studies, Central European University, Hungary

Diane Stone

University of Canberra, Australia and University of Warwick, UK

NEW HORIZONS IN PUBLIC POLICY

 Edward Elgar
PUBLISHING

Cheltenham, UK • Northampton, MA, USA

Published by
Edward Elgar Publishing Limited
The Lypiatts
15 Lansdown Road
Cheltenham
Glos GL50 2JA
UK

Edward Elgar Publishing, Inc.
William Pratt House
9 Dewey Court
Northampton
Massachusetts 01060
USA

A catalogue record for this book
is available from the British Library

Library of Congress Control Number: 2017950475

This book is available electronically in the **Elgar**online
Social and Political Science subject collection
DOI 10.4337/9781785367496

ISBN 978 1 78536 748 9 (cased)
ISBN 978 1 78536 749 6 (eBook)

Typeset by Servis Filmsetting Ltd, Stockport, Cheshire
Printed and bound in Great Britain by TJ International Ltd, Padstow

Contents

v

Contributors

Dragos Adascalitei holds a PhD from the University of Mannheim, Germany and is a researcher at the Central European University Center for Policy Studies in Budapest, Hungary. His research interests include pension reforms in Central and Eastern Europe, industrial relations and labour markets.

Agnes Batory is a professor of public policy at Central European University, Hungary. Her research interests include: party politics and populism; corruption; and regulation and various aspects of compliance and policy implementation in the EU context. Her recent publications have appeared in *Public Administration, Democratization, Governance* and the *Journal of European Public Policy*.

Andrew Cartwright is a research fellow and co-director of the Center for Policy Studies at Central European University, Hungary. His research interests include development policy in Central and Eastern Europe, particularly focusing on transitions in the rural areas. He is currently chairman of PASOS, an association of think tanks and policy centres from Central, Eastern and Southern Europe.

Daniela Craciun is a Yehuda Elkana Fellow at Central European University, Hungary, where she is pursuing a PhD. Her teaching and research interests lie in the areas of methodology and higher education public policy, specifically internationalization and international student mobility. Currently, she is a visiting scholar at the Center for International Higher Education at Boston College, USA.

Stefan Domonkos is a researcher at the Institute of Economic Research of the Slovak Academy of Sciences and advisor to the State Secretary of the Ministry of Finance of the Slovak Republic. His research concerns the political economy of pension reforms in Central and Eastern Europe as well as public preferences towards redistribution. His work has been published in *Global Social Policy*, the *International Journal of Social Welfare, Governance* and *East European Politics and Societies*, among others. He earned his PhD at Mannheim University, Germany.

Heather Grabbe is director of the Open Society European Policy Institute, Belgium. From 2004 to 2009 she was senior advisor to European Commissioner for Enlargement Olli Rehn, responsible in his Cabinet for the Balkans and Turkey. Before joining the Commission, she was deputy director of the Centre for European Reform. Her academic work includes research at the European University Institute, Italy, Chatham House, UK, and Oxford and Birmingham universities, UK (from which she earned her BA and PhD respectively), and teaching at the London School of Economics, UK. Her publications include *The EU's Transformative Power: Europeanization through Conditionality in Central and Eastern Europe* (Palgrave, 2006).

Achim Kemmerling is associate professor of political economy at the Department of International Relations and the School of Public Policy, Central European University, Hungary. He has published on issues of tax policy, social and labour market policies, and fiscal federalism. His monograph *Taxing the Working Poor* (Edward Elgar Publishing, 2009) deals with the political and economic trade-offs between redistribution and job incentives for poor workers. He has worked as a consultant to the German parliament, the German Society for Technical Cooperation and the European Investment Bank.

Andrea Krizsan is research fellow at Central European University, Budapest, Hungary. Her research focuses on equality policy change in countries of Central and Eastern Europe. Her publications include articles in journals such as *Violence against Women, European Journal of Women's Studies, Ethnic and Racial Studies, Social Politics, European Integration Online Papers*, and *Journal for Ethnic and Minority Studies*, and chapters in several edited volumes. She edited a volume on ethnic monitoring and data collection (2001) and co-edited one with J. Squires and H. Skjeie on the changing nature of European equality regimes (2012).

Kristin Makszin is a researcher at the Institute for Political Science, Hungarian Academy of Sciences Centre for Social Sciences. She completed a PhD in political science at Central European University, Hungary in 2013 on 'Reforming East Central European welfare states: Governments, technocrats, and the patterns of quiet retrenchment'.

Liviu Matei is the provost and pro-rector of Central European University, Hungary and a professor of higher education policy at the university's School of Public Policy. He directs the Yehuda Elkana Center for Higher Education at the university.

Gergő Medve-Bálint is a research fellow at the Centre for Social Sciences, Hungarian Academy of Sciences, and an assistant professor at the Department of Comparative and Institutional Economics at Corvinus University of Budapest, Hungary. His main research interests include regional development and regional disparities, with a particular focus on the territorial effects of foreign investments and the EU's cohesion policy on the Eastern member states.

B. Guy Peters is Maurice Falk Professor of American Government at the University of Pittsburgh, USA. He has written extensively in the areas of public administration and public policy, both for the United States and comparatively. Among his recent publications are *Comparative Governance: Rediscovering the Functional Dimension of Governing* (Cambridge University Press, 2016), with Jon Pierre, and *Contemporary Approaches to Public Policy* (Macmillan, 2016), with Philippe Zittoun.

Diane Stone is Centenary Professor in the Institute of Governance and Policy Analysis at the University of Canberra, Australia. She is also a professor in politics and international studies at Warwick University, UK. From 2004 to 2008, she was European Commission Marie Curie Chair and Foundation Professor of Public Policy at Central European University, Hungary, where she remains a visiting professor. Currently, she is consulting editor of the journal *Policy and Politics* and a vice president of the International Public Policy Association.

Sara Svensson is a research fellow at the Center for Policy Studies and visiting professor at the School of Public Policy at Central European University, Hungary. She has also taught courses and supervised BA theses at four Swedish universities: Orebro University, Karlstad University, Halmstad University and University West. Her academic research focuses on policy formation and governance structures in European cross-border regions. She holds a PhD in public policy and political science from Central European University.

András Tétényi is an assistant professor of economics at the Institute of World Economics of the Corvinus University of Budapest, Hungary. He is programme managing director for the International Economy and Business (IEB) Master's Programme and academic coordinator for the International Master's in Economy, State and Society (IMESS) double degree with University College London, UK. His research interests are in the field of official development assistance policies of Visegrad countries and asylum policies of Hungary.

Simona Torotcoi is a PhD candidate at Central European University, Hungary's Doctoral School of Political Science, Public Policy and International Relations. Her main research interests include the study of higher education policies, especially access and participation policies. Currently she is conducting research on the implementation of the Bologna Process in a comparative perspective.

Violetta Zentai is a cultural anthropologist with a PhD from Rutgers University, USA. She serves as co-director of the Center for Policy Studies at Central European University, Hungary. She is engaged in research focusing on ethnic and gender inequalities and European equality policies, and debates on post-socialist capitalisms and social exclusion and inclusion. She has served as team leader or lead coordinator of a number of larger comparative European research projects. Her recent publications discuss Roma inclusion and social exclusion in Central and Eastern Europe.

Foreword

Heather Grabbe

How do policies and norms grow after being transplanted into another context? This volume surveys a variety of Central and East European experiences over a quarter-century of post-communist transition. Many of the policies were imports from the EU, which was the largest single foreign influence in the region during this period. The scale of the transfer was remarkable: thousands of pages of legislation and regulation, as well as models for the institutions to implement and enforce them.

The United States has never been able to boast having such a direct and immediate influence outside its borders through soft power. After 1989, the desire to move as quickly as possible away from state socialism and to become normal, Western, European countries motivated wholescale adoption of policy and institutional frameworks from abroad. EU models became especially attractive once membership became a possibility, and later their adoption became essential criteria for advancing in the accession process.

Viewed from 2017, the lack of competition from alternative models is striking. Russia was busy with its own transition, while the US generally supported the goal of moving Central and Eastern Europe towards EU membership. The years after 1989 also saw the peak of the unquestioned belief in liberalism – both political and economic – following the 'end of history' in terms of competing ideologies (Fukuyama 1992). This period was very different from the contemporary contestation of liberal norms in domestic politics by Hungarian prime minister Viktor Orbán, US president Donald Trump's 'alternate facts', or Russian criticism of 'degenerate' European values under titles such as 'Eurosodom'.

The power of the EU's appeal came from the combination of stability, prosperity, security, and the personal freedoms it seemed to offer. Open markets and open societies were extremely attractive to people who had lived under state socialism. The previous political and economic systems were thoroughly discredited, and the EU provided a successful alternative model, combined with a framework of support for the reforms to get there, and crowned with the achievement of joining a powerful and rich regional club. This goal united people across the political spectrum and society, creating little political opposition until years after their countries had joined the EU.

However, the EU's agenda for Central and Eastern Europe was never intended to be a full plan for democracy and development. Rather, the enlargement policy was intended to ensure that potential members could meet the core requirements for EU membership, which are a much narrower set of goals focused on ensuring that the incomers could participate in a common market, a shared budget and policies, and a community of law. No wonder that so many of the detailed policies analysed in this volume fell on to stony ground, or were reshaped to local circumstances.

The EU's approach has been criticised as 'institutional monocropping', whereby uniform policies were applied without due regard to the economic, social or regional contexts on the receiving end – and in the absence of regional mechanisms to synchronise EU requirements and domestic demands (Bruszt 2015). In the sphere of regulation, one of the EU's most advanced areas of integration, it produced some extreme examples of 'monocultures' resulting from transnational harmonisation (Bronk and Jacoby 2016). Yet the case studies in this volume of areas of the transfer of mainly 'soft' EU law highlight the many ways in which policies were adapted by local actors to local circumstances, opportunities and cultures. Even if the EU prescribed monocultural models, that was not necessarily the result – especially in areas where it was less prescriptive and where implementation was intended to happen at regional or local level.

However, the EU was not neutral about the form of government that its transferred policies and norms were supposed to work within. What happened to the liberal democratic ideals that these laws, policies and institutions were supposed to support and be supported by? The Copenhagen conditions set for membership started with the requirement that a country must have achieved 'stability of institutions guaranteeing democracy, human rights, rule of law, and respect for and protection of minorities' (European Council in Copenhagen 1993).

This condition worked with the second condition (on being a market economy that could cope with competition in the Single Market) and the third on adopting the body of EU law called the '*acquis communautaire*'. The third Copenhagen condition also included the goals of 'economic, monetary and political union'. Put together, these conditions promoted a particular vision of what it meant to be a European country. The transfer of policies was supposed to be part of a package deal of governance.

Parts of the package have since withered – no longer does any member have to join the monetary union as soon as it can meet the Maastricht criteria for public finances and currency. Other parts have fallen by the wayside because history did not take the EU to the stated goal of political union, indeed, the decade following the eastward enlargements of 2004 and 2007 took European integration much further away from it. The failure of the Constitutional Treaty in 2005 and the series of crises over the euro that started in 2008 and migration in 2015 increased the use of inter-governmental deals among the member states rather than political integration.

Nonetheless, the process of domestication of EU policies and models continued in Central and Eastern Europe during these years – even though it was no longer driven by accession conditionality (Sedelmeier 2012). The 2004 entrants' compliance with EU norms has been remarkably durable – even in Hungary, where the rhetoric at the top level of government became very anti-EU and anti-liberal after the return to power of Fidesz in 2010. Continued compliance cannot have happened only because of the threat of material sanctions such as infringement proceedings, which apply to all members, or the desire to avoid losing EU structural funds. It must also be the result of the transfer of norms through social learning and persuasion during the accession process (Epstein and Sedelmeier 2009). Yet, although the effects went deep into policies, laws and institutions, the limits of EU influence on political culture became evident after accession, when populist xenophobic politics emerged in several countries.

This volume provides valuable insights into how the political dynamics worked in local contexts. By showing the details of how policies and models have been translated, filtered, exploited, resisted and reshaped, the chapters give a picture of Europeanisation on the receiving end, enriching the literature on this extraordinary period in the history of Europe.

REFERENCES

Bronk, R. and W. Jacoby (2016), *Uncertainty and the Dangers of Monocultures in Regulation, Analysis and Practice*, MPIfG Discussion Paper No. 16/6, Köln: Max-Planck-Institut für Gesellschaftsforschung.

Bruszt, L. (2015), 'Regional normalization and national deviations: EU integration and transformations in Europe's eastern periphery', *Global Policy*, 6, 38–45.

Epstein, R.A. and U. Sedelmeier (eds) (2009), *International Influence beyond Conditionality: Postcommunist Europe after EU Enlargement*, Abingdon: Routledge.

European Council in Copenhagen (1993), *Conclusions*.

Fukuyama, F. (1992), *The End of History and the Last Man*, New York: Free Press.

Sedelmeier, U. (2012), 'Is Europeanisation through conditionality sustainable? Lock-in of institutional change after EU accession', *West European Politics*, 35 (1), 20–38.

Acknowledgements

The Central European University and its Open Society mission

Conceived during the 15th anniversary of the Center for Policy Studies at Central European University, most of the chapter contributors have a connection with the Center or the University.

This book came to completion when the Hungarian government passed a law that imposed restrictions on foreign universities and threatened academic freedoms in Hungary, which has been CEU's home for over 25 years. The book is dedicated to CEU's future in Budapest as a free, self-governing institution devoted to the pursuit of academic excellence, critical thinking, and the values of open society.

Abbreviations

BGRF	Bulgarian Gender Research Foundation
CEDAW	Convention on the Elimination of All Forms of Discrimination against Women
CEE	Central and Eastern Europe
CEEC	Central and Eastern European countries
CESCI	Central European Service for Cross-Border Initiatives
CODEV	Council Working Group on Development
CoE	Council of Europe
ČSSD	Czech Social Democratic Party
DC	Democratic Convention
DKK	Danish krone
EAFRD	European Agricultural Fund for Rural Development
EC	European Commission
ECTS	European Credit Transfer System
EGTC	European Grouping of Territorial Cooperation
EHEA	European Higher Education Area
EMFF	European Maritime and Fisheries Fund
ERDF	European Regional Development Fund
ESF	European Social Fund
ESG	Standards and Guidelines for Quality Assurance in the EHEA
EU	European Union
EUMAP	European Union Monitoring and Advocacy Program of the Open Society Institute
EUR	euro
FRA	Fundamental Rights Agency
G8	Group of Eight major industrial democracies
GDP	gross domestic product
GNI	gross national income
HAND	Hungarian Association of NGOs for Development and Humanitarian Aid
HPI	Health Policy Institute
IATI	International Aid Transparency Initiative
IFIs	international financial institutions
IMF	International Monetary Fund

LAGs	Local Action Groups
MAHR	Minnesota Advocates for Human Rights
MBA	Master of Business Administration
MDGs	Millennium Development Goals
MLG	multi-level governance
NDP	national development plan
NGO	non-governmental organization
NPM	new public management
NRIS	National Roma Integration Strategies
NUTS	Nomenclature of Territorial Units for Statistics
ODA	official development assistance
ODS	Civic Democratic Party
OECD	Organisation for Economic Co-operation and Development
OMC	open method of coordination
OSCE	Organization for Security and Co-operation in Europe
OSF	Open Society Foundations
OSI	Open Society Institute
PAYG	pay-as-you-go
PHARE	Poland and Hungary: Assistance for Restructuring their Economies
PUMA	Public Management Programme
QA	quality assurance
QUING	Quality in Gender+ Equality Policies in Europe
RDF	Regional Development Fund
ROP	regional operational programme
SDP	Social Democratic Party
SIDA	Swedish International Development Cooperation Agency
SIGMA	Support for Improvement in Governance and Management
UN	United Nations
UNDP	United Nations Development Programme
UNFPA	United Nations Population Fund
USA	United States of America
USAID	United States Agency for International Development
USD	United States dollar
V4	Visegrad Four
VAT	value added tax
WAVE	Women Against Violence in Europe
WB	World Bank

1. Trial and error: Policy experiments, failures and innovations in Central and Eastern Europe

Agnes Batory, Andrew Cartwright and Diane Stone

1.1 INTRODUCTION

In the early part of the last decade, a new European Union funding programme was introduced for rural areas in Central and Eastern Europe (CEE). Originating in 1980s France, the LEADER programme was widely seen by the EU as a central policy tool for bottom-up innovation and growth, especially in areas struggling to adapt to out-migration and the decline of agricultural employment. Project funding was available for implementing local territorial development plans, which would be overseen by 'Local Action Groups' (LAGs) made up of representatives from businesses, civic groups and local authorities (Macken-Walsh 2009). The policy goals were ambitious: sustainable development, mitigating climate change, countering social exclusion and promoting economic revival in the countryside. Yet there was a problem which both confused and frustrated the implementing agencies: the actual amount of project funding available was relatively modest, particularly in the light of the scale of rural problems in the regions. Rather than helping maintain strained public services and creating widespread opportunities that could halt out-migration, the LAGs sponsored projects that appeared more modest and marginal, even eccentric, such as reviving local dance festivals, erecting public notice boards, establishing wildlife trails and publishing local recipe books.

Despite the slightly bombastic rhetoric of the programme, in a number of areas of Central and Eastern Europe LAGs came to be understood locally as a kind of folk preservation society, familiar from socialist times, which would help preserve local cultural traditions but would be almost wholly irrelevant to more pressing questions of rural development. Thus LAGs were reinterpreted as something similar to old socialist era institutions that ran so-called 'cultural houses' – state sponsored village halls for official and social events which functioned as meeting places for choir practice, Friday night discotheques for the young, and drawing lessons for children. Such an outcome was in stark contrast with the original plan, and may have come as somewhat of a disappointment to EU officials who saw LAGs in the vanguard of social innovation and rural revival. In their reinterpreted form, LAGs were certainly meaningful and useful, but not in the sense that was intended.

Such processes of recognition and reinterpretation characterized many projects and programmes, and sometimes entire policy fields, in the EU's 'new' member states. For instance, as András Tétényi shows in Chapter 8 of this volume, the idea that the CEE countries should be providing development assistance for poorer countries came as somewhat of a surprise to both the European Commission, which assumed such a policy was already in place, and the individual candidate countries themselves, which were more used to their status as aid recipient rather than donor (Szent-Iványi and Tétényi 2008). Despite the lack of relevant institutions, expertise and legislation, the accession countries were expected to sign up to offering 0.7 per cent of their GDP, for instance, committing themselves to fulfilment of the United Nation's (UN) Millennium Development Goals, and administering aid in line with the latest best practices with their concern with equal partnerships, efficiencies and coordination. In this regard, the CEE countries received training and support from a bewildering array of actors, not least Canada, Japan, Finland, Sweden and the UK, as well as international agencies such as the United Nations Development Programme, the World Bank and of course the European Commission. In the eventual implementation of official development assistance (ODA) policies, significant differences appeared among the CEE countries in terms of the size of budgets, scope of work and political profile. In some cases, countries assumed significant responsibilities, and were quick to align themselves with the goals and mores of the international development community. In other cases, however, CEE countries reinterpreted the goals of official development policy in ways that profoundly puzzled their original advisors. For example, the largest recipients of Hungarian government bilateral ODA have not been the least developed countries in Africa and Asia, but the minority Hungarian community in neighbouring Ukraine and Serbia – thereby turning ODA into a policy tool for maintaining close links with co-ethnics divided by borders in Europe.

These examples illustrate some of the conundrums addressed in this edited volume on Central and Eastern European countries as they adopted and translated foreign ideas and policies in the path towards European Union accession and beyond. They show how policies with strong external origins go through complex processes of interpretation and implementation that can lead to outcomes that significantly diverge from the original intention, albeit retaining certain formal commonalities to the original.

The book is structured around two central themes. We address, on the one hand, the concepts of policy transfer and policy diffusion and, on the other, the concept of policy failure and success within the general context of Europeanization. The authors in the volume show many different features between those two poles, covering a range of phenomena and according a variety of labels. Around the policy success pole are terms such as 'convergence', 'compliance', 'adoption' and so forth. Around the pole of failure come terms such as 'back-sliding', 'policy reversal', 'resistance' and 'lack of political will'. The seemingly straightforward aim of assessing the success or failure of policy transfer is complicated by a wish to provide a more complex understanding of both the interpretative processes and the dynamics of translation. The central questions guiding this volume were the following:

- What is the origin of the policy/institution/idea transferred or diffused to CEE countries?
- To what degree was the policy/institution/idea transferred intact? Was it a faithful copy or was it emulated with a view to improving on the original? Was it used merely as an inspiration? Did it result in a synthesis or was it a hybrid, as Dolowitz and Marsh (1996: 351) might have labelled it?
- Did the resulting policy or institution come to be viewed as a success or failure, or somewhere in between? Could the process of adoption/adaptation be a success, but seen as a failure when it came to implementation and application?

As these questions imply, while the contributors in this volume are interested in the sources of policy ideas, this is balanced with an analytical concern to address what happened to those ideas and policies in the processes of transmission and transplantation and eventual application on the ground.

The focus on CEE requires little explanation. The process of social, economic and political change provides fertile soil for empirical inquiries on the transfer, diffusion and fate of external models. In the 1990s and early 2000s, the EU, but also almost every other major international organization, was present with policy advice, technical assistance, conditionalities and ideas. International civic groups, from global NGOs to private philanthropy, promoted a wide range of 'goods', from election campaign techniques to know-how in enforcing freedom of information legislation, helping civic group start-ups or working for minority protection. The original moments of transfer attracted considerable scholarly attention, and yet it is our contention that after over a decade of EU membership we need to revisit these processes and analyse whether the 'implants' have taken root, grown and perhaps borne fruit, or whether they have morphed into something quite distinct from what was originally intended and envisaged.

The chapter is structured into a further four sections. Section 1.2 covers some of our key concepts regarding policy diffusion, transfer and translation as well as the various understandings of policy failure and success. Section 1.3 focuses on the specific context of Central and Eastern Europe and the experiences of accession countries. Section 1.4 provides an overview of the subsequent chapters. Finally, in section 1.5 we briefly offer some thoughts as to the main findings we can draw from the chapters in the volume (a task that Chapter 10, the concluding chapter, by B. Guy Peters will undertake in greater detail).

1.2   THEORETICAL FOUNDATIONS: POLICY TRANSFER/DIFFUSION AND POLICY SUCCESS/FAILURE

In this volume, we grapple with several concepts and approaches. First there is the extensive and well established literature on policy diffusion and policy transfer. This is relevant given the explicit transfers of policy that came with the transposition of the *acquis communautaire* and accession to the European Union. However, to a large degree, this literature has focused on the processes of transmission and initial adoption rather than considerations of longer term compliance and durability. There are also questions regarding the actual effectiveness of such transfers in achieving Europeanization and meeting international standards which relates to the second body of literature which features high in this volume: that of policy failure and policy success. Cross-connecting 'success' and 'failure' are related ideas of policy translation and policy mobilities (from political geography) alongside ideas of interpretation and policy *bricolage* that emerge within local contexts as part of the processes of 'enrolment' in the foreign but also locally transfigured policies.

1.2.1   Policy Diffusion and Policy Transfer

Conceptual development of the ideas of policy diffusion and policy transfer are now well established in the social science literature. This sub-section provides a brief overview looking backwards to the political science diffusion literature and cognate policy studies literature on policy transfer, and then forward to the expanding multidisciplinary literature on 'learning', 'mobilities' and 'translation'. The latter is particularly important to overcoming binary distinctions of 'success' and 'failure' to capture the nuances in policy evolution in the region, including various practices of hybridization, experimentation and *bricolage* with the international best practices, standards and policy prescriptions coming from outside the new member states, and in drawing attention to methodological and epistemological issues of interpretation.

Policy diffusion is 'the process by which an innovation is communicated through certain channels over time among members of a social system' (Berry and Berry 1999: 171). These patterns of sequential adoption of an innovation emerge incrementally. They can be propelled by: a policy community of like-minded policy thinkers and practitioners; the geographic or cultural proximity of policy arenas; the leadership effect of 'pioneer states' that prompt emulation among 'follower states' (although in this respect there can also be followers who turn into 'laggards'); or, finally, authoritative inducement from a stronger state, international organization or other persuasive actor. The 'power of global models' – liberalism or democracy – is increasingly taken for granted (Dobbin et al. 2007: 450). However, the focus on the patterns whereby 'models' spread at the macro-level to the widespread adoption of specific policy tools at the micro-level has led some to complain that there is not enough attention to how policies or practices are altered during processes of adoption. By observing and mapping policy adoption, both the political actors involved and the content of what is being spread are of less interest when the original policy is presumed to be contagious. In this regard, the outcomes of policy convergence are viewed as driven by structural forces and path dependencies.

By contrast, policy transfer studies have emphasized the role of agency and the decision-making dynamics that are internal to political systems. The logic of selecting policy ideas – whether this is by 'systematically pinching' (Schneider and Ingram 1988) or a voluntary process of 'lesson-drawing' (Rose 1993) by civil servants and politicians seeking to interpret 'best practice' by imitation and modification – was central to many analyses. In this field, greater attention is accorded to what is transferred, specifically policies, institutions, ideologies or negative lessons (see Stone 2012). The different degrees of transfer are also a common theme, from straightforward copying to investigating the power dynamics of persuasion, indirect pressure and apparent coercion whereby policy transfers may be achieved through imposition.

Clearly there are significant similarities between transfer and diffusion, and despite the different terminology each points to circumstances of 'policy interdependence' (Gilardi 2012). Emerging out of different scholarly tributaries, the terms are sometimes interchangeable, with both streams attracting similar criticisms. In the past decade, various studies of transfer or diffusion have challenged this assumption of undiluted dichotomous diffusion or unmediated 'import' of transferred ideas (*inter alia*, Lendvai and Stubbs 2007; Sissenich 2008; Tews 2009). Rather than have a linear process of transmission, it is possible to learn from more than one jurisdiction at a time, and to take away a multiplicity of lessons. This can result in selective borrowing leading to policy hybrids and adaptive innovation that can make policy development fit local conditions.

A further interpretative dynamic occurs when moving away from the official domain of policy-making where politicians and civil servants are the main channels and conduits for addressing the wider universe of policy translators. A good deal of the diffusion and transfer literature has focused on exchanges amongst government elites. A smaller but growing body addresses the role of international organizations and transnational policy communities in the spread of policy, and the role of non-state actors in broadcasting policy approaches. The latter group – a mixed cadre of NGOs, foundations, think tanks, consultancy firms and so on – have been associated with 'soft' forms of transfer, such as the spread of norms, logics and justifications via professional communities or networks, as a complement to the 'hard' or legal transfer of policy tools, structures and practices.

Similarly, the rationalist underpinnings of agent directed transfer has been criticized for neglecting the complexity of context (*inter alia*, Dwyer and Ellison 2009; Newburn 2010) and the need for interpretation or experimentalism (Sabel and Zeitlin 2012) in the assemblage of policy in local political ecologies (Prince 2009). While national decision-making can be influenced by diffusion, policy innovations elsewhere are not in themselves sufficient condition for another jurisdiction to adopt the same policy. Internal factors such as the power dynamics of political interests and a polity's socio-historical make-up can be far more persuasive than external factors. Accordingly, the concept of 'policy translation' has gained traction as an alternative perspective that places less emphasis on origins and dissemination, preferring to stress the importance of local sources of inspiration, learning among importing policy communities, and the more unpredictable processes of trial and error.

1.2.2 Translating Policy Successes and Failures

Policy failure has re-emerged as a field of analysis in comparative politics and policy studies. In its most simple rendition, 'Failure is the mirror image of success: A policy fails if it does not achieve the goals that proponents set out to achieve and opposition is great and/or support is virtually non-existent' (McConnell 2010. 356). However, as McConnell argues, not only do policy outcomes have 'multiple dimensions', but the politics of policy are more complicated: proponents are more likely to emphasize achievements, while opponents stress the limitations and flawed execution. There is also a tendency to lump together the linked but nonetheless distinct ideas of state failure, governance failure and policy failure (Peters 2015).

State failure is an extreme condition when governments have lost the capacity to deliver basic public services and public order due to war and unrest, and/or usurpation by warlords, clans or others. This is not the focus of this volume. Rather, we look at governance failure, which is 'less dramatic than state failure, albeit still significant involving the incapacity to provide systematic direction to the society and economy' (Peters 2015: 263). Governance failures arise from the inability to generate workable compromises because of ideology and politics, or through lack of cooperation and coordination between government departments and bureaucratic agencies because of the cross-sector nature of policy concerns, for example. However, the remedy for these types of failures extends well beyond the design of public policies into the realm of society and political economy.

Policy failure can occur independently from the above types. Even with governance failure, it is feasible to deliver effective policies in a range of policy arenas. While policy failures are seemingly common, and represent perverse public value, nonetheless this type of failure is 'not linked to the organic structure of the state'; instead a policy is 'an instrument that can be manipulated in order to produce better results' (Peters 2015: 264). The distinctions are important for the discussions in this volume. Awareness of these distinctions sharpens understanding of the causes of the limited successes of candidate countries in reaching policy outcomes. As Peters puts it, is the problem 'more a function of the designs of those policies and the politics involved in their implementation, or are these failures more a function of general failures within the governance systems within which policymaking is embedded, or the interactions between these possible causes?' (Peters 2015: 264). In other words, 'any specific policy failure may be only a symptom of a broader failure in governing'. Addressing an instance of policy failures *per se* may result in an analysis 'only on the proximate "causes" of observed failure rather than on more deeply seated roots of failure' (Peters 2015: 264).

By making the link to policy failure, the study of policy diffusion and transfer becomes 'the object of debate rather than facilitating analyses of the social processes that constitute policy transfer' (McCann and Ward 2012: 327). Treating policy transfer as the dependent variable entails seeking to understand processes of Europeanization or donor conditionality. Alternatively, if this phenomenon is treated as the independent variable, then the analytical focus becomes one of addressing the relationship between policy transfer/diffusion and subsequent policy outcomes (Marsh and Evans 2012: 589).

One set of dynamics contributing to policy failure concerns uninformed, incomplete or inappropriate transfers (Dolowitz and Marsh 2000: 17). Uninformed transfer happens when policies are transferred with insufficient knowledge about how and why they 'work' in their original setting. Incomplete transfer results when some features of a policy are transferred, but others are not, where success in the original jurisdiction depended at least in part on those features that were not transferred. The two chapters that address pension policy exemplify aspects of incomplete transfer. Finally, inappropriate transfer occurs when the contextual factors – cultural, political, economic – are so different, which leads to differences in policy outcomes in the countries concerned. This final type of failure has been well documented by Peter Larmour in *Foreign Flowers* (2005), which charts the failure of many Commonwealth institutional transfers to the Pacific island states since the British colonial era.

A second set of dynamics resides with importing jurisdictions and the concept of 'negative lesson-drawing'. 'Back-sliding' may represent a belated and ex post facto form of negative lesson-drawing. As the EU accession was largely characterized by an asymmetric interdependence for 'subordinate' Central and Eastern European country (CEEC) recipients, the subsequent post-accession tactics of *policy resistance* may account for the phenomenon of 'back-sliding' (Bache and Taylor 2003; also Meyer-Sahling 2011). Working with such loaded terminology helps in querying assumptions of undiluted diffusion or unmediated 'import' of transferred ideas emanating from the EU in a one-way process and remaining preserved in their original form (*inter alia*, Lendvai and Stubbs 2007, 2009; Sissenich 2008; Tews 2009).

In addition, there can be 'dysfunctional' transfer, that is, dysfunctions resulting from 'normative mimicry, or market pressures, whereby over-committed policymakers have responded to complexity and crisis by unreflectively cutting and pasting from foreign models' (Sharman 2010: 623; also Moynihan 2006). This is a form of 'satisficing' whereby the adoption of international best practice represents a 'symbolic act through which politicians seek to enhance their status, credibility or "modernity". Compared to the idea of policy learning, or even "bounded learning", this mimicry or emulation is "blind" as "it does not entail enhanced reflection"' (Meseguer 2005: 79). Emulation is *ad hoc* and piece-meal, reflective of the transfer of rhetoric and ideology.

Then there are deviations from that which was diffused. The "indigeniza-tion" of policy occurs over the long term but it might begin at the very point of adoption. Even if there are cases of linear transmission from one juris-diction to another, the transfer does not create a cryogenically preserved policy for evermore. At some point, the process ends and endogenous forces of mutation take over. Local ownership becomes more pronounced and logics of appropriateness entail a gradual adjustment and modification that lead to outcomes that may not originally have been envisaged.

A third dynamic reinterprets the absence of transfers, distortions or diffusion not as 'failure', 'back-sliding' or incompleteness, but rather as experimentation, learning and 'translation'. This valorizes the reality and extensiveness of hybridity, synthesis, tinkering and adaptation that take place when policies move from one place to the next. It contests the notion that policies are internally coherent, consensually informed 'blueprints'. Instead, unintended consequences and misconstrued policy messages are integral to the assembly and metamorphoses of policy reforms. Policy translation (see, *inter alia*, Prince 2009; McCann and Ward 2012; Stone 2012) offers a more flexible conceptual framework for comprehending and recognizing value in the learning and policy innovations that come with the trials and errors that are inherent in policy-making. Intended recipients are neither passive nor unchanging ciphers.

The perspective of policy translation also points to a common epis-temological conundrum in determining successes or otherwise, namely, the question of who or what is authoritative in making such claims. As Mosse (2005: 34–9) puts it, policy ideas, whether they are expressed in terms of objectives or outcomes, have a certain social work to perform, one that seeks at different stages to enrol, to persuade, to create agreement and to contribute towards wider policy arguments. In this regard, the reconstruction of the process of policy take-up has to consider the sources of information concerning internal hearings, presentations, debates and revisions, but also establish a common understanding as to the significant elements in the development life of the policy. Informants may be privy to inside information on account of their technical expertise, their claims to represent those affected or their position in some implementing agency (Matyas and Zentai 2012). However, their accounts might also need to be qualified to the extent that their actual access to information may be both filtered and limited. The same actor can be both observer and active participant. Empirical reconstructions need to acknowledge how these positions influence their account of the development of the policy. For external commentators, reconstruction poses different questions, requiring alternative techniques bearing in mind what part of the policy cycle is being considered.

Thus, one recurring theme in this volume is that policy success and failure ought to be seen from more than one perspective. Evaluations by non-governmental organizations (NGOs) or donors of policy reforms may diverge considerably from government reviews. Moreover, there might be shortcomings in reaching particular goals, but these might be overshadowed by additional achievements, even if they were not anticipated beforehand. Yet again, considering success and failure from political, administrative or other perspectives requires some interpretative consensus in order to come to analytical judgements and conclusions.

1.3 THE CEE CONTEXT: THE EU AS MAIN DRIVER OF 'REFORM'

The Central and Eastern European region is an eminently suitable region for studying policy transfer and translation processes and their outcomes. The pathways of post-communist transition did not follow a rational process of policy design choosing from a galaxy of potential 'best practices'. Instead, today's realities emerged through a more muddy process of adjustment and learning. The region has long been a location for radical institutional reconstruction: 'awash with imported "solutions", never perfectly replicated, it is a region in which hybrid and "recombined" policy forms have been produced with almost tectonic intensity' (Peck 2011: 780). The process was rarely about policy-makers weighing up the pros and cons of a particular model or practice. Nonetheless the process was 'targeted' in the sense that a lot of reforms were the direct result of the European Commission telling candidate countries how exactly to adopt EU law and practice. This section provides greater detail of the context and trajectories of CEE transition, democratic consolidation and European Union membership.

1.3.1 The EU as Origin of Policy Transplants

The countries that joined the EU in 2004 are still referred to as 'the new member states', despite the fact that over a decade has elapsed (Romania and Bulgaria joined later, in 2007). The term has some analytical value since it draws attention to the centrality of EU membership, first as a goal that oriented transformations away from central planning and one-party systems to capitalism and democracy, and second as a source of very concrete legal obligations stemming from membership. This alone makes the CEE countries interesting cases for studying policy diffusion/transfer and the way that external models take hold, or fail to take hold, and/or are adapted and shaped by contextual factors.

Highlighting the generic among CEE countries, the term 'new member states' obfuscates the differences that existed, and continue to exist, within the region. Communism was not 'all the same' across the Eastern bloc, ranging from severe repression in Romania, Poland and Bulgaria to Hungary's relatively lax goulash-communism, leaving behind distinct resources and liabilities for the post-communist elite. Countries differed in their ability to bring into office reform-minded new political elites, which then pursued various modernization agendas, with a resulting variance in political economy across the region (Bohle and Greskovits 2012). This variation fractured external influence, with the result that the present CEE landscape is a patchwork rather than a picture of uniformity or convergence.

The phrase 'new member states' also de-emphasizes the importance of the period since accession, as if, with membership finally secured, the CEE countries somehow reached a *finalité*. Whereas the pre-accession years are seen as a period of dynamic, linear progress towards 'graduation' and full membership, the post-accession years are characterized as simply continuing along this trajectory, albeit without the earlier guiding external influence. A wave of influential books was published around the time of enlargement (2004), taking stock of changes thus far and offering predictions about how these countries would fare once inside the Union (Cowles et al. 2001; Dimitrova 2004; Schimmelfennig and Sedelmeier 2005; Vachudova 2005; Grabbe 2006). Yet the past decade offers the conceptually most fruitful period for observing how the CEE countries have come to adapt, translate, localize and generally make their own (or fail to make their own) the policies, institutions and ideas that have been brought by the EU, sometimes 'progressing', sometimes reversing or side-stepping earlier achievements or implants.

The academic literatures most relevant to dissecting the EU's influence on the CEE countries are those dealing with Europeanization, conditionality and, particularly since accession, compliance with EU norms. 'Europeanization' as a term has often been criticized for lacking conceptual clarity (Flockhart 2010), but it is so widely accepted in the literature as to be almost inescapable. It is normally taken to mean 'different forms of diffusion processes of European ideas and practices across time and space' (Flockhart 2010: 788) or simply the EU's impact on whatever is the object of study: member states (polity), party systems, policies or normative frameworks (Sedelmeier 2011). Europeanization is also seen as 'the "downloading" of EU policy into the national polity' (Grabbe 2006: 4). Common to these definitions is the idea of the EU as the origin of models, templates and obligations, and of the CEE countries (and other member states) as addressees, recipients and (willing) takers. Embedded in such definitions is a perception of structural and linear processes of policy diffusion/transfer rather than a reciprocal agent-driven negotiation of policy translation. Europeanization in the latter sense is seen as the reverse of 'uploading' processes, whereby the member states shape EU policies and institutions.

The first noteworthy feature of the Europeanization of the CEE countries is the sheer scale of the process: that is, the extraordinary scope of institutions, processes and ideas that have been diffused/transferred, primarily in the years prior to accession, and the generally high degree of influence these have had. This has been observed, on the one hand, in relation to the very nature of the CEE countries' political regimes. In the early 1990s, as these countries emerged from four decades of communism, the aspiration to 'return to Europe' symbolized a desired end-goal for macro-level transformations. The wish to join the club of Western European countries was a strong pull factor and enjoyed widespread support among political elites in CEE countries – partly because in the early 1990s, in marked contrast with today's post-Brexit context, European integration enjoyed a period of dynamic expansion. At this stage, primarily diffusion processes were at play, with CEE political elites driven by a desire to emulate the socio-political arrangements of the more successful Western half of the continent.

Soon, however, the EU insisted that respect for liberal democratic principles was a formal requirement for aspiring members. From 1992, progress in democratic reforms was a condition for receiving financial assistance under what was originally Poland and Hungary: Assistance for Restructuring their Economies (PHARE) (the EU's aid programme of 'Assistance for Economic Restructuring' for the CEE countries, which widened from Poland and Hungary; Schimmelfennig et al. 2005: 30), and the 1993 Copenhagen European Council famously adopted 'the stability of institutions guaranteeing democracy, the rule of law, human rights and respect for and protection of minorities', the so-called Copenhagen criteria, as precondition for eventual membership. To what extent the EU has been successful in 'anchoring democracy' in the CEE countries is a matter of debate, but the ambition of the Union to effect wholesale political transformations by conscious, strategic transfer of normative requirements is beyond doubt.

The scale of Europeanization is also significant with respect to policy: the penetration of EU law, 'good practices' and procedures is observable in areas ranging from veterinary standards to public administration and the territorial organization of the state, albeit to various degrees. For the first time, prospective members were required to adopt the whole of the *acquis communautaire* prior to accession (this was not a condition in earlier rounds of enlargement). With the beginning of accession negotiations in 1998, these requirements were communicated, in great detail, in the Commission's annual monitoring reports, which essentially functioned as legislative agenda for candidate governments. For several years, the incorporation of the *acquis* into domestic legal norms dominated parliaments. The volume of legislation was at times enormous – to the extent that parliaments kept up with the timetable of accession negotiations by establishing fast-track, low scrutiny procedures (Schimmelfennig and Sedelmeier 2005: 2). As Jacoby points out, the flood of an estimated 10 000 directives or 80 000 pages of EU legislation to transpose resulted in a 'cookie-cutter method of transfer' in national ministries (1999: 65).

At this stage, the process resembled ideal-typical 'linear' policy transfer, and especially in highly technical areas the CEE countries adopted EU rules with little thought to implementation. '[A] lack of adaptation to specific circumstances in each country as well as an absence of broad consultation of affected groups during the preparation of the laws' was characteristic of pre-accession legal alignment (Falkner and Treib 2008: 298–9). As Dimitrova (2004: 8) argues, '[e]nlargement is explicitly defined by the Commission and accepted by the candidates as an "asymmetrical process" of taking over the rules of a club . . . [and consequently] political elites in CEE have limited control over the institutional changes they have undertaken to affect'. The impact this has had on the CEE countries is difficult to overestimate: EU policy influence has generally been described as strong and direct across most policy areas regulated by the *acquis* (Sedelmeier 2011: 22).

As to the mechanisms through which the EU has 'driven [the CEEs] to change', as Dimitrova (2004) put it, the key role was played by conditionality. Considerable scholarly attention has been devoted to when and under what conditions conditionality 'worked best', in the sense of eliciting the highest levels of compliance. Such accounts tend to be rooted in rationalist institutionalism, and rely on incentive structures for an explanation (see Sedelmeier 2011). Consequently, conditionality is seen as productive largely because the ultimate reward of membership was strongly desired by the CEE countries, thus offering the EU strong leverage backed up by the possibility of denying or delaying accession. Clear requirements, a credible membership perspective and strong monitoring capacities combined to put the Commission in an extremely strong position vis-à-vis the negotiating governments. This strengthened the foundations of policy transfer, in these accounts conditioned by domestic adaptation costs, operationalized as veto players inside the CEE countries (Schimmelfennig et al. 2005).

Although the CEE countries were of course always free 'to walk away', the power asymmetry was so pronounced as to give the Commission licence to ask for more from the accession countries than from existing member states. Not only did the Commission have competencies towards the CEE countries that member states had not accepted for themselves (Grabbe 2006: 36), but at times conditionality covered areas not included in the *acquis*, or obligations member states had not complied with. A prominent example is anti-corruption, an area not covered by the *acquis* yet prominently and consistently included in pre-accession conditionality (Batory 2010). Moreover, leverage gained through membership conditionality was used to reinforce standards set by other international organizations, notably the World Bank and the Council of Europe (CoE), with, for instance, candidate countries explicitly recommended to adopt various CoE conventions. 'Parallel and additive conditionality' was the case particularly in human and minority rights, where CoE and Organization for Security and Co-operation in Europe (OSCE) demands worked in tandem with the Copenhagen criteria (Schimmelfennig et al. 2005: 33).

At times, the accession countries voluntarily assumed more than that which was strictly required of them, going beyond conditionality. Instrumental rational motivations do not fully explain these cases in particular, or the scale of EU rule adoption in CEE in general. Apart from leverage, 'linkage' is pivotal to the transmission of policies and ideas (Levitsky and Way 2006). The EU is an environment that is dense with policy networks and epistemic communities to which the CEE countries have also been increasingly connected. Through these channels, emphasized in sociological and constructivist institutionalist perspectives, the accession countries 'acquired' policies, institutions and ideas through: elite socialization in EU fora; learning and persuasion; identifying with and accepting the EU as the legitimate source of authority; and the particular resonance of ideas with prevailing norms within the CEE countries (Finnemore and Sikkink 1998; Schimmelfennig and Sedelmeier 2005; Schwellnus 2005). From this perspective, supranational institutions are seen as transfer agents, facilitating and enabling transfer/diffusion rather than 'pushing' EU requirements on behalf of the existing member states, and learning also occurs in horizontal relationships, for instance in terms of lesson-drawing from the experience of one candidate/new member state by another. Rule adoption is seen as a reflective rather than mechanical exercise.

1.3.2   Other External Sources of Policy Change

It should be noted that a number of other organizations were also present in the region, acting as transfer agent and working to enable policy learning. An example is the Organisation for Economic Co-operation and Development (OECD)'s Public Management Programme (PUMA). It has

several methods for spreading information and provide 'forward thinking' on matters such as national accounting standards, human resources
management and 'OECD Best Practices for Budget Transparency' –
publications, networks of senior officials, conferences and so on (Pal
2012). Similarly, a joint initiative of the EU and OECD – Support for
Improvement in Governance and Management (SIGMA) in Central
and Eastern Europe – provided advice on improving public governance
at the central government level. Other international organizations and
bilateral development agencies – such as the United States Agency
for International Development (USAID) and the Swedish International
Development Cooperation Agency (SIDA) – sought to provide lessons
to boost capacities in public sector administration and policy reforms.
With its regional centre in Bratislava, the United Nations Development
Programme (UNDP) launched numerous initiatives to support the CEE
countries' accession. By and large these initiatives were educational and
concerned the promotion of policy learning: that is, 'soft' or persuasive
modes of policy transfer. Nevertheless, as our contributors on pension
reform (Chapter 3), domestic violence policies (Chapter 4) and Roma
initiatives (Chapter 5) discuss, these international actors also mediated
Europeanization transfer/diffusion processes and offered distinct interpretations of their own as to what constituted 'best practice'.

Conditionality is the 'hard' dimension of transfer, generally brought
about by authoritative and legitimate policy actors such as governments
and international organizations. However, the hard transfer of rules,
institutions and policy instruments is frequently underpinned by complementary soft processes of training, persuasion and consensus building.
The emphasis is on cognition and the redefinition of interests on the basis
of new knowledge which affects the fundamental beliefs and ideas behind
policy approaches. The mechanisms for such transfer include a wider
constellation of individuals, networks and organizations. Think tanks or
research institutes, management consultancies, philanthropic foundations,
university centres, law firms, scientific associations, professional societies,
training institutes and so forth help transfer the intellectual matter that
underpins policies. Ordinarily private or quasi-autonomous organizations,
many have used their intellectual authority or market expertise to reinforce
and legitimate certain forms of policy or normative standards as 'best
practice'.

For example, quasi-governmental political foundations such as the
German Stiftungen, the British Westminster Foundation for Democracy
or, in the USA, the Center for International Private Enterprise were proac-
tive in exporting the principles of market oriented democracies among
government officials, businesspeople, media and the public. Independent

philanthropies have also been important, notably the Open Society Foundations (OSF), in bankrolling exchange programmes or training initiatives for local government officials and national administrators. OSF funded the European Union Monitoring and Advocacy Program of the Open Society Institute (EUMAP) – a programme that monitored the progress of national administrations in the EU accession process on wide-ranging concerns such as minority protection, freedom of information law, and other human rights and rule of law issues. There have been policy parallels in the higher education realm with foundation, bilateral donor support and foreign university partnerships in the flowering of 'Western style' graduate public policy programmes, MBAs and law degrees to prepare new generations of leaders in government, business and the professions (Stone 2007: 547).

1.3.3   Compliance

In the decade since the CEE countries gained full membership, the literature dealing with rule adoption in these countries has moved on from Europeanization to the perspective of compliance with EU norms, considering questions such as whether the new member states remain a distinctive group or whether general patterns hold across the EU. In this literature too, compliance is a function of instrumental rationality and/or normative motivations, or a combination of the two. Accordingly, the enforcement approach emphasizes the threat of sanctions, the management approach emphasizes incentives of the 'enabling kind', and the persuasion approach shares normative commitment as a source of rule adoption/transfer processes (for a review see Hartlapp 2007). Commonly used variables, again echoing the Europeanization debate, include 'goodness of fit' as a proxy for adaptation costs, EU enforcement and sanctioning powers, and administrative/government capacity for the former two, and elite socialization, learning effects and particularly 'a culture of compliance' for the latter (for a review see Neyer and Wolf 2005; Falkner and Treib 2008; Angelova et al. 2012; Conant 2012).

As for the findings, scholarship found little evidence for a decrease in formal rule adoption rates following accession, contradicting expectations rooted in incentive-based models of Europeanization. Even in the absence of the leverage afforded to the Commission by membership conditionality, the new member states continued to transpose EU rules. In fact, as Sedelmeier (2008: 806) points out, 'far from constituting an "eastern problem", [in alignment with EU law] virtually all of the new member states outperformed virtually all of the old members during the first four years of membership'. Other studies provide a more varied picture, with a number of new member states being highly compliant with EU law after accession whereas a second group was characterized by frequent shortcomings in transposition (Knill and Tosun 2009).

However, studies of this kind tend to rely on data generated from Commission enforcement action, that is, times when the EU's 'guardian of the treaties' takes action to bring errant member states into line. Since this is largely based on formal rule adoption, the data may mask massive policy failures on the ground. Indeed, scholarship that looked into the implementation of laws originating from the EU uncovered major deficiencies: EU directives in social policy remained 'dead letters' in the new member states (Falkner and Treib 2008). Dimitrova's (2010) study found that many of the institutions supporting the functioning of the *acquis*, also 'imported' from the EU during the accession process, failed to become institutionalized, were reversed in some countries or simply remained 'empty shells'. For instance, the principles of civil service reform, notably the independence of the civil service, promoted by the EU were often reversed following accession (Meyer-Sahling 2006). This body of literature serves to remind us that policy transfer cannot be assumed to be a simple linear process of a model taken, mechanically adopted and implemented, but, as the recent experience of the CEE countries investigated in this volume shows, it is an altogether more complex phenomenon with several theoretically possible outcomes, ranging from success to failure and forms in between.

1.4 STRUCTURE OF THE BOOK AND CHAPTER CONTRIBUTIONS

Picking up on the theme of policy failure, Chapter 2 by Achim Kemmerling and Kristin Makszin considers whether too much policy transfer can be a lead cause for policy failure, in this respect via introducing extreme policy volatility. This offers an alternative perspective on the idea of the receptive environment and the importance of policy learning; it also suggests that there is a way around some of the normative problems of judging whether a policy is successful or not. If, as in the case of the privatization of pensions, their focus in the chapter, we see a complete reversal, this can be deemed a failure regardless of whether it was based on sound economic analysis or astute political bargaining; the original reform simply had no chance to mature and bear fruit. The three cases that the authors describe contain significant differences in terms of the stakes involved, the degree of domestic support and the nature of the external protagonists. As noted earlier, in this case (as in others in the volume) the EU was by no means the only instigator of policy reform. Especially in the 1990s, there were a host of individual countries and international bodies that promoted different reform directions, for instance the World Bank and the OECD in the case of pension privatization.

In Chapter 3, Dragos Adascalitei and Stefan Domonkos offer a more in-depth discussion of the vagaries of pension reform, but consider the question of policy diffusion from a temporal as well as a spatial dimension. Many former socialist countries saw the introduction of a second, mandatory private pillar as the solution to the question of ageing populations. Why then did the Czech Republic and Romania wait almost ten years after their neighbours introduced the policy? Would there not be evidence of significant peer learning advantage in coming to the party so late, avoiding the mistakes of the early adopters and maximizing the advantages promised by the World Bank? Adascalitei and Domonkos demonstrate that although policy-makers in both countries were in close contact with neighbouring countries, especially Slovak advisors, they were still unable to completely avoid some of the traps of the policy, not least its impact on the existing public pension programme and its ability to attract higher income employees. Interestingly, the late implementation of private pension schemes coincided with a marked cooling of enthusiasm on the part of the main policy protagonists themselves. This might well have led to policy reforms that were less ambitious and, as a result, less able to convince sceptical domestic populations.

In Chapter 6, Gergő Medve-Bálint focuses directly on the EU and cohesion policy as its principal means of supporting economic development and reducing income gaps between more and less wealthy EU members, and within countries themselves. One common experience following the collapse of central planning in CEE countries was a dramatic increase in income inequality within the country, especially between the capital and the rest of the country, but also along other fault lines such as areas of heavy industry and agriculture, areas closer to newer Western markets and areas where there were limited urban populations. Initially, policy-makers in both the Czech Republic and Hungary, Medve-Bálint's country cases, followed their pro-market advisors and resisted calls for strong regional policy. However, largely at the prompting of the EU, both countries later introduced mid-tier intermediate bodies to develop regional policies to help revive backward areas. Implementing the partnership principle – a key requirement in cohesion policy – meant creating new administrative models and charging them with ambitious programmes of policy formation and implementation. The chapter illustrates the unfolding contradiction between policy objectives and techniques in the run-up to accession. Although the EU insisted on regional bodies, in the end it sided with the central governments when they argued that the new entities had insufficient capacity to run complex operational programmes. The chapter also highlights policy implementation as an odd mixture of 'success' and 'failure'. On the one hand, CEE countries have secured the majority of cohesion funding; on the other, the democratic potential for decentralized planning and implementation was thwarted by external concerns for optimal resource allocation and accountability.

Not all policy interactions in this volume are at the state/supranational level. There are several examples of other policy actors that can exert influence over the interpretation and application of externally driven policies on sub-state levels. Sara Svensson in Chapter 7 investigates how local authorities understood cross-border cooperation in the framework of Euroregions, a long-standing institutional initiative of the Council of Europe. Euroregions have proliferated in Northern and Western Europe for over 50 years, but appeared in CEE only after 1989. Unlike the regional bodies effectively forced on to the accession countries, Euroregions were voluntary associations aiming to promote peaceful cooperation and mutual aid across national boundaries. With a much more modest budget and limited legal capacity, for CEE countries and Hungary and its neighbours in particular, the motivation to join was driven by, on the one hand, grant opportunities but, on the other, a desire to bolster fraternal ties with ethnic kin who happened to be on the other side of the border. In one respect, this could be seen as circumventing and even contradicting the original idea behind Euroregions: building peace and prosperity through bridging different nations and ethnicities. The question for Svensson is in what sense we can assess the contribution of this institutional transfer. In the end, the process of comprehending or, as the author puts it, reinterpreting the goals of the policy reflects the local priorities of the participants, even when those are antithetical to the pan-European politics of the protagonists.

András Tétényi in Chapter 8 introduces a perhaps unfamiliar policy story, namely the establishment of international development programmes in Hungary. In this instance, there was no single transfer agent, and the process of policy development highlights diverse signs of transfer and diffusion through an eclectic mix of advisors and supporters. At the domestic level, there were none of the high profile stakes that were evident in the privatization and welfare reforms. Development assistance registered very low in public concern and this was reflected in a general lack of interest amongst Parliament and ministries. Tétényi shows how the reluctant Ministry for Foreign Affairs spent years trying to attract law makers' interest and impress on a sceptical public the need to raise levels of ODA spending in line with the Millennium Development Goals. As with other areas of policy development, there was no shortage of advisors and, unlike in cohesion policy, EU member states did have full autonomy as to how to pursue their international development objectives. In that regard, policy outcomes did resemble international standards, for example focusing on areas of comparative advantage, working though multilateral programmes and cooperating with domestic civic associations. However, the targets for support clearly reflected Hungary's foreign policy goals and there was an unashamed bias towards ensuring that Hungarian companies benefited from enhanced market access. From this perspective, an initially unfamiliar policy field can be quickly saturated with the concerns and frameworks of related fields, even if, to outside observers, they seem to refute the original policy objective.

Andrea Krizsan in Chapter 4 shows how civil society actors have been influential in the development of new policy fields, in this case the creation of legislation and effective enforcement mechanisms to counter domestic violence in the region. As this was not an EU competence *per se*, domestic advocates used the panoply of international instruments to argue for legislative reforms, not least a combination of UN-based monitoring mechanisms, as well as the assistance of US-based human rights groups, in the context of EU accession and beyond. The five-country study shows variation in terms of inspiration for policy reform and actual progress in addressing the issue, but also highlights the different ways in which domestic and international civic groups cooperated, sometimes in a top-down, quasi-instructive relationship, in other cases in more horizontal partnerships. As Krizsan puts it, transnational policy actors can mediate between state and non-state actors and, in the absence of local sources of revenue, international foundations can become important means for ensuring civic participation in policy reform, especially when the national context might not be conducive. However, as has become increasingly clear, foreign funding for domestic groups that engage in policy reform is also highly controversial and can lead to damaging allegations of foreign agency and influence peddling.

In Chapter 9, Liviu Matei, Daniela Craciun and Simona Torotcoi make the under-appreciated point that, when it comes to assessing the achievements of the Bologna Process, it is important to be clear what exactly is being assessed. Although CEE countries tended to go for wholesale adoption of higher education reform policies covered by the Bologna Process, sometimes at the expense of national debate and experimentation, it is better to see the various policy transfers as an evolving set of values where eventual assessments are more partial and based on judgement rather than science. By disaggregating the policy process, the authors can point to areas where there are clear and relatively unambiguous achievements, whereas in other areas the score sheet is more open to interpretation and debate. They also show the strong differences in domestic support for these

European reforms. Even though the European Commission itself has relatively limited formal competencies in higher education policy, it turned out to be probably the most important driver of legislative change in the member states.

In Chapter 5, Viola Zentai provides a theoretically rich and nuanced account of the relative successes and failures of Roma inclusion policy in the region. Considering a period stretching back over 15 years, the chapter shows the different inspirations for national strategic policy frameworks, first within the internationally supported civil society and promoted by the World Bank and then taken up by the European Union. For a host of reasons, the initial promise of transforming agendas and frameworks evaporated in a climate of reluctance and avoidance, despite the very significant support that came from coupling Roma inclusion policy to cohesion fund programmes. Zentai argues that understanding policy experiments and learning in the context of social justice and equality agendas needs to bear in mind the adversarial nature of struggles to change societies. One way in which the topic remains in play is through the, albeit precariously funded, work of networks of shadow reporters, monitors and professionals. Acutely aware of the ways in which national governments can disguise inaction, these national and transnational coalitions remind governments and the EU of their obligations as well as widen the scope for Roma participation in policy formation. However, there remains no guarantee that policy experimentalism will not be used to pursue goals entirely against the original agenda of inclusion.

As bookend to this introductory chapter, Chapter 10, the last chapter, by B. Guy Peters reminds us that, notwithstanding the political appeal of policy transfer for the EU and other international organizations, it is institutional capacity that is the most important element determining whether governments have the ability to adopt and embed policies as anticipated.

1.5   KEY FINDINGS AND IMPLICATIONS

There are several themes that connect the contributions to this volume. Beyond illustrating the idea that policy 'transfer' processes are often non-linear and fuzzy and sometimes counter-intuitive, the chapters highlight the central importance of the views, interests and constellations of the domestic actors that filter and interpret international influences. In this sense, the CEE experience in the years since accession is more about active and sometimes strategic policy imports and policy distortion and less about simple receipt and incorporation of external models. While in the pre-accession years CEE countries were more or less willing and capable policy 'takers', in more recent times there are plenty of examples and abundant evidence of the reinterpretation processes central to the policy learning perspective.

A number of chapters also point to the extent to which such local reinterpretations challenge or even contradict the logic behind the original idea or model, either openly or under the surface. Medve-Bálint (Chapter 6), Svensson (Chapter 7) and Tétényi (Chapter 8) give examples of processes whereby the declared policy objective was undermined or hollowed out For instance, extending the EU's cohesion policy to CEE started out as a decentralization project aimed at decreasing regional disparities, yet these long term objectives were superseded by the short term political exigencies and pragmatism on the side of the Commission in alliance with central state authorities. The idea of Euroregions was promoted as an initiative to foster mutual understanding and economic cooperation in aid of European integration, yet, at least in the Hungarian case, they ended up aiding the 're-unification' of Hungarian-speakers divided by national borders. In a similar light, the introduction of official development policy, rather than serving the goal of redistributing resources from 'rich' European countries to developing countries, was adapted by the Hungarian government as a means of strengthening contacts with countries with Hungarian minorities.

Conversely, other contributions illustrate that CEE countries were at times 'overdoing' policy transfer and learning. This sort of excessive learning seems to have taken place in the case of pension reforms. Kemmerling and Makszin (Chapter 2) and Adascalitei and Domonkos (Chapter 3) indicate that policy-makers in the region can become more zealous defenders of ideas than the original promoters of those ideas themselves. It appears that local champions continued to promote pension privatization even when mounting evidence against the model has shaken confidence in it internationally. As Kemmerling and Makszin furthermore argue, this tendency of taking reforms too far then caused policy-makers to relapse, leaving CEE countries as victims of policy failure due to excessive volatility.

Ultimately, the volume shows that, while the region was awash with foreign models in the transition and accession years, the time since CEE countries have been full EU members often saw these 'implants' change beyond recognition. This may have been because the idea or policy adopted was never fully understood, or because somewhere along the way it became apparent that the objective was better served by other means. Important changes also occurred because policy-makers deliberately redirected a model that was more or less forced on them towards partisan goals. Whatever the case, the resulting landscape in CEE is diverse and unique to the region. As to whether transfer and diffusion processes can therefore be considered successful, there is no simple answer. This book merely confirms that policy success or failure is in the eye of the beholder; it is a question of who is asking and where that person is looking.

REFERENCES

Angelova, M., T. Dannwolf and T. König (2012), 'How robust are compliance findings? A research synthesis', *Journal of European Public Policy*, 19 (8), 1269–91.

Bache, I. and A. Taylor (2003), 'The politics of policy resistance: Reconstructing higher education in Kosovo', *Journal of Public Policy*, 23, 279–300.

Batory, A. (2010), 'Post-accession malaise? EU conditionality, domestic politics and anti-corruption policy in Hungary', *Global Crime*, 11 (2), 164–77.

Berry, F.S. and W.D. Berry (1999), 'Innovation and diffusion models in policy research', in P.A. Sabatier (ed.), *Theories of the Policy Process*, Boulder, CO: Westview Press, pp. 169–200.

Bohle, D. and B. Greskovits (2012), *Capitalist Diversity on Europe's Periphery*, Ithaca, NY: Cornell University Press.

Conant, L. (2012), 'Compliance and what EU member states make of it', in M. Cremona (ed.), *Compliance and the Enforcement of EU Law*, Oxford: Oxford University Press, pp. 1–29.

Cowles, M.G., J. Caporaso and T. Risse (eds) (2001), *Transforming Europe: Europeanization and Domestic Change*, Ithaca, NY: Cornell University Press.

Dimitrova, A.L. (ed.) (2004), *Driven to Change: The European Union's Enlargement Viewed from the East*, Manchester: Manchester University Press.

Dimitrova, A.L. (2010), 'The new member states of the EU in the aftermath of enlargement: Do new European rules remain empty shells?', *Journal of European Public Policy*, 17 (1), 137–48.

Dobbin, F., B. Simmons and G. Garrett (2007), 'The global diffusion of public policies: Social construction, coercion, competition, or learning', *Annual Review of Sociology*, 33, 449–72.

Dolowitz, D. and D. Marsh (1996), 'Who learns from whom: A review of the policy transfer literature', *Political Studies*, 44 (2), 343–57.

Dolowitz, D. and D. Marsh (2000), 'Learning from abroad: The role of policy transfer in contemporary policy making', *Governance*, 13 (1), 5–24.

Dwyer, P. and N. Ellison (2009), 'We nicked stuff from all over the place: Policy transfer or muddling through?', *Policy and Politics*, 37 (3), 389–407.

Falkner, G. and O. Treib (2008), 'Three worlds of compliance or four? The EU-15 compared to new member states', *Journal of Common Market Studies*, 46 (2), 293–313.

Finnemore, M. and K. Sikkink (1998), 'International norm dynamics and political change', *International Organization*, 52 (Autumn), 887–917.

Flockhart, T. (2010), 'Europeanization or EU-ization? The transfer of European norms across time and space', *Journal of Common Market Studies*, 48 (4), 787–810.

Gilardi, F. (2012), 'Policy interdependence: Transfer, diffusion, convergence', in I. Engeli and C. Rothmayr (eds), *Comparative Policy Studies: Conceptual and Methodological Challenges*, Basingstoke: Palgrave Macmillan.

Grabbe, H. (2006), *The EU's Transformative Power: Europeanization through Conditionality in Central and Eastern Europe*, Basingstoke: Palgrave Macmillan.

Hartlapp, M. (2007), 'On enforcement, management and persuasion: Different logics of implementation policy in the EU and the ILO', *Journal of Common Market Studies*, 45 (3), 653–74.

Jacoby, W. (1999), 'Priest and penitent: The European Union as a force in the domestic politics of Eastern Europe', *East European Constitutional Review*, 8 (1–2), 62–7.

Knill, C. and J. Tosun (2009), 'Post-accession transposition of EU law in the new member states: Across-country comparison', in F. Schimmelfennig and F. Trauner (eds), Post-accession compliance in the EU's new member states, *European Integration online Papers* (*EIoP*), 13 (Special Issue 2), Art. 18, http://eiop.or.at/eiop/texte/2009-018a.htm.

Larmour, P. (2005), *Foreign Flowers: Institutional Transfer and Good Governance in the Pacific Islands*, Honolulu: University of Hawai'i Press.

Lendvai, N. and P. Stubbs (2007), 'Policies as translation: Situating transnational social policies', in S. Hodgson and Z. Irving (eds), *Policy Reconsidered: Meanings, Politics and Practices*, Bristol: Policy Press, pp. 173–90.

Lendvai, N. and P. Stubbs (2009), 'Assemblages, translation, and intermediaries in South East Europe: Rethinking transnationalism and social policy', *European Societies*, 11 (5), 673–95.

Levitsky, S. and L.A. Way (2006), 'Linkage versus leverage: Rethinking the international dimension of regime change', *Comparative Politics*, 38 (4), 379–400.

Macken-Walsh, A. (2009), 'Community action in post-socialist Lithuania', *Journal of Community Development*, 4 (4), 515–24.

Marsh, D. and M. Evans (2012), 'Conclusion: Special issue on policy transfer', *Policy Studies*, 33 (6), 587–91.

Matyas, J. and V. Zentai (eds) (2012), *Capitalism from Outside? Economic Cultures in Eastern Europe after 1989*, Budapest: Central European University Press.

McCann, E. and K. Ward (2012), 'Policy assemblages, mobilities and mutations: Toward a multidisciplinary conversation', *Political Studies Review*, 10 (3), 325–32.

McConnell, A. (2010), 'Policy success, policy failure and grey areas in-between', *Journal of Public Policy*, 30 (3), 345–62.

Meseguer, C. (2005), 'Policy learning, policy diffusion and the making of a new order', *Annals of the American Academy of Political and Social Science*, 598, 67–82.

Meyer-Sahling, J.-H. (2006), 'The institutionalization of political discretion in post-communist civil service systems: The case of Hungary', *Public Administration*, 84 (3), 693–715.

Meyer-Sahling, J.-H. (2011), 'The durability of EU civil service policy in Central and Eastern Europe after accession', *Governance: An International Journal of Policy, Administration, and Institutions*, 24 (2), 231–60.

Mosse, D. (2005), *Cultivating Development: An Ethnography of Aid Policy and Practice*, London: Pluto Press.

Moynihan, D. (2006), 'Ambiguity in policy lessons: The agencification experience', *Public Administration*, 84, 1029–50.

Newburn, T. (2010), 'Diffusion, differentiation and resistance in comparative penality', *Criminology and Criminal Justice*, 10 (4), 341–53.

Neyer, J. and D. Wolf (2005), 'The analysis of compliance with international rules:

Definitions, variables and methodology', in M. Zürn and C. Joerges (eds), *Law and Governance in Postnational Europe. Compliance beyond the Nation-State*, Cambridge: Cambridge University Press, pp. 40–65.

Pal, L.A. (2012), *Frontiers of Governance: The OECD and Global Public Management Reform*, Basingstoke: Palgrave Macmillan.

Peck, J. (2011), 'Geographies of policy: From transfer-diffusion to mobility-mutation', *Progress in Human Geography*, 35 (6), 773–97.

Peters, B.G. (2015), 'State failure, governance failure and policy failure: Exploring the linkages', *Public Policy and Administration*, 30 (3–4), 261–76.

Prince, R. (2009), 'Policy transfer as policy assemblage: Making policy for the creative industries in New Zealand', *Environment and Planning A*, 42, 169–86.

Rose, R. (1993), *Lesson-Drawing in Public Policy: A Guide to Learning across Time and Space*, Chatham, NJ: Chatham House.

Sabel, C.F. and J. Zeitlin (2012), 'Experimentalism in the EU: Common ground and persistent differences', *Regulation and Governance*, 6 (3), 410–26.

Schimmelfennig, F. and U. Sedelmeier (2005), 'Introduction: Conceptualising the Europeanization of Central and Eastern Europe', in F. Schimmelfennig and U. Sedelmeier (eds), *The Europeanization of Central and Eastern Europe*, Ithaca, NY: Cornell University Press, pp. 1–29.

Schimmelfennig, F., S. Engert and H. Knobel (2005), 'The impact of EU political conditionality', in F. Schimmelfennig and U. Sedelmeier (eds), *The Europeanization of Central and Eastern Europe*, Ithaca, NY: Cornell University Press, pp. 29–51.

Schneider, A. and H. Ingram (1988), 'Systematically pinching ideas: A comparative approach to policy design', *Journal of Public Policy*, 8 (1), 61–80.

Schwellnus, G. (2005), 'The adoption of nondiscrimination and minority protection rules in Romania, Hungary and Poland', in F. Schimmelfennig and U. Sedelmeier (eds), *The Europeanization of Central and Eastern Europe*, Ithaca, NY: Cornell University Press, pp. 51–71.

Sedelmeier, U. (2008), 'After conditionality: Post-accession compliance with EU law in East Central Europe', *Journal of European Public Policy*, 15 (6), 806–25.

Sedelmeier, U. (2011), 'Europeanisation in new member and candidate states', *Living Reviews in European Governance*, 6, http://www.livingreviews.org/lreg-2011-1.

Sharman, J.C. (2010), 'Dysfunctional policy transfer in national tax blacklists', *Governance: An International Journal of Policy, Administration, and Institutions*, 23 (4), 623–39.

Sissenich, B. (2008), 'Cross-national policy networks and the state: EU social policy transfer to Hungary and Poland', *European Journal of International Relations*, 14 (3), 455–87.

Stone, D. (2007), 'Market principles, philanthropic ideals, and public service values in international public policy', *Political Science and Politics*, 40 (3), 545–51.

Stone, D. (2012), 'Transfer and translation of policy', *Policy Studies*, 33 (6), 1–17.

Szent-Iványi, B. and A. Tétényi (2008), 'Transition and foreign aid policies in the Visegrad countries: A path dependent approach', *Transition Studies Review*, 15, 573–87.

Tews, K. (2009), 'From law-taking to policy-making: The environmental dimension of the EU accession process – challenges, risks and chances for the SEE countries', *Environmental Policy and Governance*, 19, 130–39.

Vachudova, M.A. (2005), *Europe Undivided: Democracy, Leverage and Integration after Communism*, Oxford: Oxford University Press.

2. When does policy diffusion affect policy instability? Cases of excessive policy volatility in welfare policies in East Central Europe

Achim Kemmerling and Kristin Makszin

2.1 INTRODUCTION

The last 25 years have revealed a remarkable incongruence in Central and Eastern Europe (CEE) transition countries: while the region has seen a considerable and in many ways successful political and economic transformation, recent changes have often gone, in one way or another, 'backward'. Such changes include renationalizing programmes and sectors that were privatized, or first introducing user fees for health care and then abolishing them. Numerous examples could be found for what in our view constitutes *excessive policy volatility*. By excessive we mean that these policy changes are too extreme or too frequent to allow the policies to mature and to reap public legitimacy.

We interpret these cases of excessive policy volatility as instances of policy failure. Reforms do not seem to deliver the public satisfaction among voters or the elites and are therefore reversed. For such an understanding of 'excessive' policy volatility, it does not matter how to define an optimal, non-excessive policy. Whether you start a reform-reversal episode with a big push towards nationalization or towards privatization, if the reforms are short lived the transition and implementation costs of each reform are likely to outweigh the perceived benefits. To give an example, one does not need to take a stance on the relative merits of public versus private pension or health care systems to see that swinging radically between the two options will not resolve fundamental policy problems, but exacerbate them.

Such an understanding of policy failure will mitigate an old problem of the policy failure literature (McConnell 2010; Howlett 2012): how to make non-normative claims about policy failure, given that the underlying policy problems are always collective, controversial, and value-laden issues. We narrow down policy failures to instances of repeated or extreme reforms and re-reforms. These can come in many sorts and shapes (depending on the temporal horizon). Examples include pendulum movements and classic policy cycles, as well as policy bubbles and boom–bust cycles. To make these types of volatility analytically traceable, we relate them to the recent discussion on disproportionate policy change (Maor 2012; Jones et al. 2014; Howlett and Kemmerling 2017).

While there are many reasons for disproportionate policy responses, we argue that one of the most important sources for this volatility is 'external' in the form of cross-border processes of policy diffusion and transfer. We elaborate how different forms of diffusion can contribute to excessive volatility by making governments in the region more likely to implement reforms without the necessary requirements, knowledge, or political support. Empirically, we illustrate these claims with cases of welfare state reforms in the region. We show instances of policy volatility and non-volatility and whether and how they are related to processes of diffusion. CEE is a particularly useful example, because of the rapid speed of economic and political transition, including EU accession, that made the region very vulnerable to instability (Bohle and Greskovits 2012).

Section 2.2 starts out explaining the link between policy failures and excessive policy volatility. We borrow from the literature of disproportionate policy responses to argue that excessive policy volatility comes in various shapes and forms, but that all can be seen as problems of too much rather than too little reform. This section also links instances of excessive volatility to policy diffusion and discusses different scenarios of how the two concepts relate. Section 2.3 gives illustrations for our different scenarios from three policy areas – pensions, health, and family policies – in CEE. Section 2.4, the final section, discusses the analytical and normative implications for the politics of policy transfer in the region. In it, we advance two sets of literature – analyses of policy failure as well as diffusion studies – through application of our concept of excessive policy volatility.

2.2 POLICY FAILURE, DISPROPORTIONATE POLICY CHANGE AND EXCESSIVE VOLATILITY THROUGH DIFFUSION

The policy literature is full of examples of policy fiascos (Bovens and 't Hart 1996), policy disasters (Dunleavy 1995), or policy catastrophes (Moran 2001) as examples of large-scale policy failures. A key challenge

for this literature is to give a non-normative definition of policy failure
(Howlett 2012). McConnell (2010) defines failure as the opposite of policy
success, that is, a policy achieving its previously established goals (see also
Marsh and McConnell 2010). However, often the goals are multiple, value-
laden, and the consequence of collective decisions which make a clear
evaluation of success and failure difficult. Hence, failure has been defined
in many ways: lack of goal attainment, undesirable outcomes, or lack of
public support (Howlett 2012).

The literature shares this old underlying problem of policy valuation
(Zuckerman 2012) with the re-emerging literature on disproportionate
policy responses (Maor 2012; Jones et al. 2014). A disproportionate policy
response is a case of 'over'- or 'under'-investment in a policy relative to the
level of an 'adequate' response. In many policy areas, it is hard to define
what the adequate level of response should be (Howlett and Kemmerling
2017). Below we outline the forms of disproportionate policy responses
and utilize them to conceptualize excessive policy volatility.

The first, and perhaps classic, case of disproportionate policy reaction is an *under-reaction* in the sense that the political process cannot
generate an adequate response to policy problems. One example is the
case of climate change. The social choice literature has talked extensively
about all forms of collective action problems (Mueller 2003), calling the
result coordination failures, policy gridlock, or, less normatively, policy
stability. However, the underlying reasons for under-reaction may well go
beyond cases of rational choice. For instance, there is a large literature on
cognitive failures to perceive risks and challenges (Slovic 1992; Kahneman
2003) showing that inertia is often the result of lack of awareness and
cognitive biases.

In the second case, in recent years scholars have 'imported' the notion of
(financial) bubbles into the realm of politics as cases of policy *over-reaction*
(Jones et al. 2014; Maor 2014). These are cases of political over-investment
in a specific policy area. Examples could be exaggerated political responses
to terrorist attacks or interventions against rare but headline-grabbing
diseases, such as the 'bird flu'. In these cases a bubble can arise that for
various reasons may be sustained for a while. First, political institutions
may make it difficult to reverse the status quo and calibrate the response
early (Jones and Baumgartner 2004). Second, public sentiment might
strongly push politicians in a certain direction. Third, politicians jump on
the bandwagon of what seems to be a popular policy in other instances.
The important point is that eventually the bubble will burst, either because
the policy is self-undermining (Jacobs and Weaver 2014) or because eventually public attention rapidly shifts away from the problem (Baumgartner
and Jones 2002).

We add a third case of disproportionate policy response, *cyclical policies*. Again, this is a well-known phenomenon that has been discussed in various disciplines. Rational choice theorists (Riker 1982) see it as the classic problem of collectively incongruent preferences that lead to cyclical Condorcet instability. Public opinion scholars have long observed attention cycles (Downs 1972). Policy cycles can also be the product of neglect that accumulates problems over time (De Vries 2010) or it may be the result of political mobilization and eventual counter-mobilization by special interest groups and movements (McFarland 1991), 'election-induced' cycles, if you will.

We argue that both bubbles and cycles can be seen as instances of excessive policy volatility: bubbles are excessive in extension, the size of the change, and its eventual undoing; cycles are excessive in the sense of frequency and the instability they provoke. 'Excessive' hence has these two dimensions of *extension* and *frequency*, which can, of course, also occur at the same time. Compared to the traditional policy reform literature, in which reform has often a positive connotation, excessive policy volatility implies that there are too many rather than too few reforms. This is the flipside of the first form of disproportionate response, under-reaction, which in the normative literature often figures as policy gridlock, institutional sclerosis, or *reformstau* (Nickell 1997; Siebert 1997).

While excessive policy volatility still has to be ascertained in the specific cases, it nonetheless alleviates some of the underlying valuation problems. It is clear that large boom and bust movements (bubbles) often come at significant political and economic costs (McCarty et al. 2013). Equally, excessively frequent policy change, especially if it moves in the way of a pendulum, will generally create more costs than benefits for the underlying policy problem. In other words, while the problem of valuation still exists, as there will always be political disagreement about the utility of any single reform, the notion of excessive policy volatility appeals in a broader sense as an example of policy failure. It shrinks the range of undesired political outcomes to a subset to which more people and scholars can agree: excessive policy change that undermines the purpose of any type of reform.

We prime our intuitions with an example: CEE has seen a lot of pension reforms in the last few decades (Holzmann 2012), in the 1990s mainly in the form of privatization, and since the 2000s often as renationalization, that is, reversing the previous reforms (Orenstein 2013). However, no pension system reaches maturity in ten years. In this sense it is (relatively) safe to conclude that this type of frequent policy change constitutes excessive policy volatility. Regardless of whether your ideological predisposition leans towards privatized or public old-age security, there is too much change in the system.

2.2.1   Diffusion as a Driver of Excessive Policy Volatility

Diffusion often plays a fundamental role in causing excessive policy volatility. There are several competing definitions and variations of policy diffusion (Elkins and Simmons 2004; Kemmerling 2007). In the broadest sense diffusion means situations in which a policy change in one country affects a policy change in another country. Compared to diffusion, policy transfer focuses more on the actual transfer of specific policies, and looks more at processes and agents (Dolowitz and Marsh 1996; Marsh and Sharman 2009), and, although we prefer to use the term 'diffusion', these differences should not be overstated. Today, both literatures overlap and, in varying degrees and with different explanations.

All types of transnational learning, and the socially or cognitively biased forms in particular, can accelerate reform processes in a distinctive non-linear fashion. This idea is 'enshrined' in the sometimes misleading notion of an S curve that shows how learning accelerates slowly until a critical mass is reached, and learning takes place tremendously fast (Kemmerling 2008). Heuristically speaking, this is a good illustration of why diffusion may be related to excessive policy volatility: once many countries adopt a certain policy, peer pressure takes over and countries start adopting a policy without fully anticipating the consequences of doing so. Hence diffusion often pushes the likelihood of a government joining the bandwagon and adds another dimension to the boom and bust cycle: it generates a dynamic in which even countries adopt certain policies that don't meet the necessary requirements to make the reforms work in the long run.

This is very obvious in some forms of diffusion in which learning happens in a naïve way or is subject to severe cognitive biases (Weyland 2005). But specialized agents may also contribute to this (excessive) diffusion. Commercial lobbying groups, epistemic communities, and supranational actors can play a huge role in the promulgation of policy changes across countries. Obvious examples are the World Bank and the European Union (EU). Depending on the policy area, there may be other transnational agents of change such as epistemic communities (Haas 1992; Cross 2013), as suggested below in the case of health care user fees. Their presence is a valuable indication of diffusion processes.

Thus there are good reasons to believe that diffusion processes have the potential to catalyse excessive policy volatility. Diffusion makes countries adopt policies for which they barely have the prerequisites in terms of political support or socio-economic fundamentals. The gigantic push to privatize state owned assets in many emerging economies that did not have the social, economic, and political prerequisites to orchestrate such a privatization process, let alone design sophisticated auction models which

Table 2.1   Scenarios of reform outcomes and the role of diffusion

	No (major) reform	Classic reforms	Excessive volatility (i.e. back-and-forth reforms)
Diffusion/learning as the main reason for change or stability	Learning not to do something, by looking at other countries' experiences	Classic innovation via 'transfer' learning	Diffusion-induced bubble or cycle
Domestic processes as the main reason for change or stability	Classic case of status quo prevalence (e.g. due to legacies, institutional inertia)	Domestic policy reform	Domestic bubble or cycle

could not be corrupted in one way or another (Brown et al. 2009), is a good example.

Nevertheless, it is important not to conflate all types of policy volatility with diffusion. Excessive policy changes also happen when governments are notoriously unstable, for instance. There are cases in which volatility has primarily or predominantly domestic reasons. Table 2.1 helps to differentiate all possible combinations of reform outcomes and the role of diffusion.

Table 2.1 shows six different scenarios. We differentiate between three different outcomes: no (major) reforms, classic reforms, and excessive (policy) volatility. The first, *no (major) reforms*, still leaves room for policy dynamics, but these come mainly in the form of lower-order, smaller policy changes, possibly following an incrementalist logic. In some cases, 'no reforms' can be the consequence of trans-border policy learning. That is, if policy making elite in a country look at the 'negative' experience of other countries and decide not to follow the same reform option, this can result in not doing anything (or innovating and doing something different). The perhaps more common case is that inertia is due to national legacies, institutional stickiness, or simply the lack of need to react. In this case, no reform is the consequence of primarily domestic causes, and diffusion processes play a subordinate role.

The second set of scenarios relate to the *classic* type of reforms that require a substantial political and economic investment. In many cases we will see that cross-border learning has played an influential role in engendering the necessary reform pressure, policy ideas, and even political majorities to pass such reforms. But again, it is also possible that such events are merely the consequence of domestic processes such as shifting majorities or increasing pressure to react to some domestic problem (Collier and Messick 1975). The crucial difference from the third outcome, excessive policy volatility, is that classic reforms are stable and not easily reversible.

By contrast, *excessive policy volatility* means that either major reforms are substantively altered (and, if many countries follow this path, we might call this a diffusion bubble) or we observe a back-and-forth pattern in which countries first adopt a certain type of policy because it is pushed by some form of international learning in one direction, only to reverse it a short time later. When this happens on a recurrent basis, we may call these cyclical reforms. The following section demonstrates the occurrence of the different scenarios presented above.

2.3 DIFFUSION AND POLICY VOLATILITY IN CEE WELFARE REFORMS

This section provides examples of reform reversal, cyclical reforms, classic reforms, and no (major) reform from CEE welfare states and summarizes the role of diffusion in the different reform outcomes. We investigate the role of diffusion for promoting reforms and also observe instances where policies did not spread. We focus on three policy areas: pension privatization, introduction of fees into national health care systems, and parental leave. We choose these policy areas as they include some of the most politically salient policy debates in the countries studied. Additionally, comparing these three policy areas provides interesting variation, since a priori not all three areas were equally susceptible to the influence of international policy diffusion, as discussed below: pension is a case of high financial stakes, in which international organizations – through persuasion and hard pressure – play a major role; compared to this case, financial stakes are much lower in family policy, where diffusion and, ultimately, excessive policy volatility should occur less; health policy should fall somewhere in between.

We draw empirical evidence from welfare states in CEE, primarily the Czech Republic, Hungary, Poland, and Slovakia. For each policy area we will choose clear cases of excessive policy volatility and then briefly compare them to cases of classic reforms or even no reforms. The empirical findings suggest that policy diffusion based on more naïve forms of learning tends to increase policy volatility, whereas reforms that were developed for or significantly adapted to the local context promoted greater policy stability, as the political and economic preconditions for reform are more likely to be met.

2.3.1 Pension Privatization: A Case of Excessive Diffusion

The presence of diffusion and learning in the case of pension privatization is clear, as reforms in CEE were clearly based on the World Bank's model (World Bank 1994), were part of a global trend (Brooks 2005), and were clearly supported by the European Union (Orenstein 2013). Furthermore, the World Bank and the International Monetary Fund (IMF) actively promoted and assisted in the formation of pension privatization reforms (Müller 1999; Orenstein 2008). While the timing of the privatization reforms often depended on domestic political factors (Makszin 2013), adoption was undoubtedly a form of emulation with varying degrees of adaptation to national contexts. From 2008, in the context of the global financial crisis, when the privatized pension accounts did not perform well or seemed more insecure, many cases exhibited excessive volatility, such as Hungary, where the system was effectively disbanded, or Slovakia and Poland, where the share of contributions to the private pillar was reduced substantially. The World Bank model was not designed as a way of transitioning from a mature pensions system, and insufficient adaptation of the model implied that reforms were very costly, which certainly contributed to later reforms to reverse or curb the private pillar (Naczyk and Domonkos 2015).

In the case of Hungary and Poland, the first countries in the region to introduce pension privatization, in 1997 and 1998 respectively, reforms were largely designed under governments led by the former communist parties, which were extremely divided on this issue. The involvement of the international organizations tipped the scales in favour of privatization. The World Bank even financed reform teams and supplied members of those teams (Orenstein 2008). In Slovakia, pension privatization reforms took place in 2003 by a government closely aligned to the World Bank's agenda which was openly invited to be involved in the preparation for pension privatization (Lesay 2009). Slovakia seemed to learn from the pitfalls of the Hungarian and Polish reforms, as it introduced additional taxes to cover the transition costs of privatization (Drahokoupil and Domonkos 2012: 290), but even there partisan politics produced cyclical policy volatility.

Following the introduction of the mandatory private pension accounts in Hungary and Slovakia, when the opposition came to power the governments provided opportunities to opt out of private pension contributions. In Slovakia, after a change in power following the privatization reform, the left-wing government brought a partial backlash against the reform in 2006 by making participation optional to new entrants and offered a six-month window for any current participant to opt out. The right-wing government that returned to power in 2010 voted to make participation in the private pension system mandatory again, but the government fell even before the reform was implemented. The left-wing party returned to government and reduced the scale of contributions to the private accounts from 8 per cent to 4 per cent in 2012.

The Slovak case illustrates a cyclical form of policy volatility almost perfectly: whenever a government of a different partisan composition was elected, this government tried to undo whatever had been done by its predecessor. While conservative governments tried to strengthen the conditions for entering and staying in the new private pillar, the left-wing governments tried to persuade employees to opt out of the new system. The result was a policy cycle which greatly undermines the trust people put into the system.

The Hungarian case initially demonstrates elements of a policy cycle, only to be followed by a drastic reform reversal. Following the first change in power after the privatization, the conservative government also offered individuals the option to exit the second pillar, reduced the guarantees on the private pension pay-out, and did not follow the originally scheduled increase to the contribution rates, from 6 per cent to 8 per cent (Augusztinovics et al. 2002; Simonovits 2011). The opt-out option was then removed and the contribution rate increased to 8 per cent after the left-wing government returned to power in 2002 (but the pension guarantee was not reinstated). After the national conservative government returned to power, the mandatory private pension accounts were *de facto* renationalized in 2011, representing the most dramatic reform reversal in the region.

The decision to renationalize private pension accounts was made amidst severe pressure to reduce the fiscal deficit, which was magnified due to conditionality of the IMF bailout package that Hungary received during the crisis. It was a quick one-time relief for the existing deficit. The financial crisis emboldened the Hungarian national conservative government's opposition to the privatized pension pillar, as the performance of the mandatory private pension accounts was extremely disappointing. All in all, the Hungarian 1997 pension reform and its complete reversal in 2011 constitute one of the best examples of excessive policy volatility. Not only did the initial reforms not solve the underlying fiscal problem, but they arguably exacerbated the problems and created new difficulties of oversight, low private returns, and inequity among pensioners.

Though less drastic, in Poland the scope of the private pension contributions was significantly reduced following Hungary's reform. The extent of contributions to the private pillar was decreased from 7.3 per cent to 2.3 per cent in 2011 (Naczyk and Domonkos 2015). Another reform in 2014 transferred assets from the private to the public pension system. Unlike Slovakia and Hungary, where the opposition weakened the reform, in Poland a party that previously supported privatized pensions oversaw the partial reversal and framed it as an attempt to stabilize the private pillar (Rae 2011). This move occurred under great fiscal pressure, as debt levels approached the constitutionally mandated ceiling that triggers automatic spending cuts.

The Slovene and the Czech cases (the latter until 2013) were notable in the region for their persistence in *not* adopting mandatory private pension accounts when other countries did. Czech governments from both the left and the right openly rejected pension privatization and concluded, perhaps from 'negative lesson drawing', that the model was not appropriate for their country, even while reforms were taking place in most neighbouring countries. The introduction of a much more limited second pillar pension system in the Czech Republic in 2013 was reversed after a change in government in 2014. The reform in the Czech case came very late and, possibly as a reaction to other countries' experiences (see Adascalitei and Domonkos in this volume, Chapter 3), was relatively modest and quickly reversed after the financial crisis.

2.3.2   User Fees in Health Care: Some Diffusion, Some Volatility

Compared to pension politics, a priori there is reason to believe that international policy diffusion plays less of a role in health care. Not only do national health care systems differ massively, but they are also much more complex, bestowing organizations with powerful vested interests that are not easy to change (Immergut 1992). Furthermore international organizations were much less assertive in health care compared to pensions (Nelson 2001: 259). An alternative explanatory factor is that like-minded actors from the CEE region formed an epistemic community in which a right-wing think tank based in Slovakia, called Health Policy Institute (HPI), played a visible role in diffusion reform ideas, in particular the introduction of user fees for health services (Löblová 2015).[1] This epistemic community was composed of academics, journalists, and politicians, who advocated market-based reforms to health care systems, including user fees. HPI advisors claimed greater understanding of the current CEE health care systems and needed reforms based on similarities between Slovakia and other CEE countries. After directly advising (or working within) the Slovak government during a major health care reform, HPI advisors gained direct access to ministers of health and other governmental officials in other CEE countries who viewed their approach as modern and had a shared understanding of the need for market principles in health care (Löblová 2016).

Representatives from HPI were active in preparing the major health care reform in Slovakia between 2002 and 2004. Later, advisors from HPI served as consultants in Croatia, Hungary, and the Czech Republic before the introduction of user fees into the health care system.[2] Sometimes they worked under the auspices of the World Bank and at other times independently. Following consultations with HPI, Hungary (in 2007) and the Czech Republic (in 2008) introduced user fees into their health care systems. Both of these reforms were reversed. HPI also served as a consultant to the Polish government on its hospital privatization reform, but Poland did not introduce user fees. In this section, we demonstrate how the user fee model actively promoted by HPI was not politically sustainable.

The Slovak reform model was developed by HPI and was a part of a broader reform process. The user fees were introduced in 2003 and were generally unpopular among the public. They were challenged in the constitutional court in 2004, but the court upheld the fees as legitimate. The user fees were then abolished in 2006 after the change in government, along with many other reform reversals. The left-wing government removed most of the co-payments, but left the fee for emergency services. Despite the reversal in Slovakia, HPI functioned as a consultant to neighbouring countries and continued to advocate the introduction of user fees.

In Hungary, the introduction of user fees was part of a broader health care reform package aimed at curbing costs and restricting perceived overuse of health services (and timed together with other reforms aimed at fiscal consolidation). The reform was reversed after the opposition organized a referendum in April 2008, which motivated half of eligible voters to vote, and over 84 per cent of those who voted opposed the user fees (Baji et al. 2010). The parliament subsequently abolished the user fees for doctor visits and hospitalization. Simultaneously to the policy instability in user fees, excessive volatility characterized a reform to introduce competing health funds into the state insurance system, which was passed by the parliament in December 2007 and thereafter vetoed by the president; the veto was then overturned by the parliament three months later. Following the referendum on user fees, the opposition planned another referendum on the competition reform, but the parliament repealed its own law before the referendum took place, as the same outcome was expected (Gaál et al. 2011: 168). The debates about health care following this decision and social policy reform more broadly led the liberal coalition partner to withdraw from the government (Palonen 2009), which created greater uncertainty about the future of health care reform.

Similarly, in the Czech Republic, the reform created significant controversy and public outcry, and contributed to a sweeping victory for the social democratic opposition in the regional elections in 2009 (van Ginneken et al. 2010). While the opposition was unable to reverse the reform in the parliament or by appeals to the constitutional court in 2008, most regional governments introduced reimbursement schemes for user fees, shifting the burden from individuals to regional administrations. As a result, it was difficult to determine the effect of user fees on individual use of health care services. After the government lost a vote of no confidence, the subsequent caretaker government reduced the ceiling for the fees, but left the system intact. In 2013, when the case was again brought before the constitutional court, the user fees for hospital stays were ruled unconstitutional on the basis that they unfairly affected vulnerable groups (Alexa et al. 2015: 65). Most of the remaining fees were abolished by the new government in 2015. This is a clear example of excessive policy volatility, as between 2008 and 2015 the reform was implemented, undermined by regional governments, partially restricted by a caretaker government, partially reversed by the constitutional court, and finally reversed when the social democratic party led the government. Both the Hungarian and the Czech cases serve as examples of how introducing a reform without the political prerequisites can lead to excessive policy volatility.

In Poland, no user fees were introduced, even though HPI did serve as a consultant in Poland in 2008. At first glance, this is a case of no reform and policy stability. However, the introduction of user fees was discussed in consultations with stakeholders in 2008, but then was postponed while the liberal-conservative government focused on a hospital privatization reform (Watson 2011: 70). The hospital privatization reform was passed in 2008, but then was vetoed by the president. Given the president's clear opposition to the marketization of health care, no other major reforms were passed in parliament. Rather the government tried to find alternative methods that did not require a change of law, referred to as 'Plan B: Save Polish Hospitals'. Accordingly, Poland also experienced excessive volatility following consultations with the HPI think tank, even if not specifically in the area of user fees.

In Slovakia, Hungary, and the Czech Republic, user fees were introduced with inspiration from reformers from neighbouring countries who prioritized efficiency in health care provision, but without sufficient public and political support, leading to reversal by oppositions. The instability of user fees makes it difficult even to assess the effectiveness of these tools for generating revenue and curbing unnecessary use of medical services.

2.3.3   Parental Leave: Little Diffusion, Minor Changes

Compared to the two other policy areas we expect diffusion to matter least in the field of parental leave, as expenditure is relatively low and there are strong historical legacies behind these policies (Szikra and Tomka 2009). There are also strong ideological arguments for family leave that are hard to overturn by foreign proposals and interventions that are mainly framed in terms of 'efficiency', 'cost-effectiveness', or 'deficit reduction'. The basic structures of parental leave schemes in each of the countries have remained intact over the last 25 years. Pressure from the EU did lead to anti-discrimination measures and increased flexibility for working parents, but on the whole these policies are less susceptible to reversal, as will be explored below.

There have been two major reforms. The first, in Hungary, was part of a larger austerity package supported by the IMF and World Bank in 1995, the government removed a two-year insurance-based maternity leave, leaving a six-month generous insurance-based leave and a much less generous universal leave until the child is three years old. Even this removal of one of the three forms of parental leave generated significant public opposition, including protests, and the reform was reversed by the same government. This is another example of a reform that was backed by the IMF and World Bank, but lacked sufficient public and political support, as even the government was divided on the austerity package. This parental leave reform and quick reversal even seemed to create a precedent, and no subsequent governments have since attempted to reduce the generosity of parental leave in Hungary.

The second major reform was in the Czech Republic in 2006–2007, which doubled the level of parental leave and introduced a three-track system where parents choose to take between two and four years of leave and have financial incentives to shorten their leave. This reform was quite unique in the region. It seems a clear example of a mainly domestic process, in which diffusion played no visible role, and which has produced – so far – no evidence for future reversals. Part of the reason for its stability may lie in the fact that this reform seemed to produce minimal change in the action of parents, as most mothers still opt for the pre-existing three-year leave (Saxonberg et al. 2013).

One aspect of parental leave where diffusion played a visible role is anti-discrimination. We see that the EU played an active role in promoting formal gender equalization, and the extension of rights for parental leave to fathers occurred around the time of EU accession. However, the 'devil lies in the details' of the reform. Parental leave was made available to fathers without offering incentives for fathers to take the leave instead of mothers. Consequently, the uptake of paternity leave was negligible and made the reforms ineffective on the implementation level. In this case, diffusion (in the form of EU pressure) produced negligible change in that there was little incentive to reverse. In more recent years, further supporting gender equalization, the EU encouraged flexibilizing reforms to increase opportunities for parents to work while receiving parental leave benefits, which has brought about reforms in the region since 2010. These reforms have generally been popular and have minimal fiscal impact. Given that these also address the demographic crisis by supporting young parents, they have significant public support and their reversal seems less likely than for other reforms by diffusion.

2.3.4 Summary

Table 2.2 summarizes the case study evidence along the lines of Table 2.1. Looking at Table 2.2 we see some interesting (stylized) patterns. First of all, some policy areas really seem more prone to policy volatility, as expected. Pension policy is clearly more vulnerable than the other two areas. This comes as no great surprise given the stakes involved. But it is also important to note that diffusion pressures seemed nowhere more obvious than in this policy area. (See also Chapter 3 by Adascalitei and Domonkos in this volume.) Perhaps more interestingly, some countries are

Table 2.2   Summary of empirical cases by reform outcomes and the role of diffusion

	No (major) reform	Classic reforms	Excessive volatility
Diffusion/learning as main reason for change	Czech Republic	**Several countries' anti-discrimination in parental leave**	Hungary, Poland (reversal) Slovak Republic (cycle) *Hungary, Czech Republic (reversal)* **Hungary (reversal)**
Domestic processes as the main reason for change or stability	Slovenia *Poland* **Poland, Slovak Republic**	**Czech Republic**	*Slovak Republic (reversal)*

Note: Regular font relates to cases of pension policies, italics refer to cases of health policies, and boldface refers to cases of family policies.

also more prone to volatility than other countries. Hungary seems to be a particularly notable case of short-lived reform attempts, whereas reforms in the Czech Republic were generally more stable.

In many of these cases diffusion has played a clear role, pushing governments to the adoption of policies they could not sustain in the long run. This finding needs to be qualified in several respects. First, there are also a few, but clear, cases in which the main source of instability seemed to be more domestic than international. Second, arguably not all forms of diffusion seem equally likely to push countries to excessive volatility. Especially if a government 'keeps its cool', waits, and looks at the mid- to long-term consequences of a reform, it arguably will make a more informed decision than simply jumping on the bandwagon (e.g. the Czech Republic's pension reform compared to the Hungarian case). Finally, too much diffusion may be related to certain domestic constellations. It is well known that policy failures do not occur everywhere with equal frequency, which may be related to fundamental political stability or state capacity (Howlett and Ramesh 2016). Hence, while our empirics do not provide a clear test, the patterns corroborate the idea that very often diffusion is behind a lot of empirically discernible policy volatility.

2.4 CONCLUSIONS

This chapter first introduced the term 'excessive policy volatility' and related it to the concepts of policy failure and disproportionate policy responses. While the literature often concedes too little change and the risk of rigidities or even institutional sclerosis, the case for too much change is conceptualized less frequently or effectively. By investigating some dimensions of welfare policy in CEE, including some with higher and some with lower volatility, we were able to illustrate different scenarios in which diffusion may or may not play a role in the presence or absence of policy volatility. While we find empirical evidence for all scenarios, the most significant cases nourish our suspicion that international diffusion exacerbates policy volatility in the region.

Again, our findings do not provide a hard empirical test. Our goal was rather to use the cases to illustrate the problem and the importance of excessive policy volatility. While we have an idea about why and when certain types of diffusion lead to more volatility, much more will have to be done on this analytical front. What types of diffusion lead to volatility? What types of learning end up being short-term? What types of domestic structures facilitate this type of learning? We also saw that some policy areas are more prone to major shifts than others.

There are also important normative implications of our argument. In a general sense, international diffusion may create instances of rather too much attention than too little learning. It may prompt actions for which there is insufficient public or political support. Policy learning is not necessarily negative or perverse, but if fused with power and informational asymmetries, such as the advisory hold of an epistemic community, learning can lead down troublesome paths. It can also produce problematic outcomes if cognitive biases among change agents do not allow them to make well-informed choices about policy proposals. This is very clear in the role of specific agents such as the World Bank or the European Union that dispose of both soft and hard power. These organizations sometimes push for very complicated policy designs which require an extraordinary level of state capacity in managing both the reform process and its implementation in the long run. In this sense, accession and other forms of international policy diffusion seem to exacerbate each other, a phenomenon which is well known to scholars in other areas of policy diffusion such as tax competition (e.g. Genschel et al. 2011).

In conclusion, we find that excessive policy volatility is a serious problem in the region, and international diffusion often exacerbates the problem. While we only looked at three specific areas of welfare state policies, we think our argument has larger traction also, for instance for the privatization of utility companies or even for the reform of political institutions. From the cases where we actually see policy stability (either no reforms or classic reforms) we can also observe that broad-scale institutional transformations or policy reforms need to be done with a country-specific speed and direction. Foreign blueprints may be helpful, but only if substantively adapted and translated into the national context. This argument should hold not only for transition economies in CEE, but for different regions and contexts as well.

NOTES

1. For a list of the countries and times of HPI's consultancy, see http://www.hpi.sk/en/2011/05/references/.
2. HPI also advised before a similar Croatian reform. Policy advice in the Hungarian case from 2005 can be found at http://www.hpi.sk/cdata/Documents/Hungary_-_Fiscal_Study.pdf, p. 9 and for the Czech case from 2005 at http://www.hpi.sk/cdata/Documents/Czech_Republic_-_Fiscal_Study.pdf, p. 13.

REFERENCES

Alexa, J., L. Rečka, J. Votápková, E. van Ginneken, A. Spranger and F. Wittenbecher (2015), 'Czech Republic: Health system review', *Health Systems in Transition*,

17 (1), http://www.euro.who.int/en/about-us/partners/observatory/publications/ health-system-reviews-hits.

Augusztinovics, M., R. Gál, Á. Matits, L. Máté, A. Simonovits and J. Stahl (2002), 'The Hungarian pension system before and after the 1998 reform', in E. Fultz (ed.), *Pension Reform in Central and Eastern Europe*, Budapest: ILO, pp. 25–93.

Baji, P., I. Boncz, G. Jenei and L. Gulácsi (2010), 'The short story of co-payments for health care services in Hungary – lessons for neighbouring countries', *Zdrowie Publiczne i Zarządzanie – Zeszyty Naukowe Ochrony Zdrowia*, 8 (1).

Baumgartner, F. and B. Jones (2002), *Policy Dynamics*, Chicago, IL: University of Chicago Press.

Bohle, D. and B. Greskovits (2012), *Capitalist Diversity on Europe's Periphery*, Ithaca, NY: Cornell University Press.

Bovens, M. and P. 't Hart (1996), *Understanding Policy Fiascoes*, New Brunswick, NJ: Transaction.

Brooks, S.M. (2005), 'Interdependent and domestic foundations of policy change: The diffusion of pension privatization around the world', *International Studies Quarterly*, 49 (2), 273–94.

Brown, J., J. Earle and S. Gehlbach (2009), 'Helping hand or grabbing hand? State bureaucracy and privatization effectiveness', *American Political Science Review*, 103 (2), 264–83.

Collier, D. and R. Messick (1975), 'Prerequisites versus diffusion: Testing alternative explanations of social security adoption', *American Political Science Review*, 69 (4), 1299–1315.

Cross, M. (2013), 'Rethinking epistemic communities twenty years later', *Review of International Studies*, 39 (01), 137–60.

De Vries, M.S. (2010), *The Importance of Neglect in Policy-Making*, Basingstoke: Palgrave Macmillan.

Dolowitz, D. and D. Marsh (1996), 'Who learns what from whom: A review of the policy transfer literature', *Political Studies*, 44 (2), 343–57.

Downs, A. (1972), 'The issue–attention cycle', *Public Interest*, 28, 38–50.

Drahokoupil, J. and S. Domonkos (2012), 'Averting the funding-gap crisis: East European pension reforms since 2008', *Global Social Policy*, 12 (3), 283–99.

Dunleavy, P. (1995), 'Policy disasters: Explaining the UK's record', *Public Policy and Administration*, 10 (2), 52–70.

Elkins, Z. and B. Simmons (2004), 'On waves, cluster, and diffusion: A conceptual framework', *Annals of the American Academy*, 598 (1), 1–19.

Gaál, P., S. Szigeti, M. Csere, M. Gaskins and D. Panteli (2011), 'Hungary: Health system review 2011', *Health Systems in Transition*, 13 (5), http://www.euro.who. int/en/about-us/partners/observatory/publications/health-system-reviews-hits.

Genschel, P., A. Kemmerling and E. Seil (2011), 'Accelerating downhill: How the EU shapes corporate tax competition in the Single Market', *Journal of Common Market Studies*, 49 (3), 1–22.

Ginneken, E. van, A. Ottichova and M. Gaskins (2010), 'User fees in the Czech Republic: The continuing story of a divisive tool', *Eurohealth*, 16 (3), 1–3.

Haas, P. (1992), 'Introduction: Epistemic communities and international policy coordination', *International Organization*, 46 (1), 1–35.

Holzmann, R. (2012), *Global Pension Systems and Their Reform: Worldwide Drivers, Trends, and Challenges*, IZA Discussion Papers No. 6800, Bonn: Forschungsinstitut zur Zukunft der Arbeit.

Howlett, M. (2012), 'The lessons of failure: Learning and blame avoidance in public policy-making', *International Political Science Review*, 33 (5), 539–55.

Howlett, M. and A. Kemmerling (2017), 'Calibrating climate change policies: The causes and consequences of sustained under-reaction', *Journal of Environmental Policy and Planning*, online first.

Howlett, M. and M. Ramesh (2016), 'Achilles' heels of governance: Critical capacity deficits and their role in governance failures', *Regulation and Governance*, 10 (4), 301–13.

Immergut, E. (1992), *Health Politics: Interests and Institutions in Western Europe*, Cambridge: Cambridge University Press.

Jacobs, A. and K. Weaver (2014), 'When policies undo themselves: Self-undermining feedback as a source of policy change', *Governance*, 28 (4), 441–57.

Jones, B. and F. Baumgartner (2004), 'A model of choice for public policy', *Journal of Public Administration Research and Theory*, 15 (3), 325–51.

Jones, B., H. Thomas and M. Wolfe (2014), 'Policy bubbles', *Policy Studies Journal*, 42 (1), 146–71.

Kahneman, D. (2003), 'Maps of bounded rationality: Psychology for behavioral economics', *American Economic Review*, 93 (5), 1449–75.

Kemmerling, A. (2007), 'Diffusion und Interaktion in der Arbeitsmarktpolitik? Positive und negative Ansteckungseffekte am Beispiel zweier Reformdiskussionen', *Sonderheft der Politischen Vierteljahresschrift*, 1/2007, 153–79.

Kemmerling, A. (2008), 'The weights you choose, the odds you get: Using different spatial weights. The example of labor market policies', *Concepts and Methods*, 4 (2), 10–13.

Lesay, I. (2009), *Reforming Pensions in Central Europe: Path Dependence and Path Departure in the Pension Systems of Former Czechoslovakia*, Saarbrücken: VDM Verlag Dr. Müller.

Löblová, O. (2015), 'Three worlds of health technology assessment: Explaining patterns of diffusion of HTA agencies in Europe', *Health Economics, Policy and Law*, 11 (3), 253–73.

Löblová, O. (2016), 'Halted diffusion: Epistemic communities and the non-adoption of health technology assessment agencies in Central and Eastern Europe', Dissertation, Central European University, Budapest.

Makszin, K. (2013), 'Reforming East Central European welfare states: Governments, technocrats, and the patterns of quiet retrenchment', Dissertation, Central European University, Budapest.

Maor, M. (2012), 'Policy overreaction', *Journal of Public Policy*, 32 (3), 231–59.

Maor, M. (2014), 'Policy bubbles: Policy overreaction and positive feedback', *Governance*, 27 (3), 469–87.

Marsh, D. and A. McConnell (2010), 'Towards a framework for establishing policy success', *Public Administration*, 88 (2), 564–83.

Marsh, D. and J. Sharman (2009), 'Policy diffusion and policy transfer', *Policy Studies*, 30 (3), 269–88.

McCarty, N., K. Poole and H. Rosenthal (2013), *Political Bubbles*, Princeton, NJ: Princeton University Press.

McConnell, A. (2010), 'Policy success, policy failure and grey areas in-between', *Journal of Public Policy*, 30 (3), 345–62.

McFarland, A. (1991), 'Interest groups and political time: Cycles in America', *British Journal of Political Science*, 21 (3), 257–84.

Moran, M. (2001), 'Not steering but drowning: Policy catastrophes and the regulatory state', *Political Quarterly*, 72 (4), 414–27.

Mueller, D. (2003), *Public Choice III*, Cambridge: Cambridge University Press.

Müller, K. (1999), *The Political Economy of Pension Reform in Central-Eastern Europe*, Cheltenham, UK and Northampton, MA, USA: Edward Elgar Publishing.

Naczyk, M. and S. Domonkos (2015), 'The financial crisis and varieties of pension privatization reversals in Eastern Europe', *Governance*, 29 (2), 167–84.

Nelson, J. (2001), 'The politics of pension and health-care reforms in Hungary and Poland', in J. Kornai, S. Haggard and R. Kaufman (eds), *Reforming the State: Fiscal and Welfare Reform in Post-Socialist Countries*, New York: Cambridge University Press, pp. 235–66.

Nickell, S. (1997), 'Unemployment and labor market rigidities: Europe versus North America', *Journal of Economic Perspectives*, 11 (3), 55–74.

Orenstein, M. (2008), 'Out-liberalizing the EU: Pension privatization in Central and Eastern Europe', *Journal of European Public Policy*, 15 (6), 899–917.

Orenstein, M. (2013), 'Pension privatization: Evolution of a paradigm', *Governance: An International Journal of Policy, Administration, and Institutions*, 26 (2), 259–81.

Palonen, E. (2009), 'Political polarisation and populism in contemporary Hungary', *Parliamentary Affairs*, 62 (2), 318–34.

Rae, G. (2011), 'Poland's stalled pension reform', 9th Annual ESPAnet Conference, Valencia.

Riker, W. (1982), *Liberalism against Populism: A Confrontation between the Theory of Democracy and the Theory of Social Choice*, Prospect Heights, IL: Waveland Press.

Saxonberg, S., T. Sirovátka and M. Janoušková (2013), 'When do policies become path dependent? The Czech example', *Journal of European Social Policy*, 23 (4), 437–50.

Siebert, H. (1997), 'Labor market rigidities: At the root of unemployment in Europe', *Journal of Economic Perspectives*, 11 (3), 37–54.

Simonovits, A. (2011), 'The mandatory private pension pillar in Hungary: An obituary', *International Social Security Review*, 64 (3), 81–98.

Slovic, P. (1992), 'Perception of risk: Reflections on the psychometric paradigm', in S. Krimsky and D. Golding (eds), *Social Theories of Risk*, Westport, CT: Praeger, pp. 117–52.

Szikra, D. and B. Tomka (2009), 'Social policy in East Central Europe: Major trends in the twentieth century', in A. Cerami and P. Vanhuysse (eds), *Post-Communist Welfare Pathways*, Basingstoke: Palgrave Macmillan, pp. 17–34.

Watson, P. (2011), 'Fighting for life: Health care and democracy in capitalist Poland', *Critical Social Policy*, 31 (1), 53–76.

Weyland, K. (2005), 'Theories of policy diffusion: Lessons from Latin American pension reform', *World Politics*, 57 (2), 262–95.

World Bank (1994), *Averting the Old Age Crisis: Policies to Protect the Old and Promote Growth*, Oxford: World Bank.

Zuckerman, E. (2012), 'Construction, concentration, and (dis)continuities in social valuations', *Annual Review of Sociology*, 38, 223–45.

3. Learn from thy neighbor: Emulation and learning in Eastern European mandatory private pensions reforms

Dragos Adascalitei and Stefan Domonkos

3.1 INTRODUCTION

Following from the previous chapter, this chapter analyzes in greater detail one of the most prominent cases of policy diffusion in the post-socialist space: that of pension privatization, that is, the introduction of mandatory privately managed pension schemes with the intention of partially replacing public old-age social security programs. Pension privatization set foot in Eastern Europe in 1998, when Hungary and Kazakhstan embarked on attempts to replace their public pay-as-you-go (PAYG) defined-benefit systems with fully funded private pension schemes, also known as the second pillar of old-age social security. Inspired by the Chilean example, and brokered by the World Bank (WB), the reforms promised to solve the long-term fiscal problems created by demographic aging, while ensuring that future pensioners would be protected against poverty (World Bank 1994). With the help of the WB, which strongly endorsed the policy at the time, privatization quickly spread in most of the countries in the region, which opted for implementing national variations of the policy.

As a result, by the time the region's two pension-reform laggards, the Czech Republic and Romania, implemented their pension privatization reforms in 2013 and 2008 respectively, there was considerable experience available in their post-socialist peer nations that they could use to their benefit. As the case studies in this chapter demonstrate, the two countries indeed learned from the earlier reformers, albeit to different degrees. The Czech policymakers relied to a large extent on the examples of their peer nations from the Visegrad Four (V4) region. They quickly identified a number of obvious policy mistakes that ought to be avoided if the Czech reform were to become a success. By comparison, Romania learned policy lessons drawn particularly from the examples of Bulgaria and Poland and focused on choosing a "well-sized" funded pillar that would be fiscally sustainable.

Notwithstanding these differences between the Czech and Romanian cases, the outcomes of both reform attempts were rather unstable. The new Social Democratic government of the Czech Republic had already begun shutting down the second pillar in January 2016. While the Romanian second pillar is still functioning, its size has been curtailed. More importantly, the scheme is perceived critically for the limited amounts of pension wealth savers managed to accumulate in the first half-decade of its existence.

The two cases analyzed are examples of limited learning from peer nations. The reform-minded elites of the Czech Republic and Romania have largely ignored that Eastern European countries provided very scant evidence for the positive effect of pension privatization on economic growth and on the capital markets. They also ignored that, in several early reformers, the lack of broad consensus on the policy at the time of its introduction threatened its survival later on. However, they have paid attention to lessons about the parameters and details of the new private scheme. Particular attention was given to the size of the new scheme and the initial deficit the policy generates, but also to the regulation of marketing and of the payout phase. Although learning from the experience of earlier reformers did take place, it was rather selective and biased.

Significantly, the adoption of the policy itself, as well as the learning effort that surrounded it, happened without the direct influence of the European Union (EU). Even if strict rules in fiscal matters increased the importance of limiting the costs of the reform (Casey 2014), the EU neither promoted nor opposed pension privatization. This shows that learning can also take place when there are neither coercive means nor strong incentives offered by external influences.

3.2   THE DIFFUSION OF PENSION PRIVATIZATION IN EASTERN EUROPE

Pension privatization began to gain ground in Eastern Europe during the first half of the 1990s (see Figure 3.1), when the positive macroeconomic outcomes of the Chilean pension reforms became visible across the world (Brooks 2005). The Chilean model of pension reform was in tune with the ideological inclinations of the majority of Eastern European governments, which sought to cut back their state-managed redistributive welfare systems and assign a greater role to markets in social security provision. Besides, the Chilean model of reform promised to address the policy failures generated by *parametric* pension adjustments, which made public pension systems too expensive to be sustained, while often leaving large

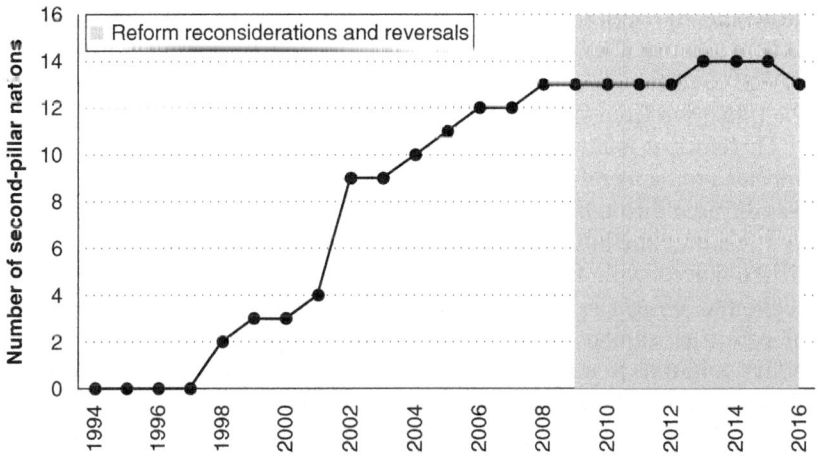

Source: Authors' own figure based on Price and Rudolph (2013) and Adascalitei and Domonkos (2015).

Figure 3.1   *The diffusion of the second pillar across Eastern Europe and Central Asia (number of countries that adopted the second pillar)*

groups of pensioners in poverty. Parametric pension adjustments denote pension reforms that do not change the institutional structure of public pension systems but adjust pension generosity levels through shifts in benefit calculation formulas, benefit indexation procedures, social security contribution rates and so forth.

Moreover, the diffusion of the privatization agenda was brokered by the efforts of the WB, which coordinated with a variety of other international actors in *campaign coalitions* that promoted the reform (Orenstein 2008). The WB has been the central player in promoting pension privatization around the world, but its efforts were also helped by other international agencies such as the Organisation for Economic Co-operation and Development (OECD) and the United States Agency for International Development. The institution linked privatization with positive economic outcomes, such as higher economic growth, higher rates of domestic savings and the development of national capital markets (World Bank 1994). These were desirable ends for governments in Eastern Europe because their transitions from state socialism were riddled by economic and debt crises. Thus, as was the case in Latin America a decade earlier, pension privatization was linked with economic development goals which represented a long-standing aspiration of East European countries

(Weyland 2009). In this context, pension privatization came with a promise to help countries in their efforts to catch up with their West European peers as well as to solve some of the social and economic problems generated by the transition from state socialism.

Therefore, it is no surprise that pension privatization was a policy that appealed to many reformers in the region. As the literature notes, the policy was diffused through learning from the experience of peer countries as well as a result of the influence exercised by international financial institutions (IFIs). Faced with the need to reform their pension systems, domestic economic reformers searched for policy solutions that were adopted in countries similar to their own. However, rather than searching for policy solutions in a fully rational manner, decision-makers used cognitive shortcuts for selecting between alternative pathways of reform (Weyland 2009). These shortcuts included the *availability*, *representativeness* and *anchoring* heuristics. The "availability" shortcut refers to the phenomenon that policy-makers prefer vivid, visible and salient cases when collecting information. The "representativeness" heuristic provides an explanation for policy-makers' overconfidence in deriving conclusions from a small amount of data: although few cases are available, policies are designed by drawing lessons from them while ignoring other relevant information. Finally, "anchoring" refers to the tendency to converge towards a benchmark given by a pre-determined baseline scenario. In the particular case of international policy diffusion, the policy pathways of peer nations can serve as such baseline scenarios (Tversky and Kahneman 1974; Weyland 2009).

These shortcuts help explain the geographical clustering of the policy, and its temporal unfolding, as well as its common features shared across a diverse set of polities. The availability shortcut helps account for the regional diffusion of pension privatization. While decision-makers sought for alternative solutions to reform, they paid attention to the policies that their neighbors used for addressing similar problems. In this respect both cultural affinity and spatial proximity mattered for the pattern of diffusion of pension privatization. Furthermore, the representativeness heuristic impacted the perceived applicability of the reform in different economic settings. In this sense, the representativeness heuristic determined a biased assessment of the effectiveness of pension privatization, based on lessons drawn from selected countries. Finally, the anchoring heuristic explains why, despite the rather different political and economic conditions that marked the transition of each country, pension privatization shared a remarkable set of commonalities across these different nations. Even so, this does not mean that second pillars are identical across countries.

However, policy-makers did not learn only from their peer nations, as the cognitive shortcuts theory may suggest at first sight, but also from IFIs, which sought to exert influence on domestic policy agendas. While the literature remains split on the magnitude of the influence of international actors on national instances of pension privatization, there is widespread agreement that these actors have relentlessly pressed for its diffusion worldwide (Orenstein 2008). In this respect, transnational actors used both hard and soft power resources to help diffuse the policy across different countries. In its most straightforward version, IFIs used the opportunities created by economic and financial crises to promote the policy through financial constraints (Müller 2003; Brooks 2005). Additionally, IFIs used soft power resources to raise awareness about the privatization agenda and ensure that it became part of the national policy debates. These resources included technical assistance to pension-reform teams, training sessions for senior government officials, financing of public relations campaigns and organization of international conferences on pension privatization. The soft power approach proved more effective in pushing for the privatization of public pensions both because policy-makers did not perceive the policy as being imposed from above and because it created a constituency in favor of privatization that, in many countries, continued to exist even after the reform was adopted.

In sum, learning from advanced reformers and from IFIs facilitated the first wave of pension privatizations in Eastern Europe. However, as the reforms that were implemented at the end of the 1990s began to take shape and make their effects visible, both national and international policy-makers began to pay attention to their own experience with pension privatization. In this regard some of the mistakes made by the early pension privatizers became visible. First, it became obvious that the fiscal burden created by shifting part of the social security contributions onto private accounts was underestimated. This became a major point of criticism against private pensions in many Eastern European countries and was used as a motivation for rolling back some of the early reforms, as shown by the examples of Poland and Hungary (Drahokoupil and Domonkos 2012; Datz and Dancsi 2013). Second, in many countries pension privatization reforms were implemented with a disregard to whether a basic regulatory and financial infrastructure was in place. This resulted in the low impact of the newly created private pillars on the domestic capital markets, and therefore also on economic growth, and in low protection of minority shareholders (Rudolph 2012). Third, administration and marketing costs were excessively high, as market competition between funds did not lead to low management fees, while in many cases the payout phase remained poorly regulated (Lindeman et al. 2000).

Nevertheless, despite the fact that the shortcomings of the reform became evident a decade after it was first adopted, some countries opted to go on with introducing private pillars. This provides a measure of the success that the international campaign to introduce private pensions had amongst domestic policy-makers. It is noteworthy that, almost two decades after the World Bank campaign started, the privatization agenda in Romania and the Czech Republic was advocated by the same national actors that promoted the policy during the first wave of reforms, but failed to implement it due to the strong political opposition that they faced at home (Adascalitei and Domonkos 2015). This is even more surprising given that the WB itself changed its position towards privatization around the mid-2000s as a result of criticism coming from external experts as well as from its own ranks (Orenstein 2011).

Against this background, the late privatizers could have benefited from the experience of their peer nations and learned from their examples as well as from the more critical positions taken by the World Bank's own experts. Importantly, they could have benefited from the experience of structurally similar countries that introduced private pillars more than a decade earlier. Yet, in the case of the two late privatizers discussed in this chapter, the domestic policy debates around the introduction of the private pillars have been only selectively informed by the experience of early reformers. As a result, this chapter argues that some of the mistakes made during the first wave of privatization have been reproduced by the late reformers. In addition, heuristic biases can lead to the adoption of unsuitable policies even in cases when domestic elites correctly identify the mistakes of earlier reformers and attempt to account for them. For instance, as will be argued in greater detail in section 3.3, excessive reliance on conclusions drawn from a small number of observations has led to the adoption of an overregulated second pillar in the Czech Republic. As the empirical discussion will show, neither financial agents nor their clients considered the new Czech pension scheme attractive.

With the exception of the double-payment problem (that is, the situation in which present tax payers have to finance current retirees while also saving for their own retirement), which in the case of the late privatizers received more attention, the framing of the policy discourse around the introduction of private pensions was strikingly similar to the debates that took place a decade earlier in other countries in the region. In particular, the policy was framed as the only sustainable solution to the problem of demographic aging. Moreover, the critics of the reform did not present pension-reform alternatives acceptable to the public, but rather advocated for reforms that remained highly unpopular amongst constituents. These comprised proposals to increase retirement ages, cut special retirement benefits or adopt less generous benefit indexation formulas. Pension privatization has thus once again gained the position of the only credible solution to the looming pension crisis, and a preferred alternative to the retrenchment measures advocated by its critics.

3.3   THE CASE OF THE CZECH REPUBLIC

Discussions about the introduction of private funding into the Czech pension system go back to the first half of the 1990s. Nevertheless, in contrast to its post-socialist neighbors, the Czech Republic maintained its pension reforms within the boundaries of the European continental tradition (Müller 1999). Instead of a paradigmatic shift, the Czech governments of the 1990s and early 2000s – several of which were center-right – managed to reform the pension system, keeping it within the confines of the public sector, and build up a moderately successful complementary private voluntary scheme.

The literature points out three reasons for this Czech exceptionalism. First, the soundness of Czech public finances and, more importantly, of the Czech social security budget in the 1990s lowered the importance of the finance ministry and the World Bank in the domestic pension-reform debate. The pension system thus stayed within the portfolio of the Ministry of Welfare, traditionally inclined towards parametric changes (Müller 1999, 2002).

Second, Czech social democracy was in a considerably better position than the social democratic movements in other post-socialist nations. The Czech Social Democratic Party (ČSSD) could rely on a distinct pre-war tradition and did not need to exert much effort distancing itself from a communist past (Grzymala-Busse 2002). As a result, ČSSD could credibly oppose all attempts at replacing the public PAYG system with private funded schemes (Adascalitei and Domonkos 2015). As a side note, the situation was different in other V4 nations. After some internal discussions, the Hungarian Socialist Party agreed to introduce a mandatory private funded system (Simonovits 2011). Similarly, the second pillar in Poland came into being as a common project of the reformed left and the free-market liberals (Guardiancich 2013; Naczyk and Domonkos 2016).

Third, opposition against mandatory private funding also came from the Czech center-right. Arguing that old-age social security is essentially an individual responsibility, Václav Klaus's Civic Democratic Party (ODS) supported a small egalitarian public scheme and voluntary, state-subsidized private pension savings (Klaus 2002). Therefore, uniquely in the region, opposition towards mandatory funding in the Czech Republic came from both sides of the political spectrum.

While the substitution of public pension provision by funding did not take place in the late 1990s and early 2000s, when regional enthusiasm for the policy was at its height, pension reform returned to the top of the political agenda in 2004. This increase in its prominence followed the publication of the first actuarial report on the social security system (Ministry of Labor and Social Affairs of the Czech Republic, 2003a), and of a comprehensive study of the Ministry of Labor and Social Affairs on the main principles of the social security system and its possible reforms (Ministry of Labor and Social Affairs of the Czech Republic, 2003b). These analyses drew attention to the consequences demographic aging may have for the soundness of Czech public pension finances. The Social Democratic government of Vladimír Špidla, who previously served as Minister of Welfare (1998–2002), in agreement with the opposition, created in 2004 an expert committee on pensions led by economist Vladimír Bezděk, whose main objective was to evaluate the pension-reform proposals of parliamentary political parties (Rudolfová et al. 2014). The committee carried out this task during 2004 and 2005 (Pensions Committee 2005), and its work did not lead to the adoption of any reform. The apparent differences between the policy preferences of the governing coalition parties were so large that no significant policy shifts could take place (Pensions Committee 2005; Večerník 2006). Nevertheless, the final report of the executive team included an expert opinion on the possible solutions to the looming Czech pension crisis. Among these solutions, the introduction of a funded defined-contribution retirement scheme was given a prominent role (Pensions Committee 2005). Part of the explanation why no significant reform took place after the publication of the report is that Czech politics sank into a period of extreme volatility between 2005 and 2009 (Adascalitei and Domonkos 2015). Therefore, no significant pension reform could take place during these years.

In 2010, a caretaker government directed by high-level technocrat Jan Fischer re-established the Bezděk pension committee, this time with a mandate to propose a pension reform. The subsequent coalition of free-market liberal parties that took over in 2010 soon agreed on the need to reform the pension system. Prime Minister Petr Nečas, who also served as Minister of Welfare between 2006 and 2009, publicly declared his willingness to respect the conclusions of the pension committee (Vašek 2010).

As the pension-reform debate among the Czech political elite began to gain momentum, it became clear that foreign experience, primarily from the Slovak Republic, would be given considerable weight. Welfare Minister Jaromír Drábek announced after a meeting with his Slovakian counterpart in June 2010 that the "[Czech government] will not follow the Slovak pension reform as such, but it will gain inspiration from the experience with implementing such a reform and its first few years of practical functioning" (*Novinky.cz* 2010).

The most important lesson learned from the Slovak case was that transition costs are to be taken seriously. By 2010, it had become increasingly clear to policy-makers, both in Prague and in Bratislava, that a large mandatory funded scheme can only be financed at the cost of immense cuts in other areas of the government or through debt financing. In reaction to the Slovak experience, the Czech government made a deliberate effort to limit the magnitude of its second pillar. Not only did the Czech reformers restrict the size of the opt-out to just three percentage points of gross wage, as opposed to nine percentage points in the Slovak Republic, but they limited the numbers of new entrants. The Czech government also made the system entirely voluntary for all cohorts, increased the compulsory contribution rate by two percentage points for second-pillar members and heavily regulated the remuneration of financial brokers promoting the new pension scheme. These measures successfully limited the number of savers. Moreover, for the first time among CEE reformers, reform-minded elites presented a viable long-term plan for the financing of the transition period, by increasing value added tax (VAT). Nevertheless, learning took place also in other, more technical areas of the reform, such as the specification of the payout phase, a lack of which was heavily criticized in Hungary and the Slovak Republic.

The first, most salient instance of learning among Czech political elites concerned the decision on the magnitude of the opt-out allowed by the pension reform. In 2010–2012, when the Czech second pillar was designed, the first reversals of the policy had already taken place in other post-socialist nations. Hungary nationalized its second pillar in 2010–2011. Poland decided to significantly limit its mandatory funded scheme in 2011. Slovakia followed suit in September 2012 (e.g. Casey 2014; Naczyk and Domonkos 2016). High transition costs were among the key reasons for these reversals.

As reports of meetings between the Czech and Slovak welfare ministries show (*Novinky.cz* 2010), the Czech government was aware of the high burden to which the double-payment problem leads in countries with a large second pillar. While some of the advisors at the Ministry of Welfare initially supported an opt-out of five percentage points (*Novinky.cz* 2011), the legislation adopted allowed only three percentage points of compulsory social security contributions to be diverted from the public to the new private scheme. In relation to this decision, Deputy Finance Minister Radek Urban noted, when presenting the paradigmatic pension reform in the media, that the Hungarian, Polish and Slovak cases were perceived as "cautionary tales" by the Czech policy-makers (*Český rozhlas* 2012).

In order to further limit the size of the second pillar, and to avoid the enrollment of individuals with low and unstable income, which was one

of the main weaknesses of the Slovak funded scheme, the Nečas government opted for a two-percentage-point increase in the compulsory social
security contribution rate of second-pillar members. A decrease in dispos-
able income was expected to dissuade low-earning groups from enrolling
into a system where the future level of pensions crucially depends on past
contributions. As a final step aimed at limiting the size of the second pillar,
the reform package adopted did not introduce automatic enrollment in the
new pension savings scheme.

In contrast to earlier reformers, some of whom expected the second
pillar to be financed by future economic growth, Czech policy-makers
have demonstrated considerably more foresight when dealing with the
long-term financing of the transition costs. The Nečas government tied
the pension reform to a significant increase in VAT, which was to cover the
deficit of the social security system. The first VAT increase took place in
2012, and was expected to yield approximately 26 billion Czech korunas
(0.9 billion euros) to the budget. This was followed by another, smaller
upward adjustment in 2013. None of the earlier reformers have shown
such effort to communicate a viable financing strategy for the reform.
The regulation of the annuity payout phase was also incorporated in the
reform package adopted in 2011–2012. In this respect, the Czech Republic
significantly differed from other countries. The Slovak Republic only
adopted its payout legislation in 2014, eight years after the start of the
reform. The Hungarian second pillar was left without a clear regulation of
the payout phase overall. Avoiding this problem, the Czech reformers gave
more credibility to their proposal by specifying most of the rules directly
influencing the expectable level of future pensions at the time of establishing the second pillar.

Nevertheless, the Czech policy-making elite tried to protect the reputa-
tion of the new pension savings scheme also in other ways. A close evaluation of the Slovak reform process convinced the Nečas government that the
size of the remuneration for financial intermediaries needed to be strictly
regulated by the state. Such regulation was not present in 2003–2004 in the
Slovak Republic, which led to heavy use of aggressive direct marketing by
brokers. In order to avoid this, the Czech legislation capped remuneration
for brokers to only 3.5 percent of the average wage (approximately 33 euros
per contract), which is a level well below the remuneration for other prod-
ucts. As pointed out by several policy-makers during a series of personal
interviews carried out by the authors, the role of financial intermediaries
in promoting the new policy was more important than expected, and the
overregulation of their activity resulted in large losses for the second pillar.

To sum up, the second pillar, as adopted by the 2010–2013 Nečas government, was a more carefully designed and less costly version of the private

pension schemes adopted by earlier reformers among the Visegrad Four countries. The Czech Republic has apparently learned its lesson. First, the second pillar should not allow a large opt-out, as this will make the reform costs unbearable for the state. Second, the policy-maker should actively shape incentives in such a way that only better-earning workers join the scheme. Otherwise, the second pillar might become overly popular even among income groups that would lose out by joining it. Third, the payout phase should be dealt with as soon as possible, in order to increase the credibility of the new scheme. While several of these policy choices were appropriate reactions to possible shortcomings of a paradigmatic pension reform, the Czech experience also demonstrates how the representativeness heuristic might lead to overconfident judgments about the public's reaction to a reform. Having witnessed several cases where the second pillar became "too" popular, and where financial brokers used aggressive marketing to sell this product, Czech policy-makers chose to cap the intermediaries' remuneration. Nevertheless, they seriously overestimated public interest in the second pillar, and underestimated the importance of direct marketing in the Czech financial industry. This contributed significantly to the failure of the new pension scheme. As of May 2014, out of the country's 4 million employees and self-employed workers, only 83 000 had enrolled in the second pillar, accumulating approximately 820 million Czech korunas (30 million euros) (Pensions Committee 2014b).

However, the Czech case also shows that it is not only the proponents that learn. So do the opponents of the reform. After the elections in November 2013, a left-of-center government assumed power. Social Democratic Prime Minister Bohumil Sobotka and his party openly pledged to reverse the reform even before its start (Mitáč 2012). Once in power, the government led by the Social Democrats created a pensions committee whose first task was to find a way of shutting down the new funded scheme (Pensions Committee 2014a). In January 2016, the second pillar was effectively closed.

The reaction of the Czech opposition to the second pillar differs in two ways from the common reaction of reform opponents in other CEE countries. While oppositions in countries that reformed earlier often declared their disagreement with the privatization of old-age social security, none of them shut down the second pillar at the first possible opportunity (Drahokoupil and Domonkos 2012). A reason behind this was the credence of the arguments used by early reformers to justify the introduction of mandatory pension savings. The new scheme was often argued to be immune to demographic aging. Pointing out the fallacies of this defense of pension privatization, the Czech Social Democrats did not accept this argumentation (*ČT24* 2013), and abolished the new private scheme as soon as possible. Second, while Sobotka and his government opposed the idea of an opt-out from the public system, they still remained in favor of the idea of voluntary and complementary pension savings that would supplement the state-run system. In fact, the end of the second pillar was coupled with an increase in subsidies for voluntary savings in the third pension pillar. In this way, pension privatization, just as some scholars have argued (e.g. Orenstein 2011), has been quickly revived. This revival, however, shifts emphasis to a private system complementary to the public one.

3.4   THE CASE OF ROMANIA

In Romania, the second-pillar reform had been on the agenda of governments since the early 1990s. However, unlike its regional peers, which had introduced private pillars by the beginning of the 2000s, Romania succeeded in implementing the reform only in 2008, after almost two decades of political conflicts over the size and the institutional architecture of the new pension system. The considerable time-span taken for the reform to be implemented allowed the Romanian reformers to draw lessons from the peer nations that already had adopted the reform and to implement institutional adjustments that would have been omitted otherwise. Still, the learning process was incomplete and was based on lessons drawn from a few neighboring countries, resulting in numerous policy mistakes that marked the adoption and implementation of the second-pillar reform.

The Romanian second-pillar reform process was challenging since there was no political consensus around it (Armeanu 2010). As was the case in other Eastern European countries, the World Bank actively supported the policy through financial aid and know-how. However, internally the policy had many opponents. The first serious attempt to introduce the reform was undertaken in 1997 by the center-right government led by the Democratic Convention (DC). The initial proposal supported by the DC was very close to the stance of the WB. The proposal demanded the introduction of a large second pillar, with an initial 8 percent contribution rate that would be introduced simultaneously with a reform that would retrench the public pension system (Adascalitei and Domonkos 2015). The new pillar would become active as of 2000 and would be adopted at once. The Bank actively promoted the second-pillar reform through financial assistance as well as through popularizing the benefits that it brought in other countries. Importantly, it presented the Chilean example of pension reform as a remarkable financial success and invited the president of the Chilean Private Pension Fund to hold talks and meet the Romanian reformers (Cashu 2002).

However, this early attempt to introduce a private pillar failed, as the DC government underwent numerous political reshufflings because of shifting political support in the legislature. Over a two-year period, the planned second-pillar reform was continuously renegotiated with the trade unions, which obtained significant concessions from the government. These included a reduction in the required minimum capital for creating a pension fund and a decrease in the minimum number of participants to a fund from 500 000 to 200 000 (see Casliu 2002). By 1999, owing to approaching elections, it was clear that the legislature would not support the reform. As a result, only months before elections, the Isărescu government passed the second-pillar law through an emergency ordinance, without the support of the Parliament. Nevertheless, the effort to force the introduction of the second pillar was short-lived. The 2000 elections restored to power the center-left Social Democratic Party (SDP), which, as one of its first actions in power, cancelled the emergency ordinance passed only a year earlier.

By this time, a number of successful second-pillar reforms had been implemented in other Eastern European countries. In Bulgaria, the right-wing reformist government that came to power in 1997 adopted the reform without much political opposition. Both the trade unions and bureaucratic elites were appeased through the appointment of a reformist Minister of Labor who came from the union ranks and through concessions in the changes introduced to the public pension system. In comparison with the proposals initially negotiated in Romania, the Bulgarian second-pillar reform was smaller, with an initial 2 percent contribution rate, and was scheduled to be phased in gradually until the contribution reached 5 percent in 2007 (Müller 2000; Adascalitei and Domonkos 2015).

During this time, the Romanian second pillar was put on hold by the SDP government. The official position of the government was summarized in its governing program, which mentioned that the second-pillar law that was passed by the previous government required "a third of the budget of the public PAYG pension system to be transferred into private accounts without specifying the sources from which the public deficit would be covered" (*Monitorul Oficial* 2000). Even though the WB campaigned for the introduction of a private pillar, political opposition made the implementation of pension privatization impossible (World Bank 2005). Still, the WB campaign maintained the possibility of reform on the political agenda and ultimately contributed to the appointment of a pension privatization commission within the Ministry of Labor and Social Affairs in 2003.

The time to put forward a legislative proposal for the introduction of the second pillar was limited due to the upcoming presidential and parliamentary elections. As a result, only a year later, the commission advanced a proposal for a second-pillar reform. Unlike the previous attempt to introduce a private pension system, which required the introduction of a large second pillar, this time the proposed private system was significantly smaller. The proposal made the private system compulsory only for those workers who entered the labor market for the first time, while introducing a contribution rate of 2 percent to be gradually increased to 6 percent over a period of eight years.

The proposal represented a significant departure from the stance of the World Bank (which at the time was still supporting the introduction of large second pillars) and built on some of the lessons learned from earlier reformers. In particular, the commission followed the Bulgarian example of two years earlier and proposed a gradual introduction of the second pillar that aimed to defuse possible political opposition. This was an essential step in ensuring that the reform would not be rejected by the Ministry of Finance, which had concerns about the fiscal impact of privatization (Adascalitei and Domonkos 2015). At the same time, the commission relied on the Polish privatization reform as a model to be followed in setting the regulatory framework for the future second pillar (Seitan 2014). The Romanian reformers were concerned with the general lack of trust in financial institutions and drew on the Polish example, putting forward a system of guarantees that would raise citizens' trust in the future savings scheme.

A year later, only a month ahead of elections, the second pillar was adopted by the Parliament in the form proposed by the Ministry of Labor and Social Affairs without much debate (Armeanu 2010). Although the Romanian private pillar constituted a significant departure from the WB model, the institution considered it to be a significant step towards privatization in Romania. The WB representative in Romania noted that "the institution is very much interested in the final shape of the law and in having the law adopted but that there is a big difference between the adoption of the law and its implementation" (*Ziarul Financiar* 2004). The position was echoed within the financial sector community, which argued that, as adopted in 2004, the pension funds did not represent an attractive business and that the law should be adjusted in order to increase the size of the market, both with respect to contribution rates and in terms of coverage levels (*Capital* 2005).

The debate over the pension privatization reform continued following the change in government brought about by the 2004 elections. The coming to power of the center-right Justice and Truth Alliance represented a major turn in the position of the government towards privatization. Ideologically the Justice and Truth Alliance championed a pro-market reform program that endorsed the privatization and individualization of social security services and the introduction of a flat tax system. As a result, the second-pillar reform came back onto the political agenda, with the government aiming to expand its size in order to make it attractive for the financial sector (*HotNews.ro* 2005b). Yet, despite endorsing the adoption of a larger second pillar, the new government relied on the lessons provided by the earlier reform attempts. In particular, as was the case several years earlier, the issue of the long-term financing of the transition costs was given particular attention. Drawing on the Bulgarian example, the Romanian reformers proposed a mix of sources for financing the deficit of the state pension system that included receipts from privatization, World Bank credits, and state bonds with long-term maturities (*HotNews.ro* 2005a).

Other aspects of the reform also indicate that learning took place. The proposal preserved the gradual raise in the contribution rates in order to minimize the fiscal impact of the reform. Furthermore, it supported the adoption of a tightly regulated second pillar that included a guarantee of return on the absolute value of savings, the establishment of a guarantee fund that supervises the financial performance of pension funds and steps in when a fund registers a rate of return that is lower than the minimum established by law, and a requirement of actuarial reserves for pension funds. A minimum rate of return on savings, adjusted for the rate of inflation, was also debated and supported by the trade unions, but the government did not accept the proposal (*HotNews.ro* 2008).

In 2007, two years after the new government took office, the pension privatization law was finally adopted, with the contributions to the second pillar planned to start in 2008. The final version of the law included the lessons learned from the neighboring countries and introduced a second pillar that was relatively small by the standards of the region, with savings guaranteed by a prudential regulatory framework. In this respect, the outcome of more than one decade of bargaining was a hybrid system that adapted the lessons learned from the early reformers to the Romanian political and economic environment.

Nevertheless, the lengthy process of reform adoption did not safeguard it from attacks similar to the ones that affected the policy in other Eastern European countries (Drahokoupil and Domonkos 2012). In fact, only a year after its adoption, the right-wing Boc government attempted a full reversal, similar to the one that took place in Hungary, arguing that the funds were necessary for supplementing the share the state budget allocated for the following years' investments (*Gandul* 2010). Discussions about the nationalization of the newly created pension fund surfaced in late 2009, when the country was affected by a deep financial and budgetary crisis. Despite the fact that the size of the accumulated funds was very small in comparison with those of other Eastern European countries, the cash-strapped Romanian government perceived it as a potential source of income that could cover the large budgetary deficit generated by the financial crisis. As a result, the government attempted to nationalize the newly created assets but failed to do so due to external pressure coming from the International Monetary Fund (IMF) and the World Bank (*Ziare. com* 2010). The maintenance of the second pillar became a central issue in the negotiations for a stand-by agreement with the IMF, which included it in the list of conditionalities attached to the loan to Romania.

Even though the private pillar was not nationalized, the increase in the contribution rate scheduled for 2010 was suspended (Adascalitei and Domonkos 2015). Furthermore, the fate of the policy remained uncertain in the aftermath of the financial crisis. Between 2010 and 2015 the second pillar was yet again contested, by the left-wing Ponta government, which perceived it to be too costly for the budget as well as too conservative in its investment policy into state bonds. While the government discarded the possibility of full nationalization of funds' assets after numerous discussions with the IMF, it did suggest that a re-evaluation of the second pillar was necessary in order to adjust it to the needs of the Romanian economy (*Capital* 2014).

Furthermore, the second pillar was impacted by the fiscal policy promoted by the government. The "fiscal relief package" adopted in 2014 and 2015 included amongst other measures a 4 percent cut in VAT levels as well as a reduction of 5 percent in the employers' social security contribution rates. While the 5 percent cut in contribution rates was criticized by both the IMF and the President, the Parliament passed the law with a significant majority (*Mediafax.ro* 2015a). With no other sources to cover the deficit of the social security system, the scheduled increase in the contribution rate to the second pillar was again postponed in 2016. As a result, contributions to the private scheme in 2016 remained at 5.1 percent of covered income instead of the planned 6 percent. The Romanian government raised the contribution rate for 2016 by only 0.1 percent in order to signal to the financial sector industry that it did not plan to nationalize the funds or introduce further cutbacks in the contribution rate (*Mediafax.ro* 2015b).

In sum, the Romanian case reveals a difficult process of learning, during which pension privatization was continuously renegotiated between competing political factions. As the reform proceeded very slowly in comparison with that of regional peers, numerous aspects regarding the implementation of the second pillar were put under discussion: the size of the contributions and the fiscal impact of the reform on the public pension system, the coverage of the future second pillars, and the supervisory mechanisms that could create trust in the private system. The main outcome of the learning process was a smaller second pillar that was planned to cover around 20 percent of pensioners' income. However, this did not safeguard it from attempts to limit even more its size or even to entirely nationalize its assets. In this respect, in the Romanian case, both the IMF and the World Bank played a key role in ensuring that the second pillar will be kept in place. Still, as the deficit of the first pillar is planned to increase in the upcoming years, the fate of the Romanian second pillar remains uncertain.

3.5 CONCLUSION

This chapter has provided a comparative analysis of the pension privatization pathways of two Eastern European reformers, the Czech Republic and Romania, which introduced the policy at a time when some other countries in the region were rolling back the reform. It showed that policy learning has played an important role in the two cases of late privatization by bringing into the debate some of the issues that were sidelined during the first wave of reforms. These concerned primarily the problem of the fiscal sustainability of the second pillars as well as the regulatory rules that would safeguard the functioning of the future private pension systems. The chapter also showed that the two late reformers have relied on lessons drawn primarily from geographically close and structurally similar nations.

However, the learning process has been uneven, with Czech and Romanian policy-makers relying on the heuristic shortcuts of availability, representativeness and anchoring. Ultimately, this biased learning process did not lead to a more coherent and sustainable policy outcome. In both cases, policy-makers acted from a position of overconfidence in their conclusions drawn from the limited number of countries. This led to a fear among Czech policy-makers that the second pillar would be too popular and, subsequently, to the implementation of overly stringent measures curtailing the new pension pillar's size. Focusing primarily on the Bulgarian example, Romanian policy-makers adopted the perception that gradual increases in the contribution size would guarantee the reform's survival.

In the case of the Czech Republic, the second pillar was abolished in 2016, after a coalition of Social Democratic and Liberal parties entered government. In Romania, the policy is heavily criticized due to its failure to generate sufficient savings for future pensioners while becoming too expensive to support in the medium term. Policy learning did not prevent a reversal in the case of the Czech Republic and generated only a partial success in the case of Romania. Despite these mixed outcomes, learning has in both cases contributed to making the shortcomings of the policy more explicit and strengthened the position of the reform opponents.

It remains to be seen whether the failure of the Czech reform attempt and the difficulties the second pillar is experiencing in Romania will provoke a reaction in other peer nations, especially those belonging to the group of early reformers. It appears that early reformers, such as Bulgaria, Poland and the Slovak Republic, are less prone to engaging in circular learning, as none of these countries are preparing an overhaul of their second pillars in reaction to the policy outcomes experienced by the two late reformers. Nevertheless, this does not rule out the possibility that the Czech and Romanian experience will be instrumentally used to justify or underpin future reforms, when fiscal pressures in the heavily aging economies of Eastern Europe increase.

ACKNOWLEDGEMENTS

This research has been financed in part by the Slovak Research and Development Agency (APVV) grant no. APVV-14-0787 and by the Grant Agency of the Slovak Republic - VEGA, grant no. 2/0158/18. We would like also to express our gratitude to the five anonymous informants interviewed in the period March 2014 to April 2015.

REFERENCES

Adascalitei, D. and S. Domonkos (2015), 'Reforming against all odds: The introduction of multi-pillar pension systems in the Czech Republic and Romania', *International Social Security Review*, 68 (2), 85–104.

Armeanu, Oana I. (2010), *The Politics of Pension Reform in Central and Eastern Europe: Political Parties, Coalitions, and Policies*, Basingstoke: Palgrave Macmillan.

Brooks, S.M. (2005), 'Interdependent and domestic foundations of policy change: The diffusion of pension privatization around the world', *International Studies Quarterly*, 49 (2), 273–94.

Capital (2005), 'Unda verde la intrarea pe o piata neatractiva: Pensiile private [Green light for entering an unattractive market: Private pensions], http://www.capital.ro/unda-verde-la-intrarea-pe-o-piata-neatractiva-pensiile-private-18587.html.

Capital (2014), 'Victor Ponta: "Am discutat de multe ori cu FMI măsura naționalizării fondurilor private de pensii"' [Victor Ponta: 'I discussed many times with the IMF the possibility of nationalizing the private pension funds'], http://www.capital.ro/ponta-am-discutat-de-multe-ori-cu-fmi-masura-nationalizarii-fondurilor-private-de-pensii.html.

Casey, B.H. (2014), 'From pension funds to piggy banks: (Perverse) consequences of the Stability and Growth Pact since the crisis', *International Social Security Review*, 67 (1), 27–48.

Cashu, I. (2002), 'Negotiating public pension reforms in Russia, Romania and Latvia: The role of compromise mechanisms', Working Paper, Center for Policy Studies, Central European University, Budapest.

Český rozhlas (2012), 'Radek Urban, náměstek ministra financí' [Radek Urban, deputy minister of finance], http://zpravy.rozhlas.cz/radiozurnal/dvacetminut/_zprava/radek-urban-namestek-ministra-financi--1137494.

ČT24 (2013), 'Špidla: Reforma penzí je nebezpečná. Vláda použila falešné argumenty' [Špidla: The pension reform is dangerous. The government used false arguments], http://www.ceskatelevize.cz/ct24/ekonomika/1088660-spidla-reforma-penzi-je-nebezpecna-vlada-pouzila-falesne-argumenty.

Datz, G. and K. Dancsi (2013), 'The politics of pension reform reversal: A comparative analysis of Hungary and Argentina', *East European Politics*, 29 (1), 83–100.

Drahokoupil, J. and S. Domonkos (2012), 'Averting the funding-gap crisis: East European pension reforms after 2008', *Global Social Policy*, 12 (3), 283–99.

Gandul (2010), 'Cum a vrut Guvernul Boc să "naţionalizeze" pensiile private' [The Boc Government's attempt to nationalize private pensions], http://www.gandul.info/stiri/cum-a-vrut-guvernul-boc-sa-nationalizeze-pensiile-private-7700980.

Grzymala-Busse, Anna M. (2002), *Redeeming the Communist Past: The Regeneration of Communist Parties in East Central Europe*, Cambridge: Cambridge University Press.

Guardiancich, I. (2013), *Pension Reforms in Central, Eastern and Southeastern Europe: From Post-Socialist Transition to the Global Financial Crisis*, Abingdon: Routledge.

HotNews.ro (2005a), 'Reforma pensiilor se face pe furis' [Pension reform is carried out in secret], http://www.hotnews.ro/stiri-arhiva-1223805-reforma-pensiilor-face-furis.htm.

HotNews.ro (2005b), 'Ministrul Muncii: "Nu stiu daca vom putea obtine resursele pentru introducerea pensiilor private in 2007"' [Minister of Labor: 'I do not know whether we will be able to gather the necessary resources for introducing the private pension system in 2007'], http://www.hotnews.ro/stiri-arhiva-1237051-ministrul-muncii-nu-stiu-daca-vom-putea-obtine-resursele-pentru-introducerea-pensiilor-private-2007.htm.

HotNews.ro (2008), 'Mai multe ONG-uri cer ca randamentele pensiilor private obligatorii sa tina cont de inflatie' [Several NGOs demand that the rate of return of private pensions has to take into account the inflation rate], http://economie.hotnews.ro/stiri-pensii_private-2167160-mai-multe-ong-uri-cer-randamentele-pensiilor-private-obligatorii-tina-cont-inflatie.htm.

Klaus, V. (2002), 'Privatizace stáří je více než potřebná' [The privatization of old age is more than necessary], http://www.klaus.cz/clanky/934.

Lindeman, D., M. Rutkowski and O. Sluchynskyy (2000), *The Evolution of Pension Systems in Eastern Europe and Central Asia: Opportunities, Constraints, Dilemmas and Emerging Best Practices*, World Free of Poverty Series, Washington, DC: World Bank.

Mediafax.ro (2015a), 'Victor Ponta: CAS scade cu 5 puncte din octombrie, fără acordul FMI. Nu creştem taxe sau impozite' [Victor Ponta: The social security contributions decrease by 5 percent starting from October, without the agreement of the IMF. We will not raise tax levels], http://www.mediafax.ro/economic/victor-ponta-cas-scade-cu-5-puncte-din-octombrie-fara-acordul-fmi-nu-crestem-taxe-sau-impozite-12742149.

Mediafax.ro (2015b), 'Dragu: Majorăm contribuţiile la Pilonul II de pensii cu 0,1 puncte în loc de 0,5 puncte, la 5,1%' [Dragu: We increase the 2nd pillar contribu tions by 0.1 points instead of 0.5 points, up to 5.1%], http://www.mediafax.ro/ economic/dragu-majoram-contributiile-la-pilonul-ii-de-pensii-cu-0-1-puncte-in-loc-de-0-5-puncte-la-5-1-14909686.

Ministry of Labor and Social Affairs of the Czech Republic (2003a), *Pojistněmatema tická zpráva o sociálním pojištení – 2002* [The actuarial report on social insurance – 2002], http://www.mpsv.cz/files/clanky/1356/zprava_2002.pdf.

Ministry of Labor and Social Affairs of the Czech Republic (2003b), *Návrh hlavních principů pokračování reformy důchodového systému* [The proposal of the main principles of continuing the pension reform], http://www.mpsv.cz/files/ clanky/663/navrh_rds.pdf.

Mitáč, S. (2012), 'Pokud budeme součástí příští vlády, druhý pilíř zrušíme, plánuje Sobotka' [If we are in the next government, we will shut down the second pillar], https://ekonomika.idnes.cz/sobotka-radi-s-penzijnim-sporenim-drl-/ekonomika. aspx?c=A121107_215541_ekonomika_ert.

Monitorul Oficial (2000), 'Program de guvernare din 28 decembrie 2000 pe perioada 2001–2004' [Governing program from December 28, 2000 for 2001–2004 period], http://www.monitoruljuridic.ro/act/program-de-guvernare-din-28-decembrie-200 0-pe-perioada-2001-2004-emitent-parlamentul-publicat-n-monitorul-oficial-nr-2 5879.html.

Müller, K. (1999), 'Pension reform paths in comparison', *Czech Sociological Review*, 7 (1), 51–66.

Müller, K. (2000), *The Political Economy of Pension Reform in Central-Eastern Europe*, Cheltenham, UK and Northampton, MA, USA: Edward Elgar Publishing.

Müller, K. (2002), 'Beyond privatization: Pension reform in the Czech Republic and Slovenia', *Journal of European Social Policy*, 12 (4), 293–306.

Müller, K. (2003), *Privatising Old-Age Security: Latin America and Eastern Europe Compared*, Cheltenham, UK and Northampton, MA, USA: Edward Elgar Publishing.

Naczyk, M. and S. Domonkos (2016), 'The financial crisis and varieties of pension privatization reversals in Eastern Europe', *Governance*, 29 (2), 167–84.

Novinky.cz (2010), 'Reforma důchodů má být inspirována slovenským systémem, který je deficitní' [The pension reform is supposed to be inspired by the Slovak system, which is in deficit], http://www.novinky.cz/finance/206782-reforma-duchodu-ma-byt-inspirovana-slovenskym-systemem-ktery-je-deficitni.html.

Novinky.cz (2011), 'Povinné úspory na penzi mají po smrti důchodce propadnout pojišťovně' [Compulsory pension savings are to be taken over by the insurance company once pensioner dies], http://www.novinky.cz/finance/225318-povinne-uspory-na-penzi-maji-po-smrti-duchodce-propadnout-pojistovne.html.

Orenstein, M. (2008), *Privatizing Pensions: The Transnational Campaign for Social Security Reform*, Princeton, NJ: Princeton University Press.

Orenstein, M. (2011), 'Pension privatization in crisis: Death or rebirth of a global policy trend?', *International Social Security Review*, 64 (3), 65–80.

Pensions Committee (2005), *Závěrečná zpráva – výkonný tým* [Final report of the executive team], http://www.mpsv.cz/files/clanky/2235/zaverecna_zprava.pdf.

Pensions Committee (2014a), 'Mandát Odborné komise pro důchodovou reformu – Příloha č. 1 k příkazu ministryně č. 9/2014' [The mandate of the Expert Committee on Pension Reforms – Annex no. 1 to Order 9/2014 of the Minister of Welfare],

http://duchodova-komise.cz/wp-content/uploads/2014/07/Mandat_Odborne_kom
sie_pro_duchodovou_reformu.pdf.

Pensions Committee (2014b), 'Počet a rozložení účastníku v II. pilíři' [The number and distribution of 2nd-pillar members], http://www.duchodova-komise.cz/wp-content/uploads/2014/08/MF-ČR-Počet-a-rozložení-účastníků-v-II.-pilíři-kvě ten-2014.pdf

Price, W. and H.R. Rudolph (2013), *Reversal and Reduction, Resolution and Reform: Lessons from the Financial Crisis in Europe and Central Asia to Improve Outcomes from Mandatory Private Pensions*, Washington, DC: World Bank.

Rudolfová, V., D. Belčev, I. Duškov, M. Potůček and V. Samek (2014), 'Historie vývoje důchodového systému v ČR: Pracovní podklad pro odbornou komisi pro důchodovou reformu' [The history of the development of the pension system in the Czech Republic: Working paper for the Pensions Commission], Ministry of Welfare of the Czech Republic, http://www.mpsv.cz/files/clanky/18251/vyvoj_2.pdf.

Rudolph, Heinz P. (2012), '2nd pillars under attack: Lessons from the financial crisis', Presented at the V Contractual Savings Conference, Washington, DC, January 9, http://siteresources.worldbank.org/FINANCIALSECTOR/Resources/session1.pdf.

Seitan, M. (2014), Authors' interview with Mihai Seitan, June 16.

Simonovits, A. (2011), 'The mandatory private pension pillar in Hungary: An obituary', *International Social Security Review*, 64 (3), 81–98.

Tversky, A. and D. Kahneman (1974), 'Judgment under uncertainty: Heuristics and biases', *Science*, 185 (4157), 1124–31.

Vašek, P. (2010), 'Petr Nečas v HN vubec poprvé přiznal: Musíme zvýšit daně' [Petr Nečas admitted to HN for the first time: We have to increase taxes], http://zpravy.ihned.cz/c1-44151960-petr-necas-v-hn-vubec-poprve-priznal-musime-zvy sit-dane.

Večerník, J. (2006), 'Changing social status of pensioners and the prospects of pension reform in the Czech Republic', *Prague Economic Papers*, 15 (3), 195–213.

Weyland, K. (2009), *Bounded Rationality and Policy Diffusion: Social Sector Reform in Latin America*, Princeton, NJ: Princeton University Press.

World Bank (1994), *Averting the Old Age Crisis: Policies to Protect the Old and Promote Growth*, New York: Oxford University Press.

World Bank (2005), 'Romania country assistance evaluation', Country Evaluation and Regional Relations Operations Evaluation Department, World Bank.

Ziare.com (2010), 'APAPR: Nerespectarea programului la pilonul II va duce la mari pierderi [APAPR: Failure to implement the second-pillar program will lead to great losses], http://www.ziare.com/pensii/pensie-privata/apapr-nerespectarea-programului-la-pilonul-ii-va-duce-la-mari-pierderi-1018470.

Ziarul Financiar (2004), 'Pensiile private: Dorite, dar putin cunoscute' [Private pensions: Wanted but little known], http://www.zf.ro/analiza/pensiile-private-dorite-dar-putin-cunoscute-2949145.

4. Translating domestic violence norms in five countries of Central Eastern Europe

Andrea Krizsan

4.1 INTRODUCTION

This chapter looks at norms translation processes in the field of domestic violence. Using data from five countries of Central Eastern Europe (CEE)—Bulgaria, Croatia, Hungary, Poland and Romania—the chapter proposes a multi-pronged cross-directional international influence model that challenges traditional top-down understandings of international influence.

Domestic violence came onto the policy agenda of these countries in the mid-1990s around the time of the Beijing Fourth Women's World Conference. The first wave of progress in policy making happened in the context of European Union (EU) accession processes during the mid-2000s (except for Croatia). This took place amidst the extensive global spread of policies on violence against women in the last two decades (Htun and Weldon 2012). It has been noted however that domestically adopted policies often diverge from the principles defined by the international framework (Kelly 2005). The translation process most often leads to domestic policies that devote far less attention to gender equality aspects compared to international norms.

In brief, international influence is not direct, linear and top-down but constructed and negotiated in processes of interaction between international actors and domestic agents, where translation processes influence the direction of policy change. International influence provides content to reforms through defining, communicating and monitoring norms, and through facilitating the production of evidence for domestic violence as a policy problem. In order to understand the nature of international influence, we have to look beyond norms transfer at two additional mechanisms through which it impacts domestic policy processes. First, international influence can create "political opportunities" to enable domestic mobilization for policy change. Second, domestic agents are key in the translation of international norms. Enabling such agency becomes critical in processes of norm translation. International influence understood along these lines contributes to variation in policy progress achieved in different contexts.

4.2 THE INTERNATIONAL NORMATIVE FRAMEWORK FOR VIOLENCE AGAINST WOMEN

Violence against women and domestic violence are part of the United Nations (UN) normative system through the Convention on the Elimination of all Forms of Discrimination Against Women (CEDAW) Recommendation 19. The text of General Recommendation 19 addresses violence against women and within that violence in the family specifically. The measures recommend that states provide laws against family violence, establish related protective and support services, provide gender sensitive training for agents involved in implementation, and work on eradicating the stereotypes that perpetuate the problem. States are expected to report on the magnitude of the problem and on action taken. Several declarations, guidelines and other soft documents developed this normative content further. The Vienna Declaration on Human Rights 1993 and the Beijing Platform for Action adopted in 1995 at the Fourth Women's World Conference are also important standard setting documents. Most recently the Council of Europe Convention on Violence against Women and Domestic Violence, the Istanbul Convention (which entered into force in 2014), established the most developed and comprehensive international standards for states to provide protection and "action against violence against women and domestic violence." Additionally, a series of good policy practices developed by pioneer countries such as the US, Austria or Spain add to the set of norms that relate to the field of domestic violence policies.

Two aspects make international norms on violence against women and their translation to domestic contexts distinct. First, standards in the field are based on general principles that guide domestic interventions but do not define policy blueprints. They revolve around a set of principles including: recognition of violence in the private sphere as human rights violation; the need for state intervention and due diligence; centrality of the victim perspective; women's empowerment; and social structural transformation towards more gender equal societies. International norms on violence against women set a framework for interventions, but do not specifically determine the content of those interventions. The Istanbul Convention brings change in this regard. However, given its recent adoption its impact cannot be determined yet. In the EU, which is the main norm setter in Europe, policy debates frame domestic violence as a component of gender inequality (Augustin 2013). Yet the EU has no strong competence with respect to domestic violence. EU-based policy responses to domestic violence, while increasing in the last decade, remain restricted to soft law documents (Augustin 2013) in which the EU explicitly uses global standards and encourages member states to do so as well.

Second, human rights regimes, including the women's rights regime, are promotional regimes, with only soft pressure mechanisms available. This means that, contrary to enforcement regimes operating in trade or security issues, they are only about establishing and negotiating norms, which allows for great flexibility in translation. The realization of these norms is basically left to each state (Zwingel 2012). Thus incentive structures attached to existent international norms on domestic violence are quite permissive of flexibility in translation. Reporting is the main monitoring instrument linked to global standards, with no strong sanctions attached other than naming and shaming, which is rarely used beyond cases of gross violation. Within the EU no hard law applies to domestic violence policy standards, and a specific policy response to domestic violence is not a formal criterion for EU membership.

More so than in many other policy fields, international influence in the field of violence against women thus has to be understood as diverse processes of translation and adaptation involving international, transnational and domestic actors. In our five cases an almost simultaneous timing of policy changes indicates that international influence cannot be disregarded. In all five countries agenda setting took place around the 1995 Beijing Women's World Conference (Bulgaria 1996, Croatia 1997, Hungary 1997, Poland 1992, Romania 1996), and specific legislation was adopted close to the time of accession to the EU or in the midst of accession negotiations (Bulgaria 2005, Croatia 2003, Hungary 2006/2009, Poland 2005, Romania 2003). Yet the extent to which progress towards domestic violence policies is sensitive to gender equality and meets the spirit of the international norms, and the extent to which domestic violence is constructed as a women's rights problem, is uneven in the five countries.

By gendered policy outputs we mean both substantive elements captured by the content of laws and policies, and procedural elements such as the ways in which policy processes incorporate women's rights advocates (McBride and Mazur 2010; Krizsan and Popa 2014). Looking at how gender equality is captured by domestic violence policies through the combination of policy framing and policy process shows important differences among the five countries (Krizsan and Roggeband 2017). In Bulgaria and Croatia, while legal texts frame domestic violence as an individual rights problem, implementation documents and inclu sive policy processes, including co-governed implementation processes in which women's organizations have the voice and capacity to contribute, make gender equality and women's rights a component of the policy. In Poland and Hungary we see policies framed in individual rights terms. However, unlike in Croatia and Bulgaria, in the absence of co-governance these policies are co-opted by meanings inconsistent with gender equality: family protection, child protection or anti-alcoholism. Domestic violence is not captured as a gender inequality problem in Polish or Hungarian policies. In Romania recent reforms initiated by women's groups amend the initial framing of the law that was oppositional to gender equality. Yet, far from co-governing, women's organizations remain external to the policy process, restricted largely to agenda setting. If looking at framing and process complementarily, gender equality issues remain marginal to domestic violence policy in Romania as well. Gendering domestic violence so that it resonates with international norms is at the core of women's movement strategies and struggles across the five countries (Krizsan 2015).

4.3 INTERNATIONAL INFLUENCE AS A TRANSLATION PROCESS

Much of international relations theory considers processes of norms diffusion as unidirectional top-down processes with a sender at the international level and passive recipients at the national level. This approach tends to disregard the role domestic actors play in negotiating and translating international norms to the domestic context, and the fact that international norms themselves are not fixed, and their content may evolve over time and in relation to the domestic context to which they are conveyed. This is especially the case in fields where norms are not specific enough to provide policy blueprints, and incentives are soft enough to allow for negotiation and adaptation of norms to the domestic context. Here bottom-up processes need to be taken into consideration that influence the content of international norms.

In the realm of violence against women norms, social constructivist approaches emphasize the importance of interactive processes of translation (Zippel 2004; Krizsan and Popa 2010; Augustin 2013; Montoya 2013). Keck and Sikkink (1998) discuss the "boomerang effect"; Zippel (2004) defines the "ping pong" effect in the context of violence to illustrate processes in which domestic non-governmental organizations (NGOs) or transnational advocacy networks shape the meanings of international requirements.

The diversity of interactive translation processes leads to diverse outputs. Levitt and Merry (2009: 446) discuss how "women's human rights ideas connect with a locality, they take on some of the ideological and social attributes of the place, but also retain some of their original formulation . . . Even though the features of the original core do not necessarily change, the new composition of elements is different." The global women's rights package is seen to create opportunities for local actors by expanding the range of options that are acceptable and good, but may also "mean abandoning explicit references to human rights language altogether and, indeed, can mean hijacking these concepts for quite different purposes" (Levitt and Merry 2009: 448).

In this understanding formal accession to international instruments is not the most important step in the process of norms diffusion. Instead, it is the realization of women's rights norms following that step that is contentious and dependent on actor constellations and domestic environments (Zwingel 2012). Adopting new instruments is not the defining moment of policy solutions but simply opening the debate on norms. Outcomes will be contingent on the how and who of these debates. Local actors are not recipients but autonomous agents in the process (Zwingel 2012: 125).

The role of norm entrepreneurs—prominent women and women's groups—whether as members of transnational advocacy networks (Keck and Sikkink 1998) or as autonomous women's rights advocates (Levitt and Merry 2009; Htun and Weldon 2012) is fundamental in this context. These actors operating in between the domestic and the international arena are "conversant with both sides of the exchange but able to move across borders of ideas and approaches" (Levitt and Merry 2009: 449). They play central roles in negotiating international standards and mediating their inroads to domestic policy processes.

Transnational advocacy actors linking international organizations and domestic state and non-state actors are also such mediators (Moghadam 2005; Ferree and Tripp 2006). Transnational advocacy is key in constructing global norms on violence against women (Keck and Sikkink 1998) and in mediating those norms to domestic women's rights groups (Johnson 2007; Montoya 2013) as well as across such groups in different European countries (Augustin 2013; Montoya 2013).

This chapter outlines three mechanisms of international influence: first, international and transnational actors providing content and direct incentives for policy reforms is the most well-known mechanism; second, international influence also occurs indirectly by creating new political opportunities; and, third, enabling and empowering domestic agency can play a critical role both in translating norms and in embarking on international political opportunities.

4.4 TRANSLATING NORMS

The creation, transmission and monitoring of international norms to the domestic context stands at the center of international influence. However, in the process of translation there is no one set of international norms that travels invariably to different contexts. It is through the input of domestic advocacy groups that international requirements are custom-fitted to national policy environments. Translation of international norms will thus vary according to the input of domestic or transnational civil society actors. Such variation is visible particularly in interactive monitoring processes such as CEDAW's but also, as argued here, in monitoring processes connected to the EU accession. The marginalization of gender equality content in domestic policy outputs in the five countries shows the significance of the process of translation.

4.4.1 Early Agenda Setting and Beijing

Some of the earliest ideas on how to address domestic violence in the five countries emerged at a regional level. Croatia, while still part of former Yugoslavia, was one of the forerunners in establishing services to women victims of domestic violence in CEE. An SOS hotline for victims of violence was established in 1988 in Zagreb, followed by a shelter, which was registered in 1992 as the "Autonomous Women's House" (Jalusic and Dedic 2007). The idea to establish a helpline for women victims of violence in Hungary came from representatives of the Belgrade hotline for battered women at a 1993 conference (Szalay 1996: 47). It was the Fourth UN Women's World Conference in Beijing (1995) that was the catalyst for women activists in the five countries to elevate their early efforts to the level of legislative and policy actions.

The Beijing process was a catalyst to policy reforms through establishing benchmarks and setting reporting requirements, by recommending states to adopt implementation strategies or national action plans on gender equality policy benchmarks set by the Beijing Platform for Action, including violence against women. Meanwhile norms set in the Platform resonated with CEDAW norms, developing further the meaning of "violence against women" by introducing an understanding of diversity among women.

Governments of all five countries had delegates at the event and they all have adopted national action plans: Bulgaria and Romania in 1996; Croatia, Hungary and Poland in 1997. These documents are particularly important in the case of Bulgaria, Croatia, Hungary and Romania, where they constituted the very first policy documents to have sections on violence against women, which specifically targeted domestic violence after transition to democracy (Dedic 2007; Stoykova 2007). The 1997 national action plan also had a significant agenda setting impact in Poland, where it initiated a new gender equality programming process (Dabrowska 2007). Despite their promising content all of these plans remained symbolic in nature, without budget allocations and implemented actions. Their importance remains in initiating policy discussions on domestic violence. The role of the Beijing process can mainly be seen in keeping domestic violence on the agenda of the states, through the drafting of national action plans, and reporting on their progress every five years at Beijing+5, Beijing+10 and Beijing+15. The other benefit of Beijing is the connections made through its NGO forum in Beijing, which was an important networking and norm diffusion site, allowing activists from the five countries to bring home not only the feminist understanding of domestic violence, but also impetus for action that the Beijing Platform for Action conveyed (Johnson and Brunell 2006).

4.4.2   The UN Process

Norms set by the UN in CEDAW and its recommendations are at the core of norms diffused globally on domestic violence. The authority of these norms has been influenced by the role of the CEDAW mechanism within the UN. Initially a relatively weak intergovernmental regime, CEDAW has progressed to become one of the core human rights related mechanisms, with an increasingly professionalized voice and a strengthened enforcement mechanism after the mid-1990s which strives for systematic inclusion of domestic NGOs in the review procedure (Zwingel 2005). Establishment of the individual complaint procedure by the optional protocol further improved the strength of the mechanism.

The CEE countries in our analysis are all signatories to the CEDAW and the 1999 optional protocol on the complaint procedure. The number of reports and the delays in reporting by countries (Zwingel 2005) indicate recognition by state parties of the Convention and its importance. Four out of the five countries we examined are "good compliers" since the regime change took place in the region in 1990 (Zwingel 2005: 406). For these countries a pattern of regular reporting has been established, including the active participation of NGOs. Bulgaria emerged as a "weak complier" between 1993 and its next report, submitted in 2012. Meanwhile Bulgaria's active NGO sector has been using the CEDAW complaint mechanism more than the others.

Analysis of country reports and their debate before the CEDAW[1] shows that domestic violence policy reforms are an important CEDAW priority for the five countries, making up about one-tenth of all Committee member questions. All concluding comments have substantive recommendations on domestic violence that are well beyond the level of abstract norm setting. Analysis also indicates convergence with domestic violence norms in CEDAW over time. Reports from the governments of Croatia, Poland, Hungary and Romania present domestic violence as a social problem and as an issue demanding policy action. Exceptions are two very early reports (the Bulgarian report submitted in 1994 and the Croatian report submitted in 1995) and the sixth Hungarian report (submitted in 2006), which argues (though not explicitly) that all necessary measures had already been taken by the state. A year later, the Hungarian delegation gave more firm recognition of domestic violence both as a social problem and as a policy issue to be acted upon.

Over time, norms promotion by the CEDAW Committee moved from requiring formal adoption to demanding measures of implementation. The Committee develops an understanding of the policy situation in the reporting country based on consultations with NGOs and shadow reports prepared by local NGO coalitions. This sets the framework for questions asked and recommendations made. Norm development is also reflected in the definition of domestic violence used, which moves from tackling different forms of violence such as trafficking and domestic violence separately in the 1990s to placing them in the common framework of violence against women in the 2000s. The increased attention paid to violence against specific subgroups of women—Roma women and others—is another line of norm development in the practice of the Committee. This is an attempt to contextualize the normative framework by responding to demands of transnational advocacy groups such as the European Roma Rights Center.

Another aspect of CEDAW influence comes through the individual complaint mechanisms. Thus far the Committee has only dealt with a few cases on their merits, but importantly four of the eight such violence cases concerned Hungary and Bulgaria and three related to domestic violence (T. v. Hungary 2/2003; V.K. v. Bulgaria 2008; Isatou Jallow v. Bulgaria 32/2011). In the Hungarian domestic violence case, the recommendations not only included measures directed to solving the specific complaint but also asserted general recommendations concerning improvement of the legal and institutional system, and enforcement of law and policy. CEDAW examination of the sixth periodic report of Hungary brought the procedure to a close due to the resolution of the victim's problems. In the debate the response of the state was dismissive of the larger structural problems raised by the case. The Hungarian state has not done anything on the merits of the case. In the Bulgarian case the Committee requested the state to introduce immediate protection measures, which the state introduced, but in ways that were inefficient in their implementation and subsequently drew further criticism from the Committee. Recommendations included the need to amend the legal framework, an increase in the number of shelter places, and mandatory training on domestic violence for providers.[2] The half-hearted responses given by both states to CEDAW criticisms reveal the limitations of this CEDAW mechanism.

In sum, both the CEDAW and the Beijing process made contributions to domestic violence policy development in the five countries, particularly in agenda setting, rather than defining the details of the specific policy solutions. Overall, states are good formal compliers. Four of the five countries are overall consistent in reporting to CEDAW, with Bulgaria being in serious delay with the second round of reporting. Bulgaria and Hungary emerge as the most active users of the individual complaint mechanism of the CEDAW. Generally domestic women's rights' advocates' involvement in shadow reporting is quite prominent, even if at some points it puts an extreme burden on the under-resourced women's organizations active in the countries.

4.4.3   The EU Process

The European Union is not a norm setter in the field of domestic violence, but rather an amplifier of global and regional norms. Nevertheless the EU becomes a crucial actor in providing normative content for countries of the region through Europeanization. The EU accession process and attached conditionality constituted major international leverage on the five countries. Their accession negotiations took place in three waves: Hungary and Poland before 2004, Bulgaria and Romania before 2007, and Croatia before 2014. Albeit not formally part of the hard conditionality criteria, domestic violence had at times become part of the requirements and incentives of EU accession in the case of the five countries. Individual negotiations and consultation processes of the Commission with local NGOs created opportunities for the inclusion of fields that are not part of the core criteria.

The analysis of regular reports, issued by the Commission annually from 1998 to each country, found that the accession criteria were widened occasionally to include domestic violence policy related elements. This was particularly the case when the problem of domestic violence was somehow linked to core conditionality criteria and backed by NGO advocacy. Once the issue of domestic violence reached the agenda of the monitoring exercise, it persisted there and became part of the regular criteria. As a result, while for some countries the Commission disregarded domestic violence entirely, for others the issue stayed on the agenda. Reports for Hungary and Bulgaria did not mention domestic violence at all, whereas at the same time the issue recurred in most Romanian and Polish reports.

These differences are not explained by the presence or absence of debates around domestic violence in national contexts, because debates were taking place in all four countries at the time the reports were written. For Poland, the integration of the issue in the reports was triggered by the government's suspension in 1998 of a program with the United Nations Development Programme (UNDP) aimed at improving the shelter system for victims of domestic violence. The decision came in the context of the opposition of the new right-wing government to EU-driven gender equality policy developments, amidst the loud advocacy of activists to stop this backlash. In Romania, the inclusion of domestic violence was connected to a larger set of amendments to the Penal Code that included the decriminalization of homosexuality—a highly contentious issue that raised protracted debates among civil society and decision makers. Criminalization of domestic violence was included in the accession agenda on the back of this more politicized issue.

Attention to domestic violence endured once it emerged on the monitoring agenda. In Poland, following its initial inclusion in 1999, lack of response from the government to spousal violence was included in two more regular reports. Yet there is reason to be skeptical about the full commitment of the European Commission to the issue, since Poland actually became a member of the EU without having specific legislation against domestic violence, which was passed only in 2005. For Romania, reports subsequent to the first 1999 report not only reiterated concern with the governmental response to the issue but also included monitoring of the legislation against domestic violence that was passed in 2003 and its implementation.

The case of Croatia is quite different from that of the other four countries. By 2004, when Croatia became a candidate country for EU membership, specific legislation against domestic violence had been passed (2003) and domestic violence had been recognized as a crime in the Criminal Code (2000). Croatia was ahead of other European countries in the field. The positive tone of the progress reports on Croatia is therefore not surprising.

Differences in how the Commission approached the issue of domestic violence within the framework of accession monitoring is an illustration of the adaptation by the Commission of EU norms and requirements to domestic politicization of the policy issue at stake. The inclusion of assessments of the response to domestic violence in the regular reports on progress towards accession was shaped by the interaction of EU institutions and domestic advocacy actors. Importantly, in the absence of EU norms in the field, the process of regular reporting set no clear domestic violence policy benchmark but referenced UN and other international norms. Post-accession EU influence is mainly in the form of support for networking and exchange of good practices between NGOs and local level actors, which ultimately allows for the coordinated development of an EU normative framework on violence.

4.4.4   Beyond the UN and the EU

Aside from the normative framework embedded in international organizations, several domestic violence policy models gained currency as "best practices" among activists from Bulgaria, Croatia, Hungary, Poland and Romania. In particular, the US-based "Duluth model" has been used by activists in Bulgaria and Romania, while activists in Hungary and Poland favored the Austrian model of intervention, which is widely recognized as the European best practice in the field. Furthermore innovative practices were generated in the five countries, and networking among activists ensured that these ideas were disseminated at least region-wide. Transnational advocacy actors were mediators in bringing these norms to the region alongside international norms enshrined in the CEDAW and Beijing documents. Importantly, transnational networks mostly engaged with domestic advocacy groups rather than states. Contributions of transnational actors proved important for agenda setting and for implementation, but also in developing specific laws and policies. Differences in the capacities and policy connections of domestic advocacy groups that serve as domestic niches for transnational advocacy groups can condition the importance of international influence in a specific country.

Transnational advocacy groups working on domestic violence had come to the region by the early 1990s with the objective of bringing feminist ideas to the region and shaping emergent forms of feminism. Minnesota Advocates for Human Rights (MAHR) and the Women Against Violence in Europe (WAVE) network were the two most important, but others intervened in this role as well. MAHR (later Advocates for Human Rights), a US-based organization of lawyers aiming to promote human rights worldwide, brought to the region mainly US-based expertise. While they engaged in regional networking, MAHR represented a top-down model of knowledge transfer, which was increasingly challenged throughout the years as local expertise developed. WAVE was created in the aftermath of Beijing in response to the realization that "women from the South were better organized than women from Europe."[3] As a network, WAVE is based on a horizontal knowledge transfer model. Its funding members include organizations from West as well as East and Central Europe, including the Polish Center for Women's Rights.

Public exposure of data and information about domestic violence in order to gain recognition of the problem was one of the first key early contributions of MAHR in countries of the region. Their expertise for collecting information on domestic violence and the absence of policy responses to it was realized in early policy reports in Romania, Bulgaria and Poland. The first report on domestic violence in Romania was compiled by a team of lawyers and other professionals from MAHR in 1994 (MAHR 1994). In 1996, many from the same team went to Bulgaria to prepare a similar report (Tisheva 2005). Both reports found that domestic violence was a pervasive problem that had not received any appropriate response from the respective governments. These early reports were produced with minimal contribution from local women's groups and experts, though they became important strategic tools for women's groups in their advocacy efforts. In 2002, MAHR published a report on domestic violence about Poland. An essential difference from the previous two reports was that it was co-written with a Polish organization, the Women's Rights Center (MAHR et al. 2002). Another set of co-authored implementation reports was produced by MAHR a decade later when domestic violence policies were already in place. The 2008 Bulgarian implementation report and a 2012 Croatian implementation report were once again orchestrated by MAHR with substantial contributions from local experts (MAHR and Bulgarian Gender Research Foundation 2008; MAHR et al. 2012). Crucial recommendations formulated by these reports were integrated in amendments to the existent policy frameworks both in Bulgaria and in Croatia.

Other transnational or international actors contributed to policy relevant fact finding. In Romania, the United Nations Population Fund (UNFPA) was a leading agency in a 1999 program which resulted in the elaboration of a study on violence against women commissioned by the Ministry of Health that provided the first ever nationally representative data on domestic violence in Romania. Later this became part of the Reproductive Health Survey, thus keeping the issue on the public health agenda. The UNFPA program coordinator lauded the positive impact of the study on mobilizing political will for domestic violence policy reforms, and for inspiring a spirit of cooperation among NGOs (UNFPA 2007).

Involvement in the policy drafting processes was one of the most outstanding patterns of transnational contribution that emerged in countries of the region. A rather exceptional case is that of Bulgaria, where the Bulgarian Gender Research Foundation (BGRF) closely cooperated with MAHR starting from 1997 to develop domestic violence legislation. The collaboration continued until the very last stages of drafting the Bulgarian Law on Protection against Domestic Violence (Tisheva 2005; Ivancheva 2015). In other countries there is comparatively less involvement of transnational networks in the process of drafting national legislation. In Romania, US legislation inspired the drafting of the Romanian Law on Family Violence, both through the background of the legal experts involved and through the direct assistance of the American Bar Association. Later, in 2012, Romania took the Bulgarian policy as its model for introducing amendments to the Law on Family Violence and invited Bulgaria's leading BGRF advocate Tisheva as a consultant. The Austrian model inspired Polish and Hungarian women's rights advocates. However, the involvement of transnational advocates was not substantive in these drafting processes.

Even when specific good practice models were used, the process of norm diffusion entailed adaptation, with a strong intermediary role played by domestic women's rights advocates. The definition of domestic violence used by MAHR for their reports on domestic violence evolved from a strongly gendered definition in line with international norms to a more nuanced and diluted one saying that "there was no simple explanation for violence against women in the home" (MAHR 1996: 5). Domestic women's rights advocates emerge as crucial to translation processes and to securing the resonance of domestic policies with the objectives of international norms in the field. When models from other countries were used in the drafting of national legislation, their adaptation was much more thorough and contentious. For example, in the Hungarian and Romanian cases, the gender dimension that featured in the Austrian and US models was downplayed even by women's rights advocates. The final policies and laws adopted did not speak about violence against women, but about violence in the family.

4.5   ENHANCING OPPORTUNITIES FOR ACTION

International developments can provide openings for mobilization for both domestic and transnational actors (della Porta and Tarrow 2005) by changing options available and creating new opportunities for action (Levitt and Merry 2009). International components of political opportunity structures are particularly relevant in the context of democratizing states that may be resistant to following international norms unless skillfully manipulated into doing so (Sperling 1999). International monitoring processes which often integrate advocates' input into recommendations delivered to states (for example the CEDAW process) may generate more openness of governments to act. The inclination of states to avoid critical comments from international organizations may generate more political willingness closer to reporting deadlines.

But international factors may also be used domestically to induce political opportunities. The EU accession can be seen as a process, which importantly changed domestic political opportunities in accession states and facilitated the openness of governments to a whole range of policy reforms, some of which were not necessarily required as part of the EU accession. The instrumental use of the accession process by rights advocates as a stick as well as a carrot to push governments to embark on policy reforms was frequently the case (Krizsan and Popa 2010).

4.5.1   EU Accession Impact on Opportunity Structures

The EU accession emerges as an intriguing example of how the international context can open political opportunities for reform even if relevant norms are weak and not binding, as is the case with domestic violence norms at the EU level. Earlier research distinguishes between different invocations of the EU in the accession process: either in the sense of institutional requirements, to which the country has to accede, or in a more abstract sense, of "Europeanness" (Dombos et al. 2007: 250). The latter designates an identity that creates no institutional demands yet is perceived as the direction of progress. These types of EU references qualify as a "legitimizing usage" by actors seeking to garner public acceptance of policy reforms (Jacquot and Woll 2003). Drawing on the EU funded QUING project,[4] analysis of domestic violence policy debates in the five countries shows that the EU and "Europe" more broadly have been referred to widely, especially in three of the five countries—Bulgaria, Hungary and Romania. In these debates, references to the EU and to European norms were used to legitimize policy change.

References to Europe or the EU specifically are conditioned by the proximity of the EU accession date. As accession dates neared, related debates stretched to include domains of policy not formally within the purview of accession negotiations. "EU accession" tended to become a general framing for issues not core to the accession process, such as domestic violence. The most evident examples of this stretching were the parliamentary debates on the proposals for specific domestic violence laws in Bulgaria (2004) and Romania (2003). Analysis shows that the EU was invoked only in deliberations that took place close to the EU accession date. The aggregate picture of domestic violence debates in Bulgaria (2004–2006), Croatia (2003–2004), Hungary (1997, 2003 and 2006–2007), Poland (2004–2006) and Romania (2002–2005) shows that the only direct references to the EU appear in Bulgaria and Romania, where these debates took place in the midst of EU accession and in one debate in Hungary that took place in 2003, just before Hungary became a member of the EU. There are no direct references to the EU in Poland, where the sampled domestic violence debates took place after the country became a member of the EU, in the much later acceding Croatia, or in those Hungarian debates that took place much before (1997) or after the accession date (2006–2007) (Krizsan and Popa 2010). Ideas about shared European norms, and a desired Europeanness were also important for advocates in these contexts.

In all three countries where Europeanization played an important role—Hungary, Romania and Bulgaria—"strategic framing" (Benford and Snow 2000) of domestic violence became part of European integration criteria, regardless of whether or not it was included among the formal conditionality criteria. Women's rights advocates and their allies strategically integrated the development of domestic violence policies into a larger context of Europeanization. They did this to seek resonance with an accepted mainstream frame of "Europeanness": a consistent but somewhat unspecified aspiration, in which references to the EU and Europe are used as internal incentives to legitimize action against domestic violence. In short, the international framework is appropriated by domestic policy actors in response to women's rights advocates' use of political opportunities provided by the EU accession context.

4.5.2   UN Impact on Opportunity Structures

While the EU accession provided an outstanding political opportunity for policy reforms, smaller scale and shorter timeframe opportunities can be connected to periods when countries are due to report to international and particularly UN agencies. CEDAW reporting is one such opportunity.

In Romania a moment of political opportunity emerged at the beginning of 2000 when CEDAW examined the combined fourth and fifth periodic report of Romania. In its concluding comments, the Committee called on the government "to place highest priority on the adoption of the proposed legislation on equal opportunities and on domestic violence and trafficking in women." The national action plan on equality of opportunities between women and men 2001–2004 was adopted in December 2000. The action plan called for specific measures to combat domestic violence against women (Popa 2015: 201).

In Poland the 2007 reporting process was an important push in initiating the amendment process of the Domestic Violence Act (finally amended in 2009). The shadow report prepared by a coalition of Polish women's NGOs which widely discussed weaknesses of state interventions in domestic violence resonated well with CEDAW's concluding comments in discrediting the official state report. Criticisms channeled into the 2008 governmental report on the National Program of Counteracting Violence in the Family. Following this in 2008 the government was pressured to revisit the law by several state and non-state actors (Gruziel 2015:148–9).

In Croatia CEDAW reporting can also be linked to moments of mobilization and policy progress. The country's reporting in May 1998 took place amidst family law reform. While initially the proposed amendments only introduced protection against domestic violence for children, domestic women's groups' mobilization resulted in extending protection to other family members as well, mainly women. No direct evidence is available to show how the CEDAW process facilitated progressive policy change. However, the date of adopting the amendment is quite indicative, coming just one week after CEDAW delivered its concluding comments and recommendations, including recommendations on the need to improve the situation of victims of domestic violence (Dedic 2007). Similarly the 2005 CEDAW reporting was shortly followed by the amendment of the definition of family used in the Criminal Code to also cover perpetrators who do not live in the same household as the victim of domestic violence.

Hungary's most important policy reform moment, the adoption of the Parliamentary Decision on the National Strategy for the Prevention and Efficient Handling of Domestic Violence in 2003, also took place in the immediate aftermath of Hungary's 2002 reporting to the CEDAW. The reporting was surrounded by intensive policy debates partly connected to domestic violence and the publication of an NGO shadow report which was highly critical of the absence of policies addressing domestic violence. This was also the period immediately preceding EU accession. The most effervescent domestic violence policy moment in Hungary took place in a period of very favorable international political opportunities.

Overall, both the EU accession and UN and particularly CEDAW mechanisms were used by women's groups as political opportunities to promote domestic policy change. While the EU accession provided a relatively prolonged and intense favorable period, CEDAW reporting and Beijing emerge as one-time opportunities with relatively limited long-term impact.

4.6   ENHANCING THE CAPACITY OF DOMESTIC WOMEN'S GROUPS

International and transnational actors further influence translation processes through enhancing the capacity of critical domestic actors: women's groups. This is particularly important in the CEE context. Creating identity, facilitating networking and providing resources (funding and expertise) are the main mechanisms of influence here.

The role of identity and expertise formation was particularly crucial in the 1990s and early 2000s when CEE-based women's rights advocacy groups formed and integrated into European networks. Becoming part of a global feminist network beyond state boundaries through networking and identity formation contributed to the emergence of an arena of increasingly self-conscious and knowledgeable women's rights advocates in the five countries (Johnson 2009). Crucial input came from Beijing (the years around 1995), the Network of East West Women, and the WAVE network. All of these platforms facilitated identity formation though networking, as well as transfer of expertise. Travelling international repertoires of action like the 16 Days of Activism against Gender Violence campaign also contributed to strengthening identity for regional women's rights advocates (OSI 2002: 26).

Providing technical expertise to different aspects of domestic violence policy was another contribution of transnational advocacy groups to these countries. Transferred expertise covered international norms together with successful policy models such as the "Duluth model" and the Austrian model. Training programs and expertise transfer for practitioners working on women's rights and domestic violence were supported primarily by the Open Society Institute (OSI), the American Bar Association, Minnesota Advocates for Human Rights and WAVE network.

Alongside identity and expertise formation, funding for organizations advocating for women's rights proved particularly important in the region. In the absence of consolidated civil society funding mechanisms either from states or from domestic charities, international funds were often the only source for women's rights advocates. In the 1990s international organizations as well as development programs targeted CEE countries with extensive funding which proved particularly important for promoting domestic violence policy reforms. Main donors included different UN agencies, particularly the UN Trust Fund, UNFPA and UNDP, but also national consulates and development agencies from the Netherlands, Canada and the United States. The OSI through its national foundations and its different network programs was one of the most important and most stable donors in the region, and funded projects as well as institutional grants for NGOs.

Funding from international organizations and development aid organizations was intensive until the early 2000s. Following accession to the EU a serious decrease in funding resulted (Roth 2007). This was especially notable in the case of Poland and Hungary, which acceded in 2004, but reached Romania and Bulgaria as well after their accession in 2007. Croatia benefited from development funds for a longer time given its late accession to the EU in 2014. Funding from the EU was meant to replace the withdrawing donors. EU funding however could never really replace the lost funding. The reasons for this were multiple: EU funding was primarily project oriented funding; it did not primarily support policy advocacy but rather placed the emphasis on networking, awareness raising and diffusion of good practices, and it did not target violence against women specifically. Daphne, the core anti-violence program of the Commission, contributed to enabling agency by facilitating transnational cooperation among NGOs and the exchange of good practice models. No other funding came from the EU to any of the five countries that could have progressed domestic violence policies. Unlike in many other human rights related fields the main funding mechanism of the EU in the field of violence was meant to enable women's rights advocates' agency and support norm diffusion through them rather than to push member states to act.

While international sponsoring of civil society capacities in democratizing countries has drawn criticism about the NGO-ization of civil society, recent work reiterates the importance of international funding in creating dense and diverse networks of NGOs in the region and shows that transformative movement work and policy advocacy can originate from these externally funded networks (Irvine 2013; Helms 2014). Prior to EU accession, patterns of funding for organizations fighting domestic violence against women were more favorable in Bulgaria and Croatia, and were particularly unfavorable in Hungary and in Romania. Bulgaria and Croatia, and to some extent Poland, also managed to replace international funding with state funding for the relevant organizations, thus maintaining sustainability of some advocacy capacity. In the other countries domestic violence norm brokers were visibly weakened.

4.7 CONCLUSION

In the absence of easily transferable policy blueprints and weak enforcement mechanisms in the field of domestic violence, this chapter went beyond top-down unidirectional approaches to international influence and identified three alternative influence mechanisms that work in this realm. These are: (i) providing a normative framework for translation to the domestic context; (ii) enhancing political opportunities for reforms; and (iii) enabling domestic women's rights advocacy.

All of these mechanisms have at their center the domestic agency of women's rights advocates and show that international norms and political opportunities generated by international processes will translate to domestic policy practice through the engagement and mediation of domestic women's rights advocates. The role played by these norm entrepreneurs has an impact both on the formulation of international norms by international actors and on how they are understood and translated to the local context. It has an impact on the opening of opportunities as well as on how those are used. Intervention into norm translation processes, the mediation and diffusion of norms, and how political opportunities are embarked upon depend on the capacity and resources of these actors. The chapter has discussed how international actors, intergovernmental as well as transnational, contribute to forming the capacity of domestic actors and enable them to act as agents for international norms translation through facilitating identity formation and providing resources and expertise. Understanding policy transfer in "soft" fields such as domestic violence policy has to be captured in terms of these three mechanisms.

While not aiming for a systematic comparative analysis, the chapter pointed to differences among the five countries in all three mechanisms of influence. Bulgaria emerged as a relatively poor complier with CEDAW reporting in comparison with the four other countries. Croatia and Bulgaria as well as Hungary emerge as the main litigators of their respective states before CEDAW as well as the European Court of Human Rights in Strasbourg. Further difference appears in expertise transfer models: Bulgaria followed a more top-down model initiated by MAHR, while Poland, Croatia and to some extent Hungary followed a more horizontal cross-learning approach. The variations point to the importance of understanding the domestic context and domestic mobilization patterns of women's rights advocates. Ultimately, while international influence contributes to defining the normative framework and shaping the policy agenda as well as to creating political opportunities for pursuing change, the domestic context will have to be analyzed to find the main explanations as to why policies on domestic violence are more or less in line with the gender equality content of the internationally defined standard.

NOTES

1. We examined two sets of reporting documents for all five countries. Analysis included, beyond the country reports, the questions and comments of CEDAW to the reports, state responses, the debate sessions before the Committee and the concluding comments issued at the end. Analysis focused on reports written after 1989.
2. See http://www.worldcourts.com/cedaw/eng/decisions/2011.07.25_VK_v_Buglaria.pdf.
3. Phone interview with the co-founder of WAVE, Rosa Logar, August 29, 2007.
4. For this purpose, we used data gathered in the QUING project (Quality in Gender+

Equality Policies in Europe, www.quing.eu), complemented by further documents from policy debates around the period of reforms. For our five countries the QUING database covers policy debates through the text of the law, text of a policy plan, the minutes of parliamentary debates on the draft bills and at least one civil society text. In the coding process, references to the EU were understood to include relevant actors, documents or events.

REFERENCES

Augustin, Lise Rolandsen (2013), *Gender Equality, Intersectionality and Diversity in Europe*, New York: Palgrave Macmillan.

Benford, Robert and David Snow (2000), 'Framing processes and social movements: An overview and assessment', *Annual Review of Sociology*, 26, 611–39.

Dabrowska, Magda (2007), *Series of Timelines of Policy Debates in Selected Topics: Poland*, QUING Project, Vienna: IWM, www.quing.eu (accessed May 5, 2016).

Dedic, Jasminka (2007), *Series of Timelines of Policy Debates in Selected Topics: Croatia*, QUING Project, Vienna: IWM, www.quing.eu (accessed May 5, 2016).

Dombos, Tamas, Anna Horvath and Andrea Krizsan (2007), 'Where did gender disappear? Anti-discrimination policy in the EU accession process in Hungary', in Mieke Verloo (ed.), *Multiple Meanings of Gender Equality: A Critical Frame Analysis of Gender Policies in Europe*, Budapest: CEU Press, pp. 233–52.

Ferree, Myra Marx and Aili Mari Tripp (eds) (2006), *Global Feminism: Transnational Women's Activism, Organizing, and Human Rights*, New York: New York University Press.

Gruziel, Dominika (2015), 'Polish women's movements' efforts to change domestic violence state policies between 2001–2012', in Andrea Krizsan (ed.), *Mobilizing for Policy Change: Women's Movements in Central and Eastern European Domestic Violence Policy Struggles*, Budapest: CPS Books, pp. 123–84.

Helms, Elissa (2014), 'The movement-ization of NGOs? Women's organizing in post war Bosnia-Herzegovina', in Victoria Bernal and Inderpal Grewal (eds), *Theorizing NGOs: States, Feminisms, and Neoliberalism*, Durham, NC: Duke University Press, pp. 21–49.

Htun, Mala and Laurel Weldon (2012), 'The civic origins of progressive policy change: Combating violence against women in global perspective 1975–2005', *American Political Science Review*, 106 (3), 548–69.

Irvine, Jill (2013), 'Funding empowerment: Lessons from the Balkans', Paper presented at the 3rd European Conference on Politics and Gender, Barcelona, March 22–25.

Ivancheva, Mariya P. (2015), 'The spirit of the law: Mobilizing and/or professionalizing the women's movement in post-socialist Bulgaria', in Andrea Krizsan (ed.), *Mobilizing for Policy Change: Women's Movements in Central and Eastern European Domestic Violence Policy Struggles*, Budapest: CPS Books, pp. 45–84.

Jacquot, Sophie and Cornelia Woll (2003), 'Usage of European integration – Europeanization from a sociological perspective', *European Integration online Papers (EIoP)*, 7 (12), http://eiop.or.at/eiop/texte/2003-012a.htm (accessed May 5, 2016).

Jalusic, Vlasta and Jasminka Dedic (2007), 'Framing gender-based violence after the break-up of Yugoslavia: Croatian and Slovenian case', Paper presented at the ECPR General Conference, Pisa, September 6–8.

Johnson, Janet Elise (2007), 'Domestic violence politics in post-Soviet states', *Social Politics*, 14 (3), 380–405.

Johnson, Janet Elise (2009), *Gender Violence in Russia: The Politics of Feminist Intervention*, Bloomington: Indiana University Press.

Johnson, Janet E. and Laura Brunell (2006), 'The emergence of contrasting domestic violence regimes in post-communist Europe', *Policy and Politics*, 34 (4), 575–95.

Keck, Margaret and Kathryn Sikkink (1998), 'Transnational networks on violence against women', in *Activists beyond Borders: Advocacy Networks in International Politics*, Ithaca, NY: Cornell University Press, pp. 165–98.

Kelly, Liz (2005), 'Inside outsiders: Mainstreaming gender violence into human rights discourse and practice', *International Feminist Journal of Politics*, 7 (4), 471–95.

Krizsan, Andrea (ed.) (2015), *Mobilizing for Change: Women's Movements in Central and Eastern European Domestic Violence Policy Struggles*, Budapest: CPS Books.

Krizsan, Andrea and Raluca Popa (2010), 'Europeanization in making anti-domestic violence policies in Central and Eastern Europe', *Social Politics*, 17 (3), 379–406.

Krizsan, Andrea and Raluca Popa (2014), 'Frames in contestation: International human rights norms and domestic violence policy debates in five countries of Central and Eastern Europe', *Violence against Women*, 20 (7), 758–82.

Krizsan, Andrea and Conny Roggeband (2017) *The Gender Politics of Domestic Violence. Feminists Engaging the State in Central and Eastern Europe*, New York: Routledge.

Levitt, Peggy and Sally Engle Merry (2009), 'Vernacularization on the ground: Local uses of global women's rights in Peru, China, India and the United States', *Global Networks*, 9 (4), 441–61.

MAHR (Minnesota Advocates for Human Rights) (1994), *Lifting the Curtain: A Report on Domestic Violence in Romania*, Minneapolis: MAHR.

MAHR (Minnesota Advocates for Human Rights) (1996), *Domestic Violence in Bulgaria*, Minneapolis: MAHR.

MAHR (Minnesota Advocates for Human Rights) and Bulgarian Gender Research Foundation (2008), *Implementation of the Bulgarian Law on Protection against Domestic Violence: A Human Rights Report*, http://www.theadvocatesforhuman rights.org/uploads/final_report_2_3.pdf (accessed May 5, 2016).

MAHR (Minnesota Advocates for Human Rights), Women's Rights Center and International Women's Rights Clinic at Georgetown University (2002), *Domestic Violence in Poland*, Minneapolis: MAHR.

MAHR (Minnesota Advocates for Human Rights), Autonomous Women's House Zagreb and Bulgarian Gender Research Foundation (2012), *Implementation of Croatia's Domestic Violence Legislation: A Human Rights Report*, http:// www.theadvocatesforhumanrights.org/uploads/croatia_final_report_2012.pdf (accessed May 5, 2016).

McBride, Dorothy E. and Amy Mazur (2010), *The Politics of State Feminism: Innovation in Comparative Research*, Philadelphia, PA: Temple University Press.

Moghadam, Valerie (2005), *Globalizing Women: Transnational Feminist Networks*, Baltimore, MD: Johns Hopkins University Press.

Montoya, Celeste (2013), *From Global to Grassroots: The European Union, Transnational Advocacy, and Combating Violence against Women*, New York: Oxford University Press.

OSI (Open Society Institute) (2002), *Bending the Bow: Targeting Women's Human Rights and Opportunities*, New York: OSI.

Popa, Raluca (2015), 'A decade-long struggle for change: Women's mobilization and domestic violence legal and policy reform in Romania', in Andrea Krizsan (ed.), *Mobilizing for Policy Change: Women's Movements in Central and Eastern European Domestic Violence Policy Struggles*, Budapest: CPS Books, pp. 185–222.

Porta, Donatella della and Sidney G. Tarrow (eds) (2005), *Transnational Protest and Global Activism*, New York: Rowman & Littlefield.

Roth, Silke (2007), 'Sisterhood and solidarity? Women's organizations in the expanded European Union', *Social Politics*, 14 (4), 460–87.

Sperling, Valerie (1999), *Organizing Women in Contemporary Russia: Engendering Transition*, New York: Cambridge University Press.

Stoykova, Elena (2007), *Series of Timelines of Policy Debates in Selected Topics: Bulgaria*, QUING Project, Vienna: IWM, www.quing.eu (accessed May 5, 2016).

Szalay, Kriszta (1996), 'Domestic violence against women in Hungary', in Chris Corrin (ed.), *Women in a Violent World: Feminist Analyses and Resistance across Europe*, Edinburgh: Edinburgh University Press, pp. 41–52.

Tisheva, Genoveva (2005), *The Law on Protection against Domestic Violence in Bulgaria: Insights and History*, http://www.stopvaw.org/31May20055.html (accessed May 5, 2016).

UNFPA (2007), 'Romania. Tackling domestic violence from many angles', in *Programming to Address Violence against Women: 10 Case Studies*, http://www.unfpa.org/upload/lib_pub_file/678_filename_vaw.pdf (accessed May 5, 2016).

Zippel, Kathrin (2004), 'Transnational advocacy networks and policy cycles in the European Union: The case of sexual harassment', *Social Politics*, 11 (1), 57–85.

Zwingel, Susanne (2005), 'From intergovernmental negotiations to (sub)national change: A transnational perspective on the impact of CEDAW', *International Feminist Journal of Politics*, 7 (3), 400–424.

Zwingel, Susanne (2012), 'How do norms travel? Theorizing international women's rights in transnational perspective', *International Studies Quarterly*, 56, 115–29.

5. National Roma inclusion policies in Central and Eastern Europe: Diverging learning paths with residual outcomes

Violetta Zentai

5.1 INTRODUCTION

The European Union's (EU) post-accession Roma inclusion[1] policies in Central and Eastern Europe (CEE) are viewed primarily as failures, pseudo-successes, or at best fragile and fragmented developments. This is the case both within the trend-setting policy debates in wider Europe and within scholarly and civil society reflections. The complex field of Roma inclusion policy is composed of a variety of sector based and cross-cutting policy measures ranging from education, housing, and employment to anti-discrimination and regional development policies. Since 2011, an ambitious strategic framework has been launched and is supposed to guide Roma inclusion related domestic policies in the EU member states: the European Union Framework for National Roma Integration Strategies (European Commission 2011) and the national strategies. The process of production of these strategies, the quality of these strategies, and their use in policy formations make up a policy package that is less than the full complexity of Roma inclusion policies but arguably amounts to more than what is outlined in the texts of the national Roma inclusion strategies.

The EU accession process and the Decade of Roma Inclusion (2005–2015) mechanism pushed several Central and Eastern European polities with significant Roma populations to develop national strategies or action plans for Roma inclusion. The scope and quality of these strategy documents diverged to a large degree, as did the implementation drives and capacities of the governments concerned. In 2011, as a unique political and policy move within the European Union, an EU Framework was established in support of comprehensive Roma inclusion policies for all EU member states (European Commission 2011). The Framework laced together policy paradigms of social inclusion, poverty reduction, and anti-discrimination in four major policy arenas: education, employment, housing, and health care. All EU member states were obliged to elaborate their national strategic documents within the same year and to include Roma inclusion priorities in the planning of the European structural funds for 2014–2020.

The chapter will examine the policy formations that are driven by the EU Framework and the national Roma inclusion strategies in 2011–2015 in four new member states of the EU: Bulgaria, Hungary, Romania, and Slovakia. The analysis will draw on ideas of experimental policy making and policy learning (Eckert and Börzel 2012). It will argue that, although Roma inclusion policies have fallen short in delivering transformative societal changes, they have created recognition for particular "problem" framings of societal concerns, mobilized new encounters and alliances between different modes of policy making, and repositioned actors maintaining commitment to social inclusion policy agendas in the new EU member states.

The chapter first will address the idea of experimental policy making and policy learning in the specific policy field and explore the multilevel context in which European Roma inclusion policy paradigms have emerged. It will then discuss the main narratives of policy failures in the field, against which residual outcomes will be identified as a result of diverse modalities of policy learning. Owing to word constraints, it is not possible to give a full account of the roles of specific advocacy groups forming opinions on policy successes and failures in the field. Nevertheless, some important groups or high-profile coalitions include: the Secretariat of the Decade of Roma Inclusion, the European Roma Rights Center, and the Open Society Foundations. They are complemented at national and local levels by an array of domestic civil society coalitions, expert groups, and think tanks of differing professional competences and resources and hence varying degrees of interaction with regional and international coalitions.

5.2 THEORETICAL CONSIDERATIONS ON POLICY EXPERIMENTS AND LEARNING

The field of Roma inclusion belongs to the larger cluster of social policies which are always entangled with political debates on good life, fairness, and the distribution of benefits and burdens in society (Friedman 2015). Norms and wider moral considerations that are always subject to contestation in any policy field here saturate not only agenda setting but the very process of decision making and implementation as well. When pressing inequalities and social justice matters make up the core of a policy field, experiments are often expected, because zero intervention cannot be easily legitimated and "off-the-shelf" master plans do not offer obvious courses of action. Accordingly, this chapter resonates with the position of the editors of this volume that experimentation and learning often better capture the observed disjunctures of policy formations than do claims of failures, shortcomings, and backwardness against models of systematic, rational decision making and interventions. The notion of failure, however, will not be excluded from this analysis.

The guiding concept of *experimentalism* has developed to capture governance practices, innovations, and modalities in conditions of uncertainty. The concept refers to political structures in which decision makers do not know exactly how to respond to emerging challenges, no dominant power center drives the policy thinking, and there is no single source of knowledge. Importantly, policy actors are connected by "dynamic accountability" ensured by institutionalized learning. Sabel and Zeitlin propose that, when transparent processes ensure the cooperation of multilevel actors, they will be interested in pursuing the public good without blocking decision making (Sabel and Zeitlin 2010: 5). This vision fits primarily to circumstances in which public actors have the capacities and willingness to deliberate, that is, in stable democracies. Other policy scholars warn that compliance with horizontal rules of the game is ensured in the "shadow of hierarchy" as a penalty default mechanism (Eckert and Börzel 2012). This chapter will consider the applicability of the concept of experimentalism under the conditions of social and political resistance and struggles that characterize the Roma inclusion arena and the often unstable governance structures in CEE, which in many respects are similar to the conditions of uncertainty understood by the concept of experimentalism.

The Roma inclusion field is embedded in the European multilevel policy mechanisms in which learning is a key component of policy changes. The open method of coordination (OMC) relies on peer pressure, socialization, and trial and error, with results in incremental or messy forms of knowledge formation. Policy theorists stress that policy learning is most likely to occur in collaborative policy domains rather than adversarial or intractable ones (Weible et al. 2012). The European Roma inclusion policy frame, however, is established as a political compromise on a transnational level. Thus its entanglements with domestic politics entail struggles and conflicts in the public sphere, or often the opposite: erasing the political content of the issue and turning it to technical mastering of policy programs. As Roma inclusion policy is an often adversarial agenda in the domestic settings, prospects for policy learning are unlikely to be smooth.

It is also relevant to this chapter to distinguish between modalities of policy learning. When policy makers learn how to cope with a problem without changing their preferences, they participate in "thin" learning. This may become entangled with the dispositions and experiences of "muddling through" approaches to public affairs that are widely discussed in the literature on post-socialist transformations. Political learning, largely seen as thin learning, makes policy makers more potent in the power game with the EU institutions or domestic competitors, but it does not necessarily produce policy change (Radaelli 2008). "Thick" learning implies that policy actors ultimately change their preferences, norms, or agendas.

Theorists also make a distinction between hierarchical and bottom-up learning which is pertinent to the open method of coordination. In the former case, domestic policy makers learn how to cope with proposals coming from above, in particular the EU level. In the latter, policy formations rely on the participation of civil society, expert voices, and local knowledge to develop policy-relevant knowledge. Some scholars highlight the significance of the "nudge" from horizontal cooperative networks towards both "push" and "pull" forces (Börzel and Buzogány 2010). In anti-discrimination and equality matters, governmental actors face dual pressure for learning and adaptation by "push" from above and "pull" from below. The metaphor of pincer to describe this double effect is compelling yet perhaps more forceful than how the influence mechanism occurs in reality. If the political and financial sanctions for non-learning are high, this pincer could be an efficient tool. Indeed, Roma inclusion policy is composed of soft and hard policy devices, yet even the hard ones (such as anti-discrimination directives and structural funds) leave a wide space for member state experimentalism.

The study of the EU Framework Strategy for Roma Integration and its national ramifications could profoundly benefit from discursive approaches to policy thinking and making. These approaches reveal that discursive transformations mirror or even induce shifts in belief systems, help to legitimate policy positions, and prepare or endorse the formations of alliances (Schmidt and Radaelli 2006). Particular styles of reasoning and representation serve negotiations, competition, and cooperation in support of or against policy positions or wider political agendas. In policy formations addressing social inequalities and marginalization, a powerful problem statement will orient a variety of actors and the wider public. A problem statement names the location, the scale, and the power holders of marginalization experiences. On the other end, "fudging" these pieces of information or narrating causal relations in which the marginalized are constituted as the "responsible" or "deviant" group also enacts an impactful discursive strategy. Combining or blurring these strategies can cover up political reluctance or lack of state capacities to translate discursive statements to national strategies and programs.

The chapter finally hopes to demonstrate a need for theoretical innovations to connect the policy change and experiment literature. Understanding policy challenges in *social justice and inequality* matters necessitates attention to two further substantive specificities of inequality related policy fields. First, any serious intervention to curb various forms of historically accumulated disadvantage and to tackle intended and unintended consequences of social practices will go in one way or another against the interest or convenience of the mainstream, at least in the short run. Moreover, tackling inequalities entails dwelling on a so-called "problem group." The problem solving efforts and policy initiatives can easily perpetuate the social perception of a group as primarily the source of the problem. These two properties of inequality matters may make experimentalist policy formations more the regular pattern rather than the exceptional manner of policy making in these fields.

5.3   THE ROMA INCLUSION FIELD AND THE EUROPEAN POLICY MAKING ENVIRONMENT

The core Roma inclusion norms in Europe have multiple sources. The Copenhagen criteria for accession to the European Union embodied the stability of democratic institutions, the rule of law, and protection of human rights and minorities. These criteria intended to shape the wholesale political transformations by strategic transfer of normative requirements. The critical assessments of the outcomes of these political conditions for accession point out that the adaptation of the EU directives resulted in the transposition of legal rules yet induced a weak or skewed implementation process (Grabbe 2006; Falkner et al. 2008: 288). These political conditions, however, helped norm alignments in CEE countries in human rights and minority protection fields. Other international organizations, such as the Council of Europe (CoE), backed the compliance pressure for the Copenhagen criteria and helped in empowering coalitions of civil society actors in framing the discussions on highly contentious social inclusion issues.

Candidate countries in CEE had to transpose the main anti-discrimination directives as part of their EU accession preparation. The transposition of the Race Directive, constitutive of the EU *acquis*, appeared to be an essential but ultimately insufficient condition for launching complex social inclusion policies in the post-accession years. The literature already discusses how the incentive structure became weakened after EU accession to maintain the effects of a conditionality based Europeanization (Schimmelfennig and Sedelmeier 2005; Armstrong 2010; McGarry 2010).

Some authors highlight, however, that adopted rules and institutions might become resilient due to institutional obstacles to relapse or to costs that may be incurred with dismantling. This "lock-in" concept goes together with a caveat: it tends to be more difficult to strengthen weak institutions after accession than it is to weaken strong institutions against the remaining EU soft power. This chapter argues that the basic anti-discrimination laws and monitoring bodies that have become part of the larger Roma inclusion policy infrastructure display country variations as well as these lock-in weaknesses (Sedelmeier 2012).

International and European policy bodies made decisive steps to establish a structured arena for Europe-wide policy formations for Roma inclusion parallel to the EU accession procedures. These efforts evolved into a particular coordination mechanism called the Decade of Roma Inclusion 2005–2015 (the Decade), which embraced transnational and domestic actors, including governments and international and civil society organizations. It mobilized the new member states of the 2004 and 2007 EU accession waves, and a number of Southeast European polities with significant Roma communities. The Decade was intended to generate horizontal learning in particular among the governmental actors in addition to bottom-up learning from civil society to governments. The lead was taken by the Open Society Institute (OSI, one of the world's largest international philanthropic foundations) and the World Bank, as the EU was not ready to act as a policy pioneer in the field in the mid-2000s. The Secretariat of the Decade was primarily supported by the Open Society Foundations, the nationally based chapters of OSI and the champion and key sponsor to civil society working on human rights and social justice in the region during the 2000s. With commissioned expert studies and orchestrated knowledge sharing, the Secretariat created in effect an epistemic-like community of civil society and expert groups with converging understandings of the underlying causes and nature of inequalities that divide the Roma and the non-Roma.

The Decade was a precursor and later a parallel structure to the EU Framework Strategy for Roma Integration. The overlap of principles, actors, and coordination mechanisms of the Decade and the subsequent 2011 Framework is paramount. The 2011 EU Framework Strategy is modelled upon the policy agenda of the Decade in its scope and complexity. The framing combines anti-discrimination and socio-economic reasoning, and laces together this problem recognition with distributive principles of equality. The key difference in the two mechanisms occurs in the role of the EU and civil society, and the availability of financial resources for policy interventions. In the current structures, the EU drives the rules of cooperation and the EU structural funds are placed as the main, though non-exclusive, sources for policy implementation and assessment. The difference in civil society actors' voice and access to policy formations is also noteworthy. The 2011 Framework mechanism offers structured opportunities mostly for civil society actors of transnational relevance in European level policy discussions, whereas the Decade was able to give voice to domestic civil society groups as well in strategic and assessment discussions. The current EU mechanism continues to be supportive of the key norm-setting actor of the Decade, the Open Society Foundations and its civil society networks, to maintain its critical assessments and monitoring role (Civil Society Monitoring Reports, 2012, 2013–14), but the agenda-setting impacts of these actors in the EU policy space have become fragile and quite weak. The legacy and impact of the Decade is contested: non-governmental participants in the Decade view the soft coordination structures as inefficient. The same actors are as proud of the complex and transformative agenda framing of the Decade as they are dissatisfied with the later EU Framework paradigm.

Receiving less academic attention is how another policy field of growing relevance to Roma inclusion advanced with its institutional structures in the post-accession period. This field is cohesion policy, which has become relevant to any major inequality and social inclusion field since the EU accession. From the 2000s, this policy domain has induced new learning environments for decision makers and bureaucrats with the initiation of largely deliberative procedures, policy innovations for Roma communities, and knowledge sharing. Strategic planning and programming of the structural funds – the main instruments of cohesion policy implementation – made it necessary for the new member states to build new or reshuffle executive structures, and hire and train new officials, to establish regulations and procedures. Senior decision makers in the new member states were dependent on a new generation of professionals with fluent English, advanced (often foreign) education, and enthusiasm with European policy and career perspectives. In some cases, as in Hungary, these professionals enjoyed the benefits of an institutional innovation which created a parallel executive structure, independent from line ministries, for cohesion policy making and EU structural funds distribution. Few of these professionals had genuine anti-discrimination and social inclusion knowledge yet they showed an interest in exploiting civil society and independent expert knowledge. This created intensive encounters among policy actors that are normally separated by fairly rigid lines in most policy domains in Central and Eastern Europe. In the newest member states with larger Roma populations (Bulgaria, Romania), some policy entrepreneurs heading units responsible for structural funds planning were effective in opening, at least at the agenda-setting stage, to the participation of non-governmental actors, and engaged in experimental policy formations.

In addition to the European Parliament's and civil society actors' political work, active EU presidencies in 2009 and 2010 and some particularly committed Commissioners facilitated the passing of two key policy documents: that is, first, the Common Basic Principles for Roma Inclusion (European Commission 2009) and, second, the EU Framework for National Roma Integration Strategies (European Commission 2011). The first statement addresses both substantive and procedural components of Roma inclusion policies with unambiguously transformative framing. The EU Framework was inspired by the Decade of Roma Inclusion initiative in designating four main policy areas for intervention and a combined framing of social inclusion (socio-economic equality) and human rights (anti-discrimination). The Framework Strategy obliged the EU member states to build their own National Roma Integration Strategies (NRIS) and present these documents to the European Commission by the end of the same year. The EU Framework emerged as a compromise among, first, differently positioned member states regarding their actual social exclusion problems, second, the inclination of these states to conform with European-level policy formations, and, third, their exposure to peer pressures or learning from other member state practices. The Framework positions the European Commission as a core agent in supporting and monitoring the member states in delivering on their commitments. However, the Framework puts the main responsibility for policy formation and implementation on the member states. Although the Framework relies on the open method of coordination, it also embodies hard *acquis* components such as anti-discrimination regulations and certain conditions attached to the structural funds spending mechanism.

All EU member states developed their own strategic plans for the inclusion of their Roma citizens and communities. The deadline was unusually short, mirroring the political urgency that backed the policy move behind the EU Framework. Member states, with the exception of Malta, had prepared their strategic documents by the end of 2011. Members of the Decade mechanism that had earlier developed their Decade Roma inclusion plans were invited by the European Commission to upgrade these documents in accord with the EU Framework. The National Roma Integration Strategies provide comprehensive understanding of the main causes of Roma marginalization, set objectives for policy interventions, define the main implementation mechanisms, assign financial sources, and outline assessment mechanisms. These strategies are supposed to guide sector based and horizontal policy measures promoting Roma inclusion. The quality of these documents, ranging from 30 to 120 pages, varies depending on the degree of policy and governance capacities, political commitments, and expert–civil society participation in the specific CEE member states. The very first version of these strategies in some countries did not meet the most basic requirements of a complex policy strategy. Several EU member states have updated their strategic documents since their inception. As discussed in detail in the following sections, the regular European Commission reviews of the implementation of the NRIS capture the most severe shortcomings in the quality of institutional arrangements, the intensity of financial commitments, and the thinness of the monitoring and assessment provisions.

Since the adoption of the EU Framework Strategy, the most recent policy developments in the cohesion policy cycle of 2014–2020 deserve special attention. In response to the Roma inclusion results of the European structural funds in 2007–2013, which were seen as poor, or modest at best, the new EU regulations stipulated that at least 20 percent of the European Social Fund (ESF) should be earmarked for social inclusion and poverty reduction purposes. The regulations also set positive duties for member states to allocate the ESF for promoting equal opportunities and non-discrimination by naming special target groups, including marginalized communities such as the Roma. In sum, whereas the experimentalist learning environment in the member state arenas of Roma inclusion had shrunk by the 2010s, the compulsory regulations in a narrow field within cohesion policy and EU funds mechanisms were being strengthened by the middle of the 2010s. One commentator also argues that the Europe 2020 mechanism for ensuring economic growth and the policy coordination within the European Semester could have spill-over effects on social policy areas (Szendrey 2014). Yet a caveat applies here, as the EU's Roma inclusion policy coordination mechanism has not established specific benchmarking targets for the national strategies.

Finally, it is also important to note that, with establishing the 2011 Framework Strategy and the NRIS, the field turned to a highly visible political question in European public affairs. This topic generates heated discussions between old member states exposed to critiques of their own human rights record yet always ready to harshly judge the new member states' capacities to keep the Roma issues within their borders. This political visibility is an opportunity as well as a challenge for experimentalism and thick policy learning.

5.4 POLICY FORMATIONS VIEWED THROUGH NARRATIVES OF FAILURE

The European Commission's annual reviews of NRIS implementation performances and coordinated civil society monitoring reports published in 2012 and 2013 noticed classical policy making deficiencies in the policy inputs of the new member state governments. Most importantly, strategies lacked concrete and measurable targets and timelines; civil society and local authorities were insufficiently engaged; governments did not earmark a budget for implementation; and data remained scarce for meaningful monitoring. In 2014, the Commission report on the implementation of the Framework Strategy offered a detailed portrayal of country performances since 2011 (European Commission 2014). The report highlighted a few promising practices, yet the overall conclusion voiced a warning that little progress had been made to respond to challenges that the EU Framework Strategy pronounced. By 2015, an almost full consensus emerged on the genuine governance and policy failure symptoms in the domestic Roma inclusion policy fields, characterized by, *inter alia*, lack of a comprehensive, systematic, and sustainable approach and inadequate institutional conditions (coordination, multidimensional approach, synergies between the national and the local level, etc.) for achieving substantive results. A lack of effective civil society, in particular Roma, participation was also noticed (Fresno et al. 2014). An expert assessment on the NRIS implementation that the European Parliament commissioned in 2015 added to the list of shortcomings the lack of ethnic data as well as a holistic approach to the multi-sector and intersectional challenges of Roma inclusion, weak alignment between policies and funds, poor monitoring and evaluation procedures, and thin communication between different layers of government (European Parliament 2015).

Civil society advocacy groups, watchdogs, independent experts, and the European Parliament also assessed the quality of NRIS and their implementation steps. These accounts make strong statements on the poor quality of policy inputs, incapacity to gauge successes and failures regarding short term impacts, and insufficient political willingness to counter and unravel the underlying causes of Roma poverty and exclusion (Sigona and Vermeersch 2012). In so doing, they form powerful narratives that coalesce into a bleak picture of the Central and East European domestic policy arenas and that portray a view of the OMC mechanisms as toothless. Fundamental differences also emerge, however, within these narratives to explain the main reasons for failures of the EU Framework mechanisms and domestic policy formations. Six main narratives have emerged in the academic and critical policy debates to provide explanations for the identified policy failures.

First, several independent experts and civil society commentators believe that a vague and "soft" social inclusion centered solely around agenda setting was doomed to failure right from the start. Anti-discrimination considerations, which are enshrined in EU *acquis* structures, are easily ignored or pushed to the back seat of policy making. A lack of explicit anti-discrimination backing and legal force to social inclusion measures was a fundamental conceptual mistake stemming from the Decade National Action Plans and imported into the NRIS from 2011. To adopt a "classroom" metaphor of learning, the original mistakes were made and instructed by the EU norm-setting bodies, with most new member states faithfully grasping the lesson. In other words, member states were provided with faulty guidelines and manuals and felt comfortable by not being asked to do too much or anything too challenging. The result was a reasonably good policy transfer of a minimalist and skewed policy framing of EU norms.

Second, the EU Framework for Roma Inclusion and its national variations are seen as policy manifestos of wider systemic paradigms for perceiving social inequality problems. More closely, a neoliberal economic and political vision is seen saturating all major policy formations in the EU and gaining hegemonic framing power. In this narrative the European policy wisdom centers on economic integration and the far-reaching and benign effect of market coordination. Consequently, economic integration of the Roma "will eliminate all discrimination based on someone's race, color, ethnic, social origin or membership of a minority" (Rorke and Usein 2015). Social inclusion framing in the European Union has become the hostage of quintessential neoliberal social policy governance (Vincze 2013). In this line of thought, the policy learning is driven again by a top-down transfer of policy norms which resonate with the discursive properties of a wider economic and ideological environment. This narrative of failure again points to efficient top-down learning of faulty policy framing that allows little or no scope for experimentalism.

Third, failures are also associated with the dearth of political will at all levels of national and sub-national government in the member states. A lack of political will, combined with the insufficient "bite" of the EU's soft power policy instruments, entails that political elites in EU member states have not had the incentives to invest in genuine implementation of their policy frameworks for Roma inclusion. The soft power mechanisms allowed the setting out of largely unrealistic targets in the EU Framework Strategy which could not be balanced by horizontal learning through the open method of coordination or the slow catch-up in the EU funds related incentives (European Parliament 2015). Accordingly, learning in the Roma inclusion field was doomed to failure due to the OMC power structures and political unpreparedness of the new member states. Regardless of the properties of the agenda framing, there is no pathway for experimental learning in this setting. Thin learning suffices.

A fourth explanation of failure argues that Roma policies often require difficult policy choices from governments that generate resentment among the public. The mainstream public opinion in the new member states is very critical about measures aimed at Roma inclusion. Stubborn prejudices, xenophobic fears, and welfare chauvinism reinforce each other in these dominantly negative societal reactions to the Roma. Rendering it either as a political support problem or as policy paradigm failures, critics conceive persistent anti-Roma prejudice and anti-Gypsyism as a prime threat to all coordinated efforts to promote Roma inclusion (Rorke and Usein 2015). Thus, dominant public opinion makes it unrealistic to expect increasing political commitment in favor of Roma inclusion (Fresno et al. 2014). In this understanding, there are political limits to trial and error policy formations, borrowing, and experimenting.

A further and fifth domain of policy failures is acknowledged in a lack of formal and less formal participation of non-governmental actors in policy formations, a prime condition of OMC driven learning. On the one hand, governments in the new member states do not feel a need for and do not support structures for involving civil society knowledge and contribution. On the other hand, civil society organizations, in particular the Roma organizations, are institutionally weak and often lack platforms, resources, and therefore meaningful opportunities for engaging in policy debates. Roma advocates and civil society coalitions are rarely able to share experience based knowledge, and to propose new frames for policy formations. Thus, the chances for bottom-up and thick learning, where the former is key to the latter, and genuine policy change are very low (Acton et al. 2013).

The sixth narrative dwells on a substantive and procedural reasoning. Among the educated pro-Roma public, anti-Gypsyism is viewed as both a cause and a consequence of policy failures, rendering the problem as a policy task suitable for European multilevel policy interventions. In these critical accounts, soft power based policy learning is not regarded as a meaningful response to the "wicked problem" of perpetual exclusion. Therefore, the "solution" to the controversy is a "hard" policy transfer based European Roma inclusion strategy and strong enforcement mechanism. This narrative connects the previous framing, political will, governance, and social resistance narratives into a meta-concept. An implicit hierarchical learning concept underlies this reasoning to discipline new member state governments and stipulate policy actions.

These main failure narratives leave little doubt about the very poor prospects for promising policy change towards wide objectives of Roma inclusion. They converge in arguing that the contemporary policy environment in CEE is fallow ground for the implementation of the NRIS. These critical commentaries uncover relevant explanatory factors for the partial or almost full failures of Roma inclusion policies when comparing the objectives and the policy outputs or even the outcomes. Nevertheless, the remainder of the chapter will examine signs of policy experiments and learning in the four countries concerned that at some point showed potential for genuine policy change towards decreasing Roma marginalization. These positive developments have occurred in spite of the ambiguities of the social inclusion concept or left at least some residual ideas, capacities, and incentives that can be reassembled for future policy formations.

5.5   TRACING EXPERIMENTALISM AND RESIDUAL POLICY CHANGES

The transformations in the political landscape of the European Union in the 2010s and their effects on some main social policy agendas and policy mechanisms are well documented (Stewart and Rovid 2012; Vermeersch 2012). It is worth depicting with broad brushstrokes the metamorphosis of incentive structures and policy learning capacity in the new member states that had already started in the second half of the 2000s. A significant number of policy makers in CEE, young and older generations alike, looked at the EU institutions and policy norms with tangible enthusiasm in the early 2000s. The EU accession created a need for at least partial renewal of the cadre of senior and mid-level decision makers in areas of direct encounter or subject to EU *acquis* transfer. Many of these new bureaucrats held a genuine interest in public affairs and willingly immersed themselves in making the most of EU requirements to enhance domestic policy reforms. Some became policy entrepreneurs in the field of Roma and broader social inclusion, either as ministers or deputies of education, labor, or social inclusion, or as commissioners of inclusion affairs or chief government advisers. For many, the EU has been a source of inspiration whereby some surpassed the EU benchmarks set in the Framework Strategy in their vision and policy creativity.

The experimentalism of the professionals involved in the "take-off" period of the cohesion policy field developed primarily into a political learning process in the second half of the 2000s, overlapping with the first full cycle of the European budget planning period (2007–2013) in the new member states. This learning unfolded through discursive adaptation to EU norms and the devaluation of the aspirations of the new generation of the EU and innovation-friendly experts. The lines became blurred between the old and the new cadres of policy makers and entangled with ideological divides over the 2008 economic crisis and the subsequent European political cleavages. By the time Roma inclusion became a pronounced EU policy field in 2011, the experimentalism of the cohesion policy field could be seen as a short-lived opportunity for policy learning towards transformative inclusion policies.

Towards the end of the 2000s, a parallel and additional learning process also began to take root. It was learning about how to take advantage of the enhanced EU resources by keeping the appearance of formal accountability and observing rules but in reality avoiding risk taking or adversarial domestic reform measures, so as to maintain the status quo in major societal affairs. At the worst, this involved reshuffled patterns of clientelism in the policy mechanisms. This kind of learning diluted the impact of enthusiastic professionals, making them less important or even redundant in the higher echelons of administration. A growing political populism – triggered by the discontent of the post-socialist changes coupled with the effects of the economic crisis of 2008 – created a space for different types of policy makers, that is, those with excellent capacities to speak the political and policy language of the EU, but who were also prepared to "fudge" decisions in controversial policy fields. In the second round of EU accession countries in the region, a sharp disconnect emerged between weak governing capacities and the policy ambitions right from the first moment of the accession. In Bulgaria and Romania, policy learning seemed to skip the stage of high enthusiasm in the 2000–2003 period pertinent to the first group of accession countries and its thick learning effect of putting a new style of bureaucrat in place.

The post-2011 learning modes in the field of Roma inclusion embrace certain well-recognized knowledge producers who generate genuine data and rigorous analysis but who remain open to policy adjustments rather than systemic reforms. This pattern de-centers the policy champions of the EU accession period but retains liaisons with some norm-setting actors, especially independent expert groups. The National Roma Integration Strategies and their recent updates extensively refer to independent and civil society research and analysis in their diagnostic statements. This remains true in the case of Hungary and Romania for example, two polities that do not exemplify progressive Roma inclusion policy inputs after 2011. In the Romanian Partnership Agreement, the key strategic planning document for cohesion policy in 2014–2020, the main sources of references include pro-Roma and Roma civil society analyses in addition to EU policy documents. In the Hungarian context, the National Roma Integration Strategy of 2011 relied on a fair selection of independent analyses of social exclusion of the Roma, authored in part by critical commentators of the government. This courage and openness disappeared from the Hungarian Partnership Agreement of 2014, which barely mentions any independent source in its problem statements. The new learning mode enhances governance sophistication in certain respects but tends to weaken accountability and participation structures. Governments in the four countries seek low to minimum encounters with civil society and domestic norm-setting groups. This particularly characterizes Hungarian policy making practices in the 2010s. Contrariwise, in the Bulgarian policy arenas, the relatively well-established interfaces of genuine policy discussions with civil society participation have survived; nevertheless, this does not translate into policy input and supporting governance capacity for Roma inclusion.

Although stemming from different EU accession conditions, and formed by different state capacities and political landscapes, policy makers in Hungary and Slovakia, as first-wave accession actors, and in Bulgaria and Romania, as second-wave accession actors, have converged in a particular learning modality from the second half of the 2000s. This modality entails developing a good command of the policy vocabulary of the EU agendas and dominant framings. All these skills are used to *selectively* affirm key norms articulated by a European policy community while leaving a wide space to govern society largely independently of this EU policy core. The protagonists and institutions of this *experimentalism* through *selective learning* do not want to please the EU authorities any more, yet they do not want to fully escape from all requirements. They do not resist introducing some pragmatic policy changes along the lines of common EU norms, while they occasionally propose changes against these norms for ideological, pragmatic, or symbolic reasons.

These new modes of policy formations have "sitting-on-the-fence" properties which allow maintaining or at least avoiding direct efforts to demolish policy coordination structures and experiments of the recent past. These modes also avoid direct confrontations with Brussels bureaucrats, with the exception of the Hungarian policy makers following 2014. Without disputing the insights of the failure narratives outlined in section 5.4, so too the fragile or residual elements of compliance with Roma inclusion policy making in the post-2011 EU should not be left unnoticed.

First, international advocacy coalitions advancing Roma inclusion continue to operate in spite of ebbs and flows in political support, recognition, resources, and institutional backing. With all its imperfections, the Roma Decade established systemic collaboration of a number of national governments, Roma and pro-Roma civil society, and the international partners. The Decade developed regular discussions on what the social movement literature calls "diagnostic statements" on policy problems by articulating the causes and the nature of Roma exclusion, proposing various policy frames in norm hierarchies, and ensuring monitoring exercises for civil society critical actors (Bojadjieva and Kushen 2014).

The horizontal discussions among governmental actors largely ceased towards the closure of the Decade, but civil society actors and independent expert groups often remained connected. By way of facilitation from the Decade Secretariat and the Open Society Foundations, monitoring coalitions for producing civil society "shadow reports" emerged in 2012 and 2013. Producers of these reports gained manifold experience in horizontal advocacy cooperation and remained on alert to windows of opportunity provided by the wider European policy and political space. In addition to complex and influential country reports, selective groups of these actors produced critical reflections of the whole Decade of Roma Inclusion in 2015 with complex accounts of governance innovations and failures (Decade of Roma Inclusion Secretariat Foundation 2015). Some of these actors are commissioned for analytical work for the World Bank, the European Roma Rights Center, and the Roma Education Fund, active international agents of Roma inclusion, thereby legitimating and broadcasting their analyses. It is essential not to be overly optimistic about these residual outcomes; many of these civil society actors struggle for sheer survival, with diminishing prospects for funding in the second half of the 2010s.

The current EU Framework, inspired and backed by the Decade mechanisms, has also generated spaces for policy deliberation and publicly acknowledged Roma advocacy coalitions in which civil society, expert groups, and occasionally policy entrepreneurs exchanged ideas and participated. Some official EU structures such as the Roma Platform still facilitate this process. Additionally, the ideological, normative, and communication ties connecting NGOs, think tanks, and consultancy firms beyond the EU Framework are also conducive to experimenting with different policy approaches. In spite of the documented policy failures, the pro-inclusion network – which has both advocacy and epistemic-like characteristics – keeps alive the policy discourses on social justice and ensures that Roma exclusion does not disappear from the public agenda in Europe. Network members continue to provide empirical analyses to map the direct and hidden impacts of social exclusion and remain committed advocates on domestic policy formations in the four CEE polities.

Second, despite bureaucratic control and co-optation, the problem statement and analysis repertoire has advanced. Central and East European governments in general have differential trust in, and relations to, independent knowledge producers depending on a government's electoral stability and style of political power practices. An OMC policy space, which does not entail "hands-on" regulations and inspections from Brussels (except for the EU structural funds), requires from the bureaucratic apparatus of the member states some analytical capacities for agenda setting, planning, and statistical reporting on Roma, even if it wants to keep the field in stasis rather than achieving major changes. The Fundamental Rights Agency (FRA) of the European Union, being assigned the role to propose policy performance indicators for the European Commission on Roma inclusion policies, works with often surprisingly forward-looking and knowledgeable experts from member state governments. Many of these officials provided substantive data and critical analysis in spite of their governments being reluctant, or resistant, to pursue genuine policy measures for Roma inclusion. It needs further investigations to understand what motivates national governments to keep these experts on board and how the mandates and professional autonomy of these experts look when they are not in the policy laboratory of the FRA.

The influence of the international advocacy coalitions can be seen in how some framing patterns have gained traction and stabilized in the CEE contexts. For example, desegregation is a central diagnostic paradigm which has been at the center of major political and policy debates in all CEE member states both prior to and after the rise of the 2011 Framework Strategy. Desegregation embodies a strong social justice based reasoning and the concept of duty based policy making on behalf of the mainstream in society. Desegregation has become the subject of struggles and bargains between the European Commission officials and member state policy makers in regular reviews of the NRIS, the European Semester, and the strategic planning of the 2014–2020 cohesion policy packages. The notion of desegregation is still often used by policy makers even if they resist their official duty to desegregate (O'Nions 2015). This persistent framing can be considered a lock-in effect of former thick learning and genuine experimentalism. The 2014–2020 Partnership Agreement of Romania is unambiguous about desegregation duties in education, housing, and regional development and about the prohibited use of funding towards segregation. By the same token, the Hungarian government's provocative support for segregating school developments in the spirit of "graceful separation" was challenged by a highly visible domestic litigation case and the recently initiated infringement process by the European Union against Hungary.

Third, the post-2011 policy making environment occasionally magnifies the Roma voice and facilitates slowly advancing empowerment via the wider political participation of this excluded social group. This is not only a residual but a paradoxical result of the last 15 years of Roma inclusion policy in addition to wider political processes whereby empowerment progresses amidst shrinking prospects for genuine policy change. Civil society critics often argue that engagement with mainstream policy groups and political parties, let alone with policy making and implementation, has more destructive than elevating effects on Roma citizenship rights and participation.

While it can be acknowledged that by engaging in policy advocacy Roma civil society actors find channels, tools, and forums through which to become part of the wider public in the post-socialist context, it is also the case that Roma participation in electoral and party structures has produced very thin results and suffered major downturns in all four polities concerned in the 2000s. Obviously, the route to participation through policy making can be a mixed blessing. It runs the risk of creating an image of those involved Roma actors seeking privilege and working in complicity with governmental interfaces. This may weaken the legitimacy of the concerned individuals or organizations. On the other hand, Roma representation and participation in advocacy coalitions and networks provides visibility, additional communication channels, and recognition to civil society organizations and civic leaders. The overall effect of engaging in the current challenges of multilevel European policy making for broader Roma participation and political inclusion has been a double-edged one.

5.6 CONCLUSIONS

The review of the learning modalities, experimentalism, and residual outcomes of the Roma inclusion policies in four new member states of the EU revealed that the disjuncture between the wider social and political conditions for addressing pressing inequalities and the gestation period of establishing a common policy arena for Roma inclusion with robust involvement of the new member states made the European Framework Strategy for Roma Integration a brave yet fragile undertaking. In a simplified account, by the time the EU Framework was adopted, weakened EU level governance capacities partly due to the consequences of the 2008 economic crisis turned EU-wide horizontal deliberation and coordination on social inclusion into a "hard sell." Further, by 2011 the new member states had moved to selected learning modalities and pragmatic experimentalisms in their European integration and policy learning paths. Against these conditions stood the enthusiasm of a few policy champions, the legacies and parallel existence of the Decade, a multitude of issue or value driven non-governmental networks, and general governmental interest in the member states in avoiding large-scale and systemic governance failures.

This account of residual success should not be seen to discredit or replace the critical narratives of the pressing problems of on-going marginalization. These residual outcomes emerged through diverging learning modalities. In the field of Roma inclusion policies, the grand scheme of the common Framework has not yet fallen apart, yet trust is significantly diminished in its power to induce policy change. Accordingly, smaller-scale

policy development may emerge to improve the life of particular populations. New narratives and interventions may be assembled from already
available techniques and practices of diverse provenance. Larger shifts may
occur as outcomes of national or local struggles rather than resulting from
international master plans once policy actors are placed in asymmetrical
power relations (Li 2005; Clarke at al. 2015).

Some critics believe that there is wide recognition that Roma exclusion
is one of Europe's biggest democratic deficits, ethically dubious and
economically unsustainable (Rorke and Usein 2015). Contrariwise, this
opinion is nurtured by mostly pro-equality and pro-Roma experts and civil
society groups. It is clearly not a view shared widely within the political
elites of the member states. Thus, a democratic space for all European
Roma citizens could be envisioned as an outcome at best rather than
a precondition for Roma inclusion policies. But what are the possible
scenarios for policy transformations in the field of Roma inclusion in CEE
given that only residual outcomes are being achieved and experimentalism
has stalled?

A pessimistic account by scholars of Roma politics uncovers that
new *social order* inspired agenda framings are gaining recognition and
authority. A case in point is the concept of securitization, which strives
to regulate the movement, the space, and the encounters of Roma and
non-Roma in pursuance of public safety. While not unknown before
2011, today the concept has been elevated to a highly legitimate policy
framing in contemporary European political discourses. There are good
reasons to believe that securitization will spread as an appealing frame
for governing society among the CEE political elites. As portrayed by
recent inquiries, there is an intimate conceptual connection between
evicting (in the new member states) and deporting (in the old member
states) the poor, visibly different, and undeserving others in society (van
Baar 2012). Experimenting and horizontal deliberation capacities, partly
learned through the EU social inclusion policy coordination mechanisms,
could be used paradoxically to pursue policy objectives going against the
current inclusion paradigms.

An optimistic position ponders that support for pursuing Roma inclusion and renewal of the instrumental learning space might come from
the societal mainstream. It is not the marginalized minority but the
mainstream majority who could alter major societal institutions and
practices. Potentially, a de-stabilized and often disoriented mainstream
in post-crisis European polities could build pressure for social solidarity
in self-interested thinking for the sake of non-adversarial social spaces
and community relations. This remains problematically dependent on
the galvanization of political forces that might embrace and support

non-exclusive societal visions in contemporary European publics against the current political extreme that has mobilized enemy seeking and anti-establishment approaches to social problems.

NOTE

1. The naming of the particular policy field is part of the policy discussions that the field encompasses. In this chapter, there is no space for critical analysis of the connotations and uses of the terms of inclusion, integration, equal citizenship, equality, and so on. *Roma inclusion* is used to refer to the complexity of contemporary policy discussions in Europe concerning the unfair inequalities that most Roma face.

REFERENCES

Acton, T., A. Ryder and I. Rostas (2013), 'Empowerment and the European Framework for National Roma Integration Strategies', *Roma Rights*, 2013, 11–14.

Armstrong, K.A. (2010), *Governing Social Inclusion: Europeanization through Policy Coordination*, Oxford: Oxford University Press.

Baar, H. van (2012), 'Socioeconomic mobility and neoliberal governmentality in postsocialist Europe: Activation and the dehumanization of the Roma', *Journal of Ethnic and Migration Studies*, 38 (8), 1289–1304.

Bojadjieva, A. and R. Kushen (eds) (2014), *Decade Intelligence Report: Factors for Success or Failure of Roma Inclusion Projects*, Budapest: Decade of Roma Inclusion Secretariat Foundation.

Börzel, T. and A. Buzogány (2010), 'Environmental organisations and the Europeanisation of public policy in Central and Eastern Europe: The case of biodiversity governance', *Environmental Politics*, 19 (5), 708–35.

Clarke, J., D. Bainton, M. Lendvai and P. Stubbs (2015), *Making Policy Move*, Bristol: Policy Press.

Eckert, S. and T. Börzel (2012), 'Experimentalist governance: An introduction', *Regulations and Governance*, 6 (3), 371–7.

Falkner, G., O. Treib and E. Holzleithner (2008), *Compliance in the Enlarged European Union: Living Rights or Dead Letters?*, Burlington, VT: Ashgate.

Fresno, J.M., C. Rauchberger and A. Chahin (2014), *Advocacy Brief on Roma Inclusion Policies*, Brussels: UNHCR.

Friedman, E. (2015), 'Introduction to the Special Issue, Talking about Roma: Implications for social inclusion', *Social Inclusion*, 3 (5), 1–4.

Grabbe, H. (2006), *The EU's Transformative Power: Europeanisation through Conditionality in Central and Eastern Europe*, London: Palgrave Macmillan.

Li, T. (2005), 'Beyond "the state" and failed schemes', *American Anthropologist*, 107 (3), 383–94.

McGarry, A. (2010), *Who Speaks for Roma? Political Representation of a Transnational Minority*, New York: Continuum.

O'Nions, H. (2015), 'Narratives of social inclusion in the context of Roma school segregation', *Social Inclusion*, 3 (5), 103–14.

Radaelli, C.M. (2008), 'Europeanization, policy learning, and new modes of governance', *Journal of Comparative Policy Analysis*, 10 (3), 239–54.
Rorke, B. and O. Usein (2015), *A Lost Decade? Reflections on Roma Inclusion 2005–2015*, Budapest: Decade Secretariat.
Sabel, C.F. and J. Zeitlin (eds) (2010), *Experimentalist Governance in the European Union: Towards a New Architecture*, Oxford: Oxford University Press.
Schimmelfennig, F. and U. Sedelmeier (2005), 'Introduction: Conceptualizing the Europeanization of Central and Eastern Europe', in F. Schimmelfennig and U. Sedelmeier (eds), *The Europeanization of Central and Eastern Europe*, Ithaca, NY: Cornell University Press, pp. 1–28.
Schmidt, Vivien A. and Claudio M. Radaelli (2006), 'Policy change and discourse in Europe: Conceptual and methodological issues', *West European Politics*, 27 (2), 183–210.
Sedelmeier, U. (2012), 'Is Europeanisation through conditionality sustainable? Lock-in of institutional change after EU accession', *West European Politics*, 35 (1), 20–38.
Sigona, N. and P. Vermeersch (2012), 'The Roma in the new EU: Policies, frames and everyday experiences', *Journal of Ethic and Migration Studies*, 38 (8), 1189–93.
Stewart, M. and M. Rovid (ed.) (2012), *The Gypsy Menace: Populism and the New Anti-Gypsy Politics*, London: Hurst.
Szendrey, O. (2014), 'Prospects and challenges of EU level Roma inclusion governance', MA thesis, Central European University, Budapest.
Vermeersch, P. (2012), 'Reframing the Roma: EU initiatives and the politics of reinterpretation', *Journal of Ethnic and Migration Studies*, 38 (8), 1195–1212.
Vincze, E. (ed.) (2013), 'Spatialization and racialization of social exclusion: The social and cultural formation of Gypsy ghettos in Romania in a European context', *Studia Universitatis Babes-Bolyai Sociologia*, LVIII (2), 5–21.
Weible, C., T. Heikkila, P. deLeon and P. Sabatier (2012), 'Understanding and influencing the policy process', *Policy Science*, 45, 1–21.

Policy Documents

Civil Society Monitoring Reports of National Roma Integration Strategies, 2012, 2013–14, http://www.romadecade.org/civilsocietymonitoring.
Decade of Roma Inclusion Secretariat Foundation (2015), 'To be or not to be . . . Roma Decade after 2015?', http://www.romadecade.org/contributions-from-decade-partners/to-be-or-not-to-be-roma-decade-after-2015/9283.
European Commission (2009), *Vademecum: The 10 Common Basic Principles on Roma Inclusion*, Brussels: European Commission.
European Commission (2011), *Communication from the Commission to the European Parliament, the Council, the European Economic and Social Committee and the Committee of the Regions: An EU Framework for National Roma Integration Strategies up to 2020* (COM(2011) 173 final), Brussels: European Commission.
European Commission (2014), *Report on the Implementation of the EU Framework for National Roma Integration Strategies*, April 2 (COM(2014) 209 final), Brussels: European Commission.
European Parliament (2015), *Evaluation of the EU Framework for National Roma Integration Strategies*, Brussels: European Parliament.
National Roma Integration Strategies, http://ec.europa.eu/justice/discrimination/roma-integration/index_en.htm.

6. EU cohesion policy and the Eastern member states: A case of transnational policy convergence

Gergő Medve-Bálint

6.1 INTRODUCTION

Although the Central and Eastern European (CEE) countries represent only 20 per cent of the EU population, in the 2014–2020 programming period they receive half of the cohesion policy funds.[1] The large financial transfers give political and economic salience to the policy at both the supranational and the domestic level and, consequently, it is expected to exert notable regulatory influence on CEE.

The policy frequently goes through reforms that typically take place before the adoption of the EU's multi-annual budgetary frameworks. In the last three decades there were five such cycles (1988–1993, 1994–1999, 2000–2006, 2007–2013 and 2014–2020), and each of them brought minor or more substantial reforms compared to the previous period. Those changes reflected the shifts in the broader socio-economic agenda of the EU. The cohesion policy is therefore a compelling case for examining policy transfer from the supranational to the domestic level. How does the changing external policy context influence the regional development policies of the member states? How does the policy transfer occur and what is being transferred?

The CEE countries offer a quasi-laboratory setting for studying the above questions. On the one hand, after the regime change in 1989/90, none of these states had a systematic set of regional policies. On the other hand, CEE states have since been exposed to EU leverage; thus their regional policies developed under external influence. Tracing the evolution of those policies reveals how the interactions of the supranational and the national actors produce domestic policy outcomes.

Instead of 'policy transfer', the term 'policy translation' better captures the mechanisms discussed in this chapter, because policy translation puts a greater emphasis on agency and on the role of domestic factors. The chapter builds on a comparative study of the Czech and the Hungarian regional policies and shows how policy translation in these two countries resulted in policy convergence. Even though the two countries started from different conditions, their regional policies have become similar over time. In this process, the EU represented an external stimulus to which the subsequent Czech and Hungarian governments gave similar responses, mainly driven by domestic political interests.

The structure of the chapter is as follows. Section 6.2 outlines the theoretical expectations about how the EU's cohesion policy may affect domestic regional policies and institutional structures. Next, the core concepts are defined (section 6.3), which is followed by a discussion on how regional policies evolved in the two countries in the early 1990s (section 6.4). Section 6.5 examines how the EU's external influence was translated into the domestic contexts and identifies those factors that were responsible for policy convergence. Section 6.6 concludes.

6.2   DOMESTIC IMPACT OF THE EU'S COHESION POLICY: THEORETICAL EXPECTATIONS

The degree of sub-national involvement in the regional policy structures is one of the key issues regarding the domestic impact of the cohesion policy. This is because of the anticipated effects of the partnership principle which was introduced with the 1988 reform of the cohesion policy. The partnership principle requires national and regional authorities to jointly coordinate the planning and implementation of the EU-funded programmes. The principle thus creates an opportunity for sub-national governments to actively participate in the design and implementation of the policy (Thielemann 2002). Scholars arguing from a multi-level governance (MLG) perspective expected that the application of the partnership principle would empower sub-national administrative units (counties, districts or regions) at the expense of central governments (Hooghe 1996: 6; Hooghe and Marks 2001).

The MLG framework is about the vertical diffusion of power across multiple levels of government by which the supranational and sub-national authorities gain more powers from the central state. This is relevant for the cohesion policy because the partnership principle would potentially trigger such power sharing mechanisms as could lead to a so-called 'Type I' governance system where decision-making authority is dispersed across several territorial levels (Hooghe and Marks 2003). This may involve decentralization at the domestic level and an active presence of sub-national regions in the supranational political space.

Because regional policies were weak in CEE and the EU exercised strong regulatory influence over them especially during the accession negotiations, the CEE countries were expected to respond to the partnership principle in line with the MLG framework. However, the lack of legally binding EU rules about the 'desired' degree of regionalization reduced the strength of external pressure and gave central governments plenty of leeway to choose their own model of regional policy. Adaptation to the cohesion policy may therefore be more or less voluntary. In this respect, two competing hypotheses can be posed. Building on the argument of Brusis (2005), either policy transfer may be driven by the power asymmetry between CEE states and the EU or, conversely, domestic political considerations would be the main drivers of adaptation to cohesion policy requirements.

Scholars who have studied this issue have often reached contradicting conclusions. Some have argued that the EU's impact has been shallow (Brusis 2005; Bruszt 2008; Dąbrowski 2012) because decentralization was limited in CEE and the partnership principle was only formally and superficially applied. Others have identified notable EU effects, particularly in the strengthening of the role of the regions in domestic territorial administrations (Scherpereel 2010).

Although these findings highlight important aspects of domestic adaptation to the cohesion policy, they only consider territorial reforms and fail to capture the temporal dynamics of the policy process. However, taking into account the policy dynamics over time would be crucial for the understanding of how the interactions between shifting EU cohesion policy priorities and domestic interests shape regional policy in CEE. The contribution of this chapter lies in the exploration of how the regional policy dynamics in the Czech Republic and Hungary since the early 1990s have led to policy convergence between the two countries. While the focus is on the domestic institutional structures, the chapter also addresses territorial reforms and discusses the extent to which domestic regional policy objectives have aligned with shifting EU priorities.

6.3   POLICY TRANSFER AND POLICY CONVERGENCE

Policy convergence is a special type of policy transfer characterized by 'growing similarity of policies over time' and across countries (Holzinger and Knill 2005: 776). It is a process of becoming rather than being more alike (Bennett 1991: 219). This definition assumes different initial conditions across the examined cases. Convergence therefore should reflect trends over time. In this sense, policy convergence is a systematic approximation across cases that demonstrate markedly different starting positions.

What mechanisms may lead to policy convergence? This chapter adopts the framework of Holzinger and Knill (2005), who distinguish five main mechanisms ranging from more coercive to more voluntary transfers that can produce policy convergence: imposition; international harmonization; regulatory competition; transnational communication; and independent problem-solving. International harmonization and transnational communication are of special interest here because they are the closest to the mechanisms that were driving policy convergence between the Czech Republic and Hungary.

International harmonization involves compliance with a legal obligation articulated through international law. This refers to a 'constellation in which national governments are legally required to adopt similar policies and programmes as part of their obligations as members of international institutions' (Holzinger and Knill 2005: 782). A more voluntary transfer mechanism is transnational communication, where the main driver of transfer is domestic considerations instead of external pressure. The authors differentiate four sub-types of transnational communication, among which lesson-drawing lies closest to our observed cases. By lesson-drawing 'governments rationally utilize available experience elsewhere in order to solve domestic problems' (Holzinger and Knill 2005: 783). In the context of cohesion policy, the need to administer, manage and implement EU funds constitutes the domestic problem which requires solution. The above definitions of international harmonization and lesson-drawing show conceptual similarity to the mechanisms of obligated transfer and lesson-drawing identified by Dolowitz and Marsh (2000).

What factors may facilitate policy convergence? First, convergence is more likely if the external rule has high legal specification and it can be effectively enforced. Second, convergence is more likely if countries are exposed to the same external information and if they share similar policy legacies. At the same time, high adaptation costs or a strong political opposition decreases the likelihood of policy convergence (Holzinger and Knill 2005). As the chapter will demonstrate in the Czech and the Hungarian cases, only the designation of the cohesion regions was driven by highly specified legal requirements. Apart from that, transnational communication was the dominant transfer mechanism that led to the convergence in regional policies.

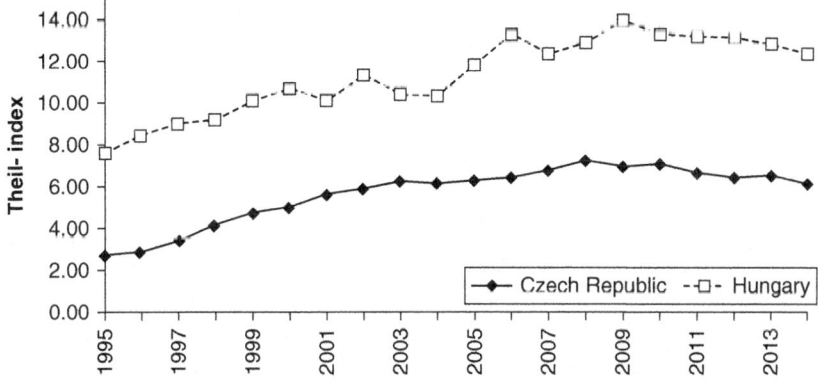

Source: The author's own calculation based on regional GDP and population data obtained from the national statistical offices.

Figure 6.1   Regional disparities (Theil-index) at the NUTS 3 level in the Czech Republic and Hungary (1995–2014)

6.4   REGIONAL POLICIES IN THE CZECH REPUBLIC AND HUNGARY IN THE EARLY 1990S

The initial Czech and Hungarian conditions differed in two important aspects. First, unlike the Czech Republic, Hungary faced high regional disparities after the regime change. Territorial inequality thus constituted a political and economic problem early on. As Figure 6.1 reveals, until recently regional disparities calculated for the NUTS 3 territorial units were rising in both countries, but inequality in the Czech Republic remained significantly below the Hungarian level in the entire period. Developed by the EU, the Nomenclature of Territorial Units for Statistics (NUTS) is a hierarchical system used for referencing the subdivisions of countries for statistical purposes and has been utilized for the delivery of EU funds. The NUTS 3 units refer to smaller territorial-administrative regions (like the *département* in France or the *Kreis* in Germany), while the NUTS 2 regions are larger entities. Regions that are eligible for support from the cohesion policy are defined at the NUTS 2 level.

Second, unlike Hungary, which has no tradition of regionalism, the Czech Republic shows strong regional identities linked to the historic lands of Bohemia, Moravia and Silesia. This is a potentially important aspect for regionalization because political demands for self-governing regions may build on such identities. Indeed, in the first democratic elections in 1990, a regional movement for Moravia and Silesia earned one-third of the votes in these two historic regions (Jordan 2001).

Aside from the above differences, the two countries shared some common legacies. Prior to 1989, a systematic, territorially focused regional policy was absent in both the former Czechoslovakia and Hungary. Even though Hungary had the most elaborate system of regional planning among the communist countries, sectoral rather than territorial considerations were dominating it (Downes 1996). The same applied to the Czech case, where central planning focused exclusively on industrial development without accounting for territorial aspects (Bachtler and Downes 2000). Another common feature was the legacy of centralized administration: the sub-national administrative units – tightly controlled by the communist parties – represented the executive arm of the central government (Blažek and Kara 1992).

It would follow from the above conditions that without intervening external influences the two countries would take different regional policy approaches. While in Hungary regional disparities would urge the government to tackle the problem, in the Czech Republic the territorial reform would take a dominant position on the political agenda. These expectations were accurate, but only in the early years of transition until the EU gained more leverage over CEE.

In the early 1990s, Hungary faced a sharp and growing east–west development divide and an excessively dominant position of the capital city. In addition, unemployment rates in the crisis-ridden, backward eastern counties were steeply rising. This situation called for policy intervention, but initially the first democratically elected centre-right government was reluctant to pursue regional policy because it was associated with the discredited practice of central planning (Horváth 2001: 390). However, owing to the pressing levels of territorial inequality, in 1991 the government established the Regional Development Fund (RDF), which subsequently became the most important tool of domestic regional policy.

Contrary to Hungary, the Czech Republic did not adopt any regional policy measures in the early 1990s: uncoordinated sectoral policies allocated limited funding to tackle isolated regional problems (Ferry and McMaster 2005). Nevertheless, the unfolding crisis of heavy industry and the rising levels of unemployment triggered a response from the central government: in 1994 a parliamentary decree created the legal basis for supporting small and medium-sized enterprises in areas of high unemployment (Červený and Andrle 2000). Yet, this measure was limited in its scope and only affected the areas of heavy industry. The absence of regional policy was partly motivated by the relatively low level of internal disparities but also by political considerations. The centre-right government led by Vaclav Klaus (1992–1996) pursued neo-liberal economic policies and did not perceive the need for any policy interventions that might distort the market (Vozáb 2007).

However, as expected, the issue of territorial reform and regionalization constituted a key part of the political debates. The 1993 Czech constitution declared that the country is 'composed of municipalities which are the basic territorial administrative units and regions which are higher territorial administrative units' (cited by LaPlant et al. 2004: 38). In spite of the constitutional mandate to create self-governing regions, the parliament did not rush to fulfil this obligation.

This is because the separation of Slovakia induced fears that decentralization would lead to further disintegration. The outbreak of the Yugoslav wars amplified those concerns. Second, the prime minister's Civic Democratic Party shared a sceptical view about regionalization because they considered it a threat to central power. At the same time, their junior coalition partners, the Christian Democrats, were in favour of decentralization also because most of their electoral support came from Moravia (LaPlant et al. 2004). There was political stalemate on the issue until the growing EU influence released the deadlock.

In the 1990s, the EU had relatively low direct influence on domestic policies in CEE, but it was active in providing development assistance through the PHARE (Poland and Hungary: Assistance for Restructuring their Economies) programme. PHARE funds became available for all the CEE countries, and contributed to the establishing of regional development agencies in the Czech Republic (Ferry and McMaster 2005) and the Ministry of Regional Development in 1996 (Marek and Baun 2002). The PHARE also funded regional development projects in northern Moravia as well as in north-east Hungary (European Commission 1998b). However, those projects were not based on the partnership principle, because their management and implementation remained the exclusive competence of the central governments and the European Commission (Marek and Baun 2002).

A major turning point came in 1996 when the Hungarian parliament adopted the Act on Regional Development and Physical Planning. EU experts heavily supported the preparation of the law, and with this piece of legislation Hungary became the first CEE state to have a comprehensive regional policy concept which was also in line with EU expectations (Downes 2000). But why did the regional development law align with EU norms given that external pressure was low in this period?

The primary reason for this lies in the fact that the 1994 Hungarian parliamentary elections gave a constitutional majority to a socialist-liberal coalition for which regional disparities represented a key concern. On the one hand, this was because the socialist party's strongholds were the most crisis-ridden, backward areas of the country. On the other hand, the socialists were the successors of the former communist party and they had to compensate for this legacy by showing commitment to democratization in general and European integration in particular. The combination of domestic political interests in regional development issues and the need to demonstrate engagement with Europe produced voluntary compliance with EU cohesion policy.

The regional development law defined mid-tier territorial units (NUTS 3 level counties or *megye*) as the basic targets for support, with which the law emulated EU practice. The four, partially overlapping categories of designated areas (socially and economically less developed areas, industrial restructuring areas, agricultural areas and areas of high unemployment) also reflected EU influence because they strongly resembled the categories of assisted regions determined in the EU's cohesion policy. Furthermore, the law delineated seven regions that corresponded to the NUTS 2 level, but their boundaries remained provisional because the creation of a regional level of state administration generated heated political debates in Hungary. However, unlike in the Czech Republic, those disputes were not related to decentralization but to the boundaries of the NUTS 2 regions, which were simply regarded as statistical planning units necessary for gaining access to EU funds (Illés 2001).

To sum up, markedly different trajectories and limited EU involvement characterized regional policies in Hungary and in the Czech Republic in the early 1990s. While with EU assistance Hungary developed an EU-compatible regional law, the Czech government was reluctant to address the issue. At the same time, unlike in Hungary, the Czech political scene witnessed fierce debates about regionalization and decentralization. After these early developments, the EU strongly influenced the regional policy responses, to which the next section turns.

6.5   CONVERGENCE OF REGIONAL POLICIES AS A RESPONSE TO EU REQUIREMENTS

The formal expectations about how the CEE countries should align their domestic regional policies to comply with the cohesion policy were communicated during the accession negotiations. The applicants had to designate territorial units in compliance with the NUTS territorial statistical system, design a national development plan, have 'appropriate administrative capacity' to implement the policy and 'ensure the implementation of the partnership principle at the different stages of programming, financing, monitoring and evaluation of Structural Funds assistance' (European Commission 2004: 67). While the application of the partnership principle would suggest regionalized structures of fund administration, even the EU emphasized that 'how the specific structures for the practical management of Structural and the Cohesion Funds look like is left to candidate countries' (European Commission 2004: 67).

The lax rules offered ample space for political manoeuvre. The *acquis* is 'thin' on the institutional requirements for the implementation of the regional policy (Hughes et al. 2004), and the EU has no legal authority to demand harmonization of the regional policy systems of the member states either (Ferry and McMaster 2013: 1505); nor is there a compulsory EU law concerning regionalization. The only coherent legal requirement was to establish territorial units that comply with the NUTS system and to draft national development plans that outline the main objectives and operational programmes.

Nevertheless, the European Commission was pushing for decentralization and the creation of regions with independent administrative powers. During the accession negotiations it revealed its preference for elected regional administrations instead of territorial units without any powers (Hughes et al. 2004). In the 1997 country opinion, the European Commission openly criticized the Czech government for the absence of regional policy and that '[t]here exists no elected body between the State and the communes although the constitution foresees the establishment of the so-called territorial units of self-administration' (European Commission 1997: 83). The direct pressure from the Commission served as an empowering factor for the social democrats, who promoted regionalization (LaPlant et al. 2004).

The criticism facilitated an agreement among the parliamentary parties that finally adopted the Constitutional Act on the Formation of Regions in December 1997. The new law established 14 regions (*kraje*) with elected self-government bodies (Brusis 2005). These mid-tier territorial units corresponded to the NUTS 3 level; thus they were too small to satisfy the criteria for the NUTS 2 regions which are the primary targets of EU funds. The agreement reflected a compromise between Klaus's party, which wanted a greater number of smaller regions to ensure that they would have low political significance, and the social democrats, who preferred a smaller number of larger regions, which would have been more effective and also more compatible with the EU's requirements (Marek and Baun 2002). In the end, the *kraje* were grouped together to form eight purely administrative NUTS 2 level 'cohesion regions'.

In 1998, a social democratic government came into power that declared regional policy as a priority. The new government created a working group of 12 governmental bodies chaired by the Ministry of Regional Development (Blažek and Boeckhout 2000). The Ministry was assigned the responsibility for coordinating the activities in the field of economic and social cohesion and it also began drafting the national development plan.

Unlike in the case of the Czech Republic, the Commission lauded Hungary in the 1997 country opinion as the first state in CEE that had introduced a regional policy framework which was in close compliance with the EU's cohesion policy. However, the 1998 progress report criticized the country because of the unsettled status of the NUTS 2 regions. By doing so, the Commission made an implicit reference to the lack of administrative powers of the NUTS 2 regions (Hughes et al. 2004). The report required that the problems 'be addressed before Hungary is ready to participate in the EU structural policy' (European Commission 1998a: 33).

To resolve the issue, the 1998 National Spatial Development Concept – adopted under the centre-right government led by Fidesz that replaced the socialist-liberal coalition – reinforced the seven NUTS 2 regions, of which boundaries were delimited only provisionally in the 1996 law. Because each NUTS 2 unit was the aggregation of self-governing NUTS 3 counties (*megye*), a mismatch – as in the Czech case – emerged between the boundaries of the cohesion regions and regions with administrative powers. Another common feature was that, like the Czech Civic Democratic Party, Fidesz was inclined to maintain central state control over regional development issues and was reluctant to engage in wide-scale decentralization (Varró and Faragó 2016).

The above developments suggest that both governments fulfilled the obligation of establishing sub-national units that corresponded to the NUTS classification. This process can be best described as international harmonization, because the main driver of the policy responses was a well-specified legal obligation articulated in European law. As for the territorial reforms, they resemble the mechanism of transnational communication, because domestic political interests determined the responses to the problem due to pressure posed by the cohesion policy requirements. In both cases, the EU triggered policy change, but its expectations were translated to the domestic context according to the interests of the governing parties. However, it would be misleading to further specify the mechanism as lesson-drawing, because it is not clear if the governments utilized external experience for designing the territorial reforms. They simply relied on the domestic legacies of centralized administration for which they did not need any external input.

After the reform of the territorial systems, both countries remained unitary states with very limited powers delegated to the sub-national level.

Although the Commission first criticized the lack of decentralization, it gradually changed its view as the accession negotiations advanced. The Prodi Commission, which entered office in 1999, realized that the weak administrative capacity of the regional actors in CEE would seriously compromise the ability of these countries to effectively manage EU funds (Bailey and De Propris 2004). The Commission had to acknowledge that 'the decentralisation of responsibilities necessary for an effective regional policy is likely to be a lengthy process' (European Commission 1999: 193)

By turning away from the regionalization agenda, the Commission also admitted that pre-accession funds failed to generate developmental capacity on the sub-national level. This also involved limited regional participation in the cohesion policy. In the end, the Commission 'wanted centralized management of funds so as to maximize efficiency, streamlining and control of expenditures' (Hughes et al. 2004: 541).

The change in the Commission's approach had direct consequences on the national development plans and the domestic decision-making structures. The national development plans (NDPs) constituted the main documents for the implementation of cohesion policy programmes in 2004–2006, the first period when the CEE countries were eligible for funding from the cohesion policy. The NDPs outlined those 'operational programmes' which the EU had to approve before funding could commence.

The Czech government presented the first draft of the NDP to the Commission in July 2001. This version of the document suggested six sectoral operational programmes and eight regional operational programmes (ROPs), one for each NUTS 2 region. In the spirit of the partnership principle, the regional councils would have managed the ROPs, while the Ministry of Regional Development would have been responsible for the sectoral programmes. However, the Commission expressed concerns about the number of operational programmes, and in the 2001 progress report it declared that '[t]he Czech authorities should urgently take a number of fundamental decisions on the implementation of Structural Funds Programmes, most notably on the number of Operational Programmes' (European Commission 2001: 82).

During the negotiations the Czech government revealed that it would prefer merging the eight regional programmes into a single operational programme, which the Commission subsequently approved. In this scenario the full responsibility for programme management would lie at the Ministry, and the regional councils would only play a consultative role in fund administration. The problem with the joint regional operational programme was that it did not take into account specific regional needs and priorities, as it only referred to common development problems.

Nevertheless, its implementation would have involved a much simpler and shorter process than the separate regional operational programmes (Sodomka 2003). The *kraj* administrations had a strong interest in the separate ROPs because they would have gained control over additional financial resources, which would have also challenged the balance of power between the central government and the regions (Baun and Marek 2006).

The regional representatives objected to the single ROP, but they failed to convince the government. By referring to the Commission's preference for efficiency over decentralization, in January 2002 the Czech government decided to include a single integrated ROP into the NDP. This caused a major disappointment for regional leaders, but they did not voice their disagreement in a coordinated manner (Baun and Marek 2006: 416).

The adoption of the Hungarian NDP for 2004–2006 shares several commonalities with the Czech case. Work on the development plan began in 1999 during the Fidesz-led conservative government. In this phase, regional actors were sidelined because an inter-ministerial committee was responsible for drafting the first version of the document (Varró and Faragó 2016). When the socialists returned to government in 2002, they aimed at strengthening the NUTS 2 regions at the expense of the self-governing NUTS 3 counties. In this vein, they planned to assign greater responsibility for the regional councils through the adoption of separate ROPs for each NUTS 2 region.

Two important developments prevented the government from executing this plan. First, after the 2002 autumn local elections the socialists began to dominate the county assemblies, which immediately toned down their idea on weakening the county level. Second, in the 2002 progress report the Commission expressed concerns about the ability of the sub-national administration to effectively participate in the cohesion policy. The document maintained that '[t]he capacity of regional and local actors as well as other relevant partners to prepare, and implement projects, needs to be considerably strengthened' (European Commission 2002: 101). Given the pressing time constraints until accession, the government decided to adopt the NDP with a single ROP (Varró and Faragó 2016).

In the end, both countries introduced similar administrative structures for the management and implementation of the EU funds. In the Czech Republic the Ministry of Regional Development became the managing authority for the whole NDP, while line ministries took care of the individual operational programmes. In Hungary, the prime responsibility for the programmes was assigned to the National Development Office and, as with the Czech arrangements, line ministries undertook the management of the operational programmes. Even in the case of the larger regional operational programmes these central government organizations performed both the management and the implementation duties (Pálné Kovács et al. 2004; Bachtler and McMaster 2007). The regional administrations were able to exert formal influence on programme management only through the monitoring committees.

The governments thus adopted centralized fund management structures with very weak involvement of the sub-national level. Although this is a 'mis-translation' of the partnership principle, it was a rational step given the limited institutional capacity of the regional administrations, the time pressure towards accession, and the goal of maximizing access to the funds. With the approval of the Commission, efficiency prevailed over the application of the partnership principle, and thereby the central state retained control over the funds and reinforced its gatekeeper position towards the sub-national level.

While the Commission gave up on decentralization in CEE, other key EU-level developments affected the cohesion policy in the early 2000s. The adoption of the Lisbon strategy in March 2000 set new mid-term strategic goals for the EU. According to this agenda, by 2010 the EU should have become 'the most competitive and dynamic knowledge-based economy in the world capable of sustainable economic growth with more and better jobs and greater social cohesion' (Council of the European Union 2000). This involved the promotion of overall economic growth through enhanced support for the metropolitan and city areas instead of the backward regions because, presumably, those urban locations are the most capable of producing knowledge and innovation (Heimpold 2008).

In line with the Lisbon strategy, the EU began to emphasize the promotion of growth and development in all the territories (Bachtler and Wishlade 2011). The shift in the cohesion policy objectives coincided with the growing global popularity of the so-called place-based approach to regional policy, which aims at stimulating growth everywhere relying on endogenous growth potentials (Barca 2009). The place-based narrative highlights under-utilized regional potentials, and it implies that 'the spatial boundaries of intervention should be open-ended and respond to the functional needs of places at different scales' (Mendez 2013: 645).

The place-based approach also requires more attention to local development needs and puts more emphasis on local ownership of the projects. In this respect, it supports the partnership principle. In line with this, the EU urged for greater involvement of the sub-national level in the management and implementation of the cohesion policy programmes for 2007–2013 and required that '[t]he partnership should be strengthened through arrangements for the participation of various types of partner, in particular regional and local authorities' (Council of the European Union 2006: Article 23).

In practice, these guidelines suggested the opening of fund management and implementation to local and regional partners and a revision of the national development goals to promote the urban and metropolitan growth poles at the expense of the backward areas. The latter is especially problematic in CEE because there is a simultaneous need to facilitate catch-up with the more developed older EU members (promotion of growth and competitiveness) and to decrease high internal regional disparities (promotion of territorial equity). The two goals, however, are hard to pursue simultaneously. In line with this, the Lisbon agenda quite openly suggests the promotion of growth rather than equalization. Being exposed to the same external expectations, both the Czech and the Hungarian governments responded in a similar way.

The new national development plans for 2007–2013 contained individual ROPs for each cohesion region (eight in the Czech Republic, seven in Hungary) as a response to the call for greater regional involvement in the programme management and implementation. In both countries, the regional councils became the managing authorities of the ROPs. This represented a substantial move towards the regionalization of EU fund management.

In spite of these developments, the new system exposed some notable weaknesses of the regional administrations, while the whole structure remained strongly centralized. First, although the ROPs were regionally managed in both countries, the control of payments remained centralized (Bachtler and McMaster 2007). This led to a dual management system that was inefficient. Furthermore, the regionally managed programmes represented only 23.2 per cent of the total funds in Hungary and 17.7 per cent in the Czech Republic. The majority of the funds therefore remained in the exclusive control of the central government.[2]

The mismatch between the boundaries of the NUTS 2 cohesion regions and the self-governing NUTS 3 counties (the *kraje* and the *megye*) posed a further problem. While the counties had a clear democratic mandate, their development function was compromised because the EU programmes and all the funds were linked to the NUTS 2 regions (Ferry and McMaster 2005). Moreover, the system inherently generated distributional conflicts between representatives of different NUTS 3 units who were sitting in the same regional councils (Scherpereel 2010).

The 'Lisbonization' of the cohesion policy also influenced the Czech and Hungarian regional policy objectives in a similar way. While the 2004–2006 national development plans emphasized balanced territorial development and promoted the equalization of regional disparities, the 2007–2013 documents represented a shift towards the place-based approach (Heimpold 2008). In line with the Lisbon goals, the new Hungary development plan adopted by the socialist government formulated a developmental pole programme. The key element of this was the promotion of pole cities as growth centres. The idea behind the designation of the development poles was to counterbalance the capital city in the country's settlement structure.

However, anticipating that the growth pole status would bring earmarked EU funds, city mayors and parliamentary representatives began to lobby for including more settlements as growth poles in the plan (Varró 2010). In the end, the original idea was diluted, although the concept of developmental poles remained in the final version of the document. The 2005 revision of the National Spatial Development Concept also incorporated the Lisbon agenda in the country's developmental objectives in that it placed the emphasis on promoting growth and competitiveness at the expense of equalization (Salamin et al. 2005).

Although the Czech development plan contained an objective of territorial equalization, the Lisbon agenda visibly influenced this document, too. Instead of placing the emphasis on lowering disparities, the plan explicitly stated that 'in compliance with the Lisbon Strategy' it promoted 'the competitiveness of regions with the highest growth potential, whose stimulation will contribute to the Czech Republic's convergence to the European average' (Ministry of Regional Development 2007: 65). Furthermore, the document indicated the need to 'support the development of urban areas, towns as poles of development and the territory in development axes whereby it spreads their development impulses into the surroundings' (Ministry of Regional Development 2007: 64, also cited in Heimpold 2008: 21).

The shift towards promoting growth instead of equity was less sharp in reality because of the adoption of ROPs that specifically aimed at lowering territorial inequality. However, as recent research has shown (Medve-Bálint 2015), the developmental pole concept prevailed in both countries because the more prosperous and more urbanized regions benefited more from the 2007–2013 funds than the most backward and rural areas.

The latest reform of the cohesion policy is strongly related to the economic crisis of 2007–2008. To tackle the crisis, member states introduced tough austerity measures. As a side-effect, net contributor countries to the EU budget, especially Germany and the United Kingdom, began to demand stricter fund spending rules (Bachtler et al. 2013). Their goal was to align the cohesion policy with the economic governance agenda, which prescribes a strict mechanism of fiscal surveillance and requires greater fiscal discipline from the member states. The efforts of the net contributors proved successful, and since 2014 the cohesion policy has been closely aligned with the EU's economic governance agenda: fiscal discipline, efficient spending and the stimulation of growth became its primary objectives.

The focus of the cohesion policy has been further oriented towards enhancing growth and competitiveness. In this vein, the Commission required the concentration of funds on a few priority areas, including a low-carbon economy, research and innovation, the competitiveness of small and medium-sized enterprises, and social inclusion (Mendez 2013). The institutional conditionalities introduced for the 2014–2020 period prescribe efficient spending and strong control over the funds.

Although these recent developments would not necessarily imply a setback for the involvement of regional partners in the management and implementation of EU funds, both the Czech and the Hungarian governments interpreted the changes in a restrictive way when designing the institutional structure for the 2014–2020 programming cycle. This occurred in spite of the generally positive experiences with the participation of local and regional actors in the monitoring committees and in the implementation of ROPs in the previous funding period (Batory and Cartwright 2011; Dąbrowski 2014). Nevertheless, because of the threat of suspended payments if institutional conditionalities are not met, central governments returned to the less risky and presumably more efficient centralized institutional arrangements.

Instead of continuing with the individual regional operational programmes for all the NUTS 2 regions, both in the Czech Republic and Hungary only a single, integrated ROP is implemented in 2014–2020. Although the Czech regions argued strongly in favour of maintaining the separate ROPs (Ferry and McMaster 2013), they failed to reach their goal. This is because the Commission expressed criticism about the irregularities and sub-optimal use of the funds which characterized the implementation of some of the regional programmes (Pelucha and Shutt 2014). Reflecting on these critiques, the Czech government decided to recentralize fund management by adopting a single ROP managed by the Ministry of Regional Development.

In Hungary, the centralization of fund management took an even sharper turn. At the 2010 elections, Fidesz gained a qualified majority in the parliament. The new government subordinated the National Development Agency to the newly established Ministry of National Development and replaced the Agency's management and even the administrators at the desk level. Following this reorganization, local and regional actors were even less involved in the decision-making structure than before. The Commission raised concerns about the restructuring, arguing that it 'may affect the absorption capacity of the Agency' (Buzogány, Áron and

Korkut 2013: 1572–3). By doing so the Commission demonstrated that it was more concerned with the administrative capacity of the bureaucracy than with the application of the partnership principle.

In 2012, the government introduced a far-reaching territorial reform which abolished the regional development councils and delegated their responsibilities to the NUTS 3 county assemblies (Hegedüs and Péteri 2015). Consequently, the NUTS 2 regions no longer play a role in Hungarian regional policy; they have become purely statistical units. The otherwise weak NUTS 3 counties remained the only intermediate partners of the central government.

Regarding the developmental goals for 2014–2020, both governments seem to have aligned with the new EU objectives: enhancing competitiveness and the stimulation of economic growth have become the main targets at the expense of lowering regional disparities. The Czech Partnership Agreement, which sets the framework for the 2014–2020 programmes, specifies the main strategic objectives as: 'developing a high-quality business environment that will support the competitiveness of the Czech Republic in the European and global markets' and '[p]roviding of an inclusive society creating conditions for full assertion of all population groups, increasing the employment rate with an emphasis on reduction of the number of excluded population groups and supporting good living conditions for the population' (Ministry of Regional Development 2014: 118). The Hungarian document is even more explicit in that it states that the overarching national developmental goal is 'sustainable economic growth based on high value added production and employment' (Ministry for National Economy 2013: 11). Clearly, the territorial aspect has been sidelined in both cases in order to maximize access to EU funds.

Domestic regional policies that are independent from the EU funds could potentially counterbalance the lack of attention to regional disparities. However, the difficulty of co-financing EU-funded projects draws domestic resources away from national programmes. This is the reason why some scholars argue that domestic regional policies have been entirely subsumed to the cohesion policy (Grosse 2006). In the Czech Republic, the government decided to abandon two domestic programmes that provided development support for the most backward three NUTS 3 districts. Currently, only a limited amount of grants are available to municipalities for regenerating lands formerly used by the army, and some funds are distributed to flood-affected areas as well (Ferry and McMaster 2013: 1521). In 2004, the Hungarian government allocated 103 million EUR for domestic regional development programmes. By 2007, the budget had been halved, and after 2010 only one domestic policy instrument remained in the state budget, with funds ranging annually between 3 million and

5 million EUR.[3] Thus in both countries EU-funded programmes have almost entirely crowded out domestic initiatives.

6.6 CONCLUSION

The massive financial transfers of the cohesion policy to CEE required policy adaptation from the target countries. This chapter has traced this adaptation process in the Czech Republic and Hungary, which in the early 1990s notably differed in terms of their internal territorial disparities and regional identities. In spite of these differences, the EU influence has shaped the regional policy trajectories of the two countries in a similar direction. The external stimulus triggered such domestic policy responses that led to policy convergence over time.

However, convergence did not follow from a coercive mechanism. With the exception of the designation of NUTS 2 regions, which was a well-specified legal requirement imposed on CEE, transnational communication has been the main mechanism that characterized the evolution of regional policies. Having been exposed to the same external incentives, the central governments adopted similar solutions that best served their domestic political interests.

Contrary to the expectations of MLG scholars, the cohesion policy, and in particular the partnership principle, did not generate decentralization processes, and the involvement of regional and local partners in the management and implementation of the programmes also remained limited. The reason for this is that the EU failed to trigger domestic changes beyond the *acquis*, and it shifted its agenda by placing greater emphasis on the efficient spending of the funds. The changes in the cohesion policy indirectly reinforced centralization tendencies in the Czech Republic and Hungary especially, because the national governments were inclined to retain central control over the funds.

The centralized institutional arrangements for fund management introduced in the early 2000s proved sticky, because with these structures the governments were able to preserve their gatekeeper roles. Also, the EU reinforced rather than challenged those arrangements. What is most interesting is the flexibility with which both governments incorporated the shifting cohesion policy priorities into the domestic development plans. Again, maximizing access to EU funds is the likely explanation for this phenomenon.

All things considered, the EU initiated the process of policy convergence, but this was mainly driven by domestic factors. In this sense, the chapter demonstrated how under the same external stimuli similar policy responses can be adopted even if domestic circumstances differ and the external influence is not coercive. Finally, the chapter has also exposed the limitations of the cohesion policy in triggering domestic policy changes: without highly specified legal requirements, member states are free to translate the external expectations according to their own interests. The low influence of the EU on domestic regional policy structures is somewhat ironic given that this policy domain represents the largest item in the EU budget.

NOTES

1. The author's own calculation based on European Commission and Eurostat data.
2. The author's own calculation based on the National Strategic Reference Frameworks.
3. The author's own calculation based on the annual budget laws of Hungary.

REFERENCES

Bachtler, John and Ruth Downes (2000), 'The spatial coverage of regional policy in Central and Eastern Europe', *European Urban and Regional Studies*, 7 (2), 159–74.

Bachtler, John and Irene McMaster (2007), 'EU cohesion policy and the role of the regions: Investigating the influence of Structural Funds in the new member states', *Environment and Planning C: Government and Policy*, 26 (2), 398–427.

Bachtler, John and Fiona Wishlade (2011), *Regional Policy in Europe: Divergent Trajectories? Annual Review of Regional Policy in Europe*, Glasgow: European Regional Policy Research Consortium, University of Strathclyde.

Bachtler, John, Carlos Mendez and Fiona Wishlade (2013), 'National interests in cohesion policy and the positions of member states', in John Bachtler, Carlos Mendez and Fiona Wishlade (eds), *EU Cohesion Policy and European Integration: The Dynamics of Budget and Policy Reform*, Farnham: Ashgate, pp. 163–200.

Bailey David and Lisa De Propris (2004), 'A bridge too Phare? EU pre-accession aid and capacity-building in the candidate countries', *Journal of Common Market Studies*, 42 (1), 77–98.

Barca, Fabrizio (2009), 'An agenda for a reformed cohesion policy: A place-based approach to meeting European Union challenges and expectations', Independent report prepared at the request of Danuta Hübner, Commissioner for Regional Policy.

Batory, Agnes and Andrew Cartwright (2011), 'Re-visiting the partnership principle in cohesion policy: The role of civil society organizations in Structural Funds monitoring', *Journal of Common Market Studies*, 49 (4), 697–717.

Baun, Michael and Dan Marek (2006), 'Regional policy and decentralization in the Czech Republic', *Regional and Federal Studies*, 16 (4), 409–28.

Bennett, Colin J. (1991), 'What is policy convergence and what causes it?', *British Journal of Political Science*, 21 (2), 215–33.

Blažek, Jiří and Sjaak Boeckhout (2000), 'Regional policy in the Czech Republic and EU accession', in John Bachtler, Ruth Downes and Grzegorz Gorzelak (eds), *Transition, Cohesion and Regional Policy in Central and Eastern Europe*, Aldershot: Ashgate, pp. 301–18.

Blažek, Jiří and Jan Kara (1992), 'Regional policy in the Czech Republic in the period of transition', in Grzegorz Gorzelak and Antoni Kukliński (eds), *Dilemmas of Regional Policies in Eastern and Central Europe*, Warsaw: European Institute for Regional and Local Development, University of Warsaw, pp. 78–94.

Brusis, Martin (2005), 'The instrumental use of European Union conditionality: Regionalization in the Czech Republic and Slovakia', *East European Politics and Societies*, 19 (2), 291–316.

Bruszt, László (2008), 'Multi-level governance – the Eastern versions: Emerging patterns of regional developmental governance in the new member states', *Regional and Federal Studies*, 18 (5), 607–28.

Buzogány, Áron and Umut Korkut (2013), 'Administrative reform and regional development discourses in Hungary: Europeanisation going NUTS?', *Europe–Asia Studies*, 65 (8), 1555–77.

Červený, Miloš and Alois Andrle (2000), 'Czech Republic', in John Bachtler, Ruth Downes and Grzegorz Gorzelak (eds), *Transition, Cohesion and Regional Policy in Central and Eastern Europe*, Aldershot: Ashgate, pp. 85–97.

Council of the European Union (2000), *Lisbon European Council Presidency Conclusions*, Brussels: European Council, http://www.europarl.europa.eu/summits/lis1_en.htm#a (accessed 6 July 2016).

Council of the European Union (2006), Council Regulation (EC) No. 1083/2006 of 11 July 2006, *Official Journal of the European Union*, L 210/25, http://eur-lex.europa.eu/legal-content/EN/TXT/HTML/?uri=CELEX:32006R1083&from=EN (accessed 6 July 2016).

Dąbrowski, Marcin (2012), 'Shallow or deep Europeanisation? The uneven impact of EU cohesion policy on the regional and local authorities in Poland', *Environment and Planning C: Government and Policy*, 30 (4), 730–45.

Dąbrowski, Marcin (2014), 'EU cohesion policy, horizontal partnership and the patterns of sub-national governance: Insights from Central and Eastern Europe', *European Urban and Regional Studies*, 21 (4), 364–83.

Dolowitz, David P. and David Marsh (2000), 'Learning from abroad: The role of policy transfer in contemporary policy-making', *Governance*, 13 (1), 5–23.

Downes, Ruth (1996), 'Economic transformation in Central and Eastern Europe: The role of regional development', *European Planning Studies*, 4 (2), 217–24.

Downes, Ruth (2000), 'Regional policy evolution in Hungary', in John Bachtler, Ruth Downes and Grzegorz Gorzelak (eds), *Transition, Cohesion and Regional Policy in Central and Eastern Europe*, Aldershot: Ashgate, pp. 331–44.

European Commission (1997), *Commission Opinion on the Czech Republic's Application for Membership of the European Union*, Country Opinion, Brussels: European Commission, http://ec.europa.eu/rapid/press-release_DOC-97-13_en.pdf (accessed 6 July 2016).

European Commission (1998a), *Regular Report from the Commission on Hungary's Progress towards Accession*, Brussels: European Commission, http://ec.europa.eu/enlargement/archives/pdf/key_documents/1998/hungary_en.pdf (accessed 6 July 2016).

European Commission (1998b), *The Phare Programme Annual Report 1996*, Brussels: European Commission.

European Commission (1999), *Sixth Periodic Report on the Social and Economic*

Situation and Development of the Regions of the European Union, Brussels: Commission of the European Communities.

European Commission (2001), *Regular Report from the Commission on Czech Republic's Progress towards Accession*, Progress Report, Brussels: European Commission, http://aei.pitt.edu/44559/1/czech 2001.pdf (accessed 6 July 2016).

European Commission (2002), *Regular Report on Hungary's Progress towards Accession*, Progress Report, Brussels: European Commission, http://ec.europa. eu/enlargement/archives/pdf/key_documents/2002/hu_en.pdf (accessed 6 July 2016).

European Commission (2004), *Enlargement of the European Union – Guide to the Negotiations Chapter by Chapter*, Brussels: European Commission, http:// ec.europa.eu/enlargement/archives/pdf/enlargement_process/future_prospects/ negotiations/eu10_bulgaria_romania/negotiationsguide_en.pdf (accessed 7 July 2016).

Ferry, Martin and Irene McMaster (2005), 'Implementing Structural Funds in Polish and Czech regions: Convergence, variation, empowerment?', *Regional and Federal Studies*, 15 (1), 19–39.

Ferry, Martin and Irene McMaster (2013), 'Cohesion policy and the evolution of reg ional policy in Central and Eastern Europe', *Europe–Asia Studies*, 65 (8), 1502–28.

Grosse, Tomasz Grzegorz (2006), 'Euro-commentary: An evaluation of the regional policy system in Poland: Challenges and threats emerging from participation in the EU's cohesion policy', *European Urban and Regional Studies*, 13 (2), 151–65.

Hegedüs, József and Gábor Péteri (2015), Közszolgáltatási reformok és a helyi önkormányzatiság' [Public service reforms and local governance], *Szociológiai Szemle*, 25 (2), 90–119.

Heimpold, Gerhard (2008), 'Growth versus equalisation? An examination of strategies for regional policy in the Czech Republic, Hungary and Poland after EU accession', *Jahrbuch für Regionalwissenschaft*, 28 (1), 1–29.

Holzinger, Katharina and Christoph Knill (2005), 'Causes and conditions of cross-national policy convergence', *Journal of European Public Policy*, 12 (5), 775–96.

Hooghe, Liesbet (1996), 'Introduction: Reconciling EU-wide policy and national diversity', in Liesbet Hooghe (ed.), *Cohesion Policy and European Integration: Building Multi-Level Governance*, New York: Oxford University Press, pp. 1–26.

Hooghe, Liesbet and Gary Marks (2001), *Multi-Level Governance and European Integration*, London: Rowman & Littlefield.

Hooghe, Liesbet and Gary Marks (2003), 'Unravelling the central state, but how? Types of multi-level governance', *American Political Science Review*, 97 (2), 233–43.

Horváth, Gyula (2001), *Európai Regionális Politika* [European regional policy], Budapest: Dialóg-Campus.

Hughes, James, Gwendolyn Sasse and Claire Gordon (2004), 'Conditionality and compliance in the EU's eastward enlargement: Regional policy and the reform of sub-national government', *Journal of Common Market Studies*, 42 (3), 523–51.

Illés, Iván (2001), 'Régiók és regionalizáció' [Regions and regionalization], *Tér és Társadalom*, 15 (1), 1–23.

Jordan, Peter (2001), 'Regional identities and regionalization in East-Central Europe', *Post-Soviet Geography and Economics*, 42 (4), 235–65.

LaPlant, James T., Michael Baun, Jiri Lach and Dan Marek (2004), 'Decentralization in the Czech Republic: The European Union, political parties, and the creation of regional assemblies', *Publius: The Journal of Federalism*, 34 (1), 35–51.

Marek, Dan and Michael Baun (2002), 'The EU as a regional actor: The case of the Czech Republic', *Journal of Common Market Studies*, 40 (5), 895–919.

Medve-Bálint, Gergő (2015), 'Converging on divergence: The political economy of uneven regional development in East Central Europe after the change of regime (1990–2014)', PhD dissertation, Central European University, Budapest.

Mendez, Carlos (2013), 'The post-2013 reform of EU cohesion policy and the place-based narrative', *Journal of European Public Policy*, 20 (5), 639–59.

Ministry for National Economy (2013), *Hungarian Partnership Agreement for the 2014–2020 Programming Period*, Budapest: Ministry for National Economy, https://www.nth.gov.hu/hu/media/download/30 (accessed 7 July 2016).

Ministry of Regional Development (2007), *National Strategic Reference Framework of the Czech Republic 2007–2013*, Prague: Ministry of Regional Development, http://www.strukturalni-fondy.cz/getmedia/247dcbb4-bfc3-4ef8-9c43-4e17ec16aead/NSRF_en_170707_bez_zmen_db_fin-tabulka (accessed 6 July 2016).

Ministry of Regional Development (2014), *Partnership Agreement for the Programming Period 2014–2020*, Prague: Ministry of Regional Development, http://www.strukturalni-fondy.cz/getmedia/92b600c0-fa29-4467-a758-9696268dcefb/CZ-PA-adopted-by-EC-20140826.pdf?ext=.pdf (accessed 7 July 2016).

Pálné Kovács, Ilona, C.J. Paraskevopoulos and G. Horváth (2004), 'Institutional "legacies" and the shaping of regional governance in Hungary', *Regional and Federal Studies*, 14 (3), 430–60.

Pelucha, Martin and John Shutt (2014), 'Preparing for 2014–2020: Can the Czech Republic improve its performance by learning more from the United Kingdom?', *Regions Magazine*, 293 (1), 25–8.

Salamin, Géza, Márton Péti and Tamás Czira (2005), 'Paradigmaváltás küszöbén: Az új Országos Területfejlesztési Koncepció és a területi tervezés' [Paradigm change: The new National Spatial Development Concept and spatial planning], *Területi Statisztika*, 45 (5), 423–39.

Scherpereel, John A. (2010), 'EU cohesion policy and the Europeanization of Central and East European regions', *Regional and Federal Studies*, 20 (1), 45–62.

Sodomka, Vladimír (2003), *Regional Policy in the Czech Republic in the Period around Accession to the European Union*, Prague: Europeum – Institute for European Policy.

Thielemann, Eiko (2002), 'The price of Europeanization: Why European regional policy initiatives are a mixed blessing', *Regional and Federal Studies*, 12 (1), 43–65.

Varró, Krisztina (2010), 'Re-politicising the analysis of "new state spaces" in Hungary and beyond: Towards an effective engagement with "actually existing neoliberalism"', *Antipode*, 42 (5), 1253–78.

Varró, Krisztina and László Faragó (2016), 'The politics of spatial policy and governance in post-1990 Hungary: The interplay between European and national discourses of space', *European Planning Studies*, 24 (1), 39–60.

Vozáb, Jan (2007), 'Evolution of the Czech regional policy in the context of the EU regional policy', 2nd Regional Development and Governance Symposium, Izmir, 25–26 October, http://www.tepav.org.tr/sempozyum/2007/bildiriler/3_4_Vozab.pdf (accessed 6 July 2016).

7. Euroregions: Institutional transfer and reinterpreted norms in Central and Eastern Europe

Sara Svensson

7.1 INTRODUCTION

In the summer of 2015 the government of Hungary drastically reinforced the borders to Serbia by erecting a 170 kilometer long barbed-wire fence. This strengthening of an external European Union (EU) border was motivated by a perceived need to keep out "illegal migrants" (the label used by the Hungarian government), mainly people fleeing unrest in the Middle East. At the same time border controls with ID check-points were reinstated at the border between the Czech Republic and Germany, an example of the several internal EU borders where this would take place in the months that followed. These policy measures caused many to forecast the demise of free movement in Europe and they were seen as symbols of the failure to construct a European polity that would transcend nation-states. Less attention was paid to what happened with social and economic integration around borders at the local level, and with efforts that have been made to construct new political and administrative entities there, especially in the context of cooperation in public administration. In relation to border control, the opinion of the Banat Triplex Confinium – an organization of 50 Hungarian, Romanian and Serbian local governments located close to the borders between the three countries – was not sought and, noticeably, it did not voice any concerns in public (Banat Triplex Confinium EGTC 2016). Likewise, Egrensis, an organization of 22 regions and municipalities at the Czech–German border, was silent on the topic (Euregio Egrensis 2016).

The Banat Triplex Confinium and Egrensis are examples of Euroregions, an umbrella term for formalized cooperation initiatives among sub-national authorities, often including private and non-profit actors, located close to a border in two or more countries in Europe (see Perkmann 2002: 104; Svensson 2013a). The institution of Euroregions – the name signifying the positive connotation of hope embedded in these associations of local and regional authorities joining up across European borders to collaborate around policy issues – came to Central and Eastern Europe (CEE) in the 1990s in the wake of communism, and partly as a result Euroregions increased in number over the next two decades. While some of them are still new, especially those that were created on the basis of the EU 1082/2006 regulation on European Groupings of Territorial Cooperation (EGTCs), enough time has passed to allow an assessment. How should we view these institutions and their achievements? Are they policy successes or failures? Or should the outcome be placed on a degree scale between success and failure, where one can also talk about "resilient success," "conflicted success" and "precarious success" as the middle ground (McConnell 2010: 354)? Or should we reject these efforts at defining policy failure and success as generic concepts altogether and think of these policy transfers as a phenomenon of policy translation (Prince 2010; Stone 2017) implying different interpretations of policy ideals with differences dependent on the level of analysis and the perspective of different types of actors?

In short, the aim of this chapter is to explore why, how and to what effect Euroregions were brought to the "East," here understood in the narrow meaning of the 11 states in CEE that joined the European Union in 2004, 2007 and 2013. These are not new questions, but the novelty of the chapter consists in approaching them from a perspective relying on the key concepts of this volume, "policy transfer" and "policy success/failure," and with original data on stakeholder motivations and perspectives from the region. This leads up to the chapter's main argument that the motivations of the stakeholders at national and especially local government levels become as important, if not more important, factors to consider as are the original policy ideas behind the transferred institution. Transformations of, and deviations from, policy goals result first in the process of transfer and second as a result of the policy attitudes and ideas of implementing local stakeholders. Whether this is judged as failure or, for instance, "precarious success" is to some degree "in the eye of the beholder," be that a transnational actor or a local agent.

Among the new member states that joined the European Union in 2004 and 2007, Hungary was especially active in encouraging the set-up of such institutions, and in 2015 Hungarian borderlands had the highest number of Euroregions registered as EGTCs in Europe. This institutional growth warrants an empirical focus on Euroregions located at borderlands between Hungary and its neighboring countries, and much of the evidence brought forward in this chapter draws from several rounds of fieldwork taking place in these borderlands between 2009 and 2015, consisting of over 100 interviews and numerous site observations. The material has been analyzed using standard qualitative content analysis techniques (Patton 2002: 453; Richards 2005).

The chapter is structured in terms of the concepts of policy transfer and policy success/failure. Section 7.2 provides more detail on what was transferred, why and how, with a primary but not exclusive focus on Hungary, regarding the mechanisms and actors involved in the transmission of Euroregions to CEE. In section 7.3 the chapter seeks to assess whether this relatively straightforward example of a policy transfer can be labeled as either a policy success or a policy failure and, if so, by whom. The vantage of discussion is within the CEE Euroregion and focuses on local processes of interpretation and amendment.

7.2   THE POLICY TRANSFER OF EUROREGIONS TO EAST CENTRAL EUROPE

In discussions on policy transfer, some countries are frequently viewed as "senders," whereas others are called "receivers," or countries have been referred to as "lenders" and "borrowers" (Robertson 1991; Rose 1991; Robertson and Waltman 1992). Whereas this terminology is a simplification of a reality in many aspects – for instance by giving primary agency to one set of actors and by neglecting the existence of reverse directions in many policy areas – it is clear that Euroregions as an institution did not have any forerunners in Eastern Europe before 1989 and that they were not independently invented. It is therefore a case of the frequent West-to-East transfer. In this section, the idea is to outline what was "sent" by which actors in sub-section 7.2.1, and what "arrived" (or was "received") in sub-section 7.2.2.

7.2.1   What Was "Sent" by Whom

In Dolowitz and Marsh's (2000) seminal work on policy transfer, eight categories of policy transfer were identified (policy goals, policy content, policy instruments, policy programs, institutions, ideologies, ideas and attitudes). This content can be transferred wholesale ("copying") or partially (on a sliding scale towards "inspiration"). As will be shown, regarding the case of Euroregions, the type of transfer concerned is primarily the transfer of an institution, which was transferred in remarkable completeness. Other elements include instruments, goals, ideas and attitudes.

While the legal arrangements vary – 'Euroregion' is not a legal term and different local requirements for bilateral cooperation need to be fulfilled – the structure and policy ambitions of these organizations have showed surprisingly little variation since the 1950s. Most have operated through assemblies joining local governments and/or regions, electing a board and working groups, with usually at least one manager being hired. They have been set up for multiple purposes, but would often put special emphasis in their founding documents on cooperation around regional/economic development including infrastructure and cultural cooperation, with the possibility open for cooperation in a range of other areas, from tourism to health. Since the foundation of the first Euroregion in 1958 – the Dutch–German EUREGIO – around 150 such organizations have come into existence (see Perkmann 2003; Svensson 2013b). They first developed in Western and Northern Europe, where they numbered around 30 at the end of the 1980s, and through the active promotion by a variety of international and domestic actors that will be discussed below they spread rapidly to the East and South after 1990. For instance, during the 1990s the Erzgebirge and Elbe/Labe Euroregions at the German–Czech border were founded in 1992, and Egrensis the year after. At the German–Polish border the Spree–Neisse–Bober Euroregion was founded in 1993 and Pomerania in 1994. In 1993 the large Carpathian Euroregion covering territory of Poland, Hungary, Slovakia, Romania and Ukraine was founded (Perkmann 2003). In 2013, more than a third of the estimated Euroregions were located in Eastern or Southeast Europe, and, in 2015, 24 out of 53 Euroregions registered as EGTCs were located in CEE.

In a broader perspective, the institution can be seen as associated with certain policy goals and ideas stemming from a war-weary mid-twentieth-century Europe. These policy goals were peace and prosperity, and the interlinked policy idea that these would be reached through collaboration at all levels. Cooperation across borders, both within the larger European context and at the local level, was assumed to secure peaceful and benevolent relations between citizens of different countries and to promote growth via the establishment of open markets that would not be restricted by "arbitrary" borders, at the local level meaning that they would be based on so-called "functional regions" shaped by a combination of geography, demography and infrastructure (see de Blij and Murphy 2003 for a discussion on a functionalist perspective on regions). In modern times, the European Commission has emphasized that cross-border cooperative agreements emerge to "tackle common problems," such as manage environmental resources, respond to disadvantages stemming from locations of periphery, come up with strategies to enhance competitiveness and generally "fill the gaps" between different regulatory systems (see European Commission InfoRegio 2011, 2013).

Importantly, the same policy goals and policy ideas that were behind the emergence of Euroregions were also behind the creation of the European

Union's founding treaties in the 1950s, and it should be noted that in the early days the EU was not an independent actor pushing the creation of Euroregions. Important early international actors of policy transfer were instead the Council of Europe and the Nordic Council. They served as advocacy hubs for these positive policy ideas to overshadow earlier negative attitudes towards sub-national authority cooperation, which had often not been allowed or was viewed with skepticism as a form of "para-diplomacy" (Aguirre 1999; Aldecoa and Keating 1999) that encroached on the prerogative of the state to conduct foreign policy.

The key achievement of the Nordic Council was the inclusion of a paragraph on cross-border cooperation in the Treaty of Cooperation between the Nordic countries of Denmark, Finland, Iceland, Norway and Sweden signed on March 23, 1962. According to Article 25 of the Treaty, the countries should promote the development of "joint economic development of adjoining parts of the territories" (cited in Anderson 1967: 174) through local and regional cooperation. The Nordic Council would subsequently set up a working group for knowledge exchange among actors involved in cross-border cooperation activities, and has at times also provided funding. For instance, in 2012, 10.5 million DKK, approximately 1.4 million EUR, was given in direct support to the operation of Euroregions. In addition, other budget lines could be utilized for project applications depending on their activities (Nordic Council 2012: 5). The Council of Europe did not use the mechanisms of technical or financial support, but agreed on a landmark convention on territorial cooperation in 1980 (Council of Europe [1980] 2012), which codified the permissive and positive attitude towards cross-border cooperation by mandating signatories to promote and support cross-border cooperation between local and regional authorities. To facilitate the integration into public administration structures, model agreements on intrastate and local level were included as guidance, although they lacked treaty value (Article 3, para. 1). However, it was often not possible to use these templates due to diverging legal settings, and throughout the 1980s the Council of Europe was in dialogue with interest organizations such as the Association of Border Regions as well as the European Commission on how the European Union could step up action on this issue.

For this purpose, the European Union has used both financial and legal instruments. Funding was introduced via the program INTERREG IIIA in 1990, through which regions could apply for funding for cooperation with other regions. Throughout the 1990s INTERREG grew in scope, while a cross-border cooperation component was worked into economic assistance to CEE through the PHARE (Poland and Hungary: Assistance for Restructuring their Economies, as initially only these two countries were eligible), which was implemented with the help of the OECD, thereby introducing yet another international actor on the scene. In the 2014–2020 funding period EU support to cross-border cooperation is a part of European Cohesion Policy, linked to the goal of "territorial cohesion" (Jaschitz 2013). Within this, INTERREG constitutes a part of the umbrella program European Territorial Cooperation, which furthers territorial cooperation on different levels. Eligible regions are regions on the third level of the European territorial classification scale (NUTS III) that are located directly at national borders or close to them; the final list is decided in discussions between the Commission and the member states. Different types of actors within these regions can apply for funding, and Euroregions constitute one type of actors that can compete for the 6.6 billion EUR budget that has been set aside for cross-border cooperation at internal borders in the programming period 2014–2020 or the 876 million EUR available for the same purpose in pre-accession and neighborhood countries. The overall allocation to territorial cooperation is 10.1 billion EUR, which includes, among other things, support to external borders and cooperation across geographical distance. This is an increase in comparison with previous funding periods, but still constitutes only a small part of the overall Cohesion Policy budget of 351 billion EUR.

All European Territorial Cooperation programs have to fulfill two general objectives: (1) to strengthen territorial, economic and social cohesion; and (2) to contribute to smart, sustainable and inclusive growth of the region and the European Union. In concrete terms, four-fifths of the financial resources have to be related to the Europe 2020 strategy "for smart, sustainable and inclusive growth" (European Commission InfoRegio 2016). They also have to show coordination with other relevant policies and funding structures (for example national programs, macro-regions).

A recent Eurobarometer survey shows that one-third of people living in the border regions are aware of EU funded cross-border cooperation activities in their region, which, given that Euroregions are usually said to be invisible, is relatively high. The highest awareness can be found in the CEE member states (European Commission 2015a, 2015b). However, this may be due to the relative higher importance of European funding in the region, and that respondents are not clear which local projects are supported from the cross-border cooperation program and which ones receive support from other programs.

Through the Association of Border Regions and the Committee of the Regions, many local actors emphasized that there were legal obstacles to cooperation and, hence, that the use of financial instruments was not considered sufficient to promote cross-border collaboration. This led to the introduction of the aforementioned European Grouping of Territorial Cooperation in 2006. The 2006 EGTC regulation implied the introduction of a European legal instrument designed to facilitate and promote cross-border, transnational and interregional cooperation. It enables for instance the delivery of joint public services without requiring a prior international agreement to be signed and ratified by national parliaments. The law applicable for the interpretation and application of the convention is that of the member state in which the official EGTC headquarters are located. Early on, scholars from several disciplines paid attention to the EGTC institution and called for research on its development. For instance, articles on EGTCs appeared from a planning perspective (Janssen 2009; Zapletal 2010; Bufon 2011), appeared in journals on geography (Spinaci and Vara-Arribas 2009; Zapletal 2010; Jaschitz 2013) and were explored from a legal and political science perspective (Engl and Zwilling 2014). Coming into effect as the 2007–2013 funding cycle started, the EGTCs were however too few, too new and too little known to become actors of real importance in the implementation of Cohesion Policy. Their underutilization was pointed out by Zapletal (2010: 25), who stated that "[t]hese Groupings truly are new governance 'contracts' of multilevel cross-border cooperation, which can become creative engines for local development and deeper European integration. This provides food for thought for the EU policy and budgetary package after 2013."

In light of further modifications to the regulation in 2013 (Regulation 1302/2013) it is easy to agree with Zapletal that the 2014–2020 period will be the key test for these bodies. Furthermore, the Commission had made clear that it would like to see more EGTCs created in the 2014–2020 funding period. This can be seen for instance in the instructions regarding the European Regional Development Fund (ERDF):

> In line with the Union strategy for smart, sustainable and inclusive growth, the European Structural and Investment Funds should provide a more integrated and inclusive approach to tackling local problems. In order to strengthen such an approach, support from the ERDF in border regions should be coordinated with support from the EAFRD [European Agricultural Fund for Rural Development] and the EMFF [European Maritime and Fisheries Fund] and *should, where appropriate, involve European groupings of territorial cooperation (EGTCs)*. (European Union 2013, emphasis added)

The financial instrument led to an increased pace of transfer, with most current Euroregions tracing their cooperation back to the 1990s or early years of the 2000s. The legal instrument EGTC was expected to lead to more targeted policy transfer in the area of economic and social development, whereby EGTCs would become "strategic and functional engines for strategy-making and policy delivery" (Haselsberger and Benneworth 2010: 93). While some early work that evaluates EGTCs has been published (Evrard 2016), it is within this context that the present research should be placed.

In CEE, a number of think tanks and associations have aspired to the role of catalyzing policy entrepreneur, in recent years the most important being the Central European Service for Cross-Border Initiatives (CESCI), which was created in 2009 with the purpose of supporting the creation of "as many relations as possible between people living on each side of the border, to help removing the barriers hindering cooperation" (CESCI 2016). The founder of CESCI had managerial experience from one of the first and most prominent Euroregions in the region, the Ister-Granum EGTC, and has used his extensive personal network to promote the idea among policy-makers at national and regional level. CESCI generates revenues from both grants and consultancies on how to set up and develop EGTCs, and also serves as an information hub for EGTCs in the region through regular workshops and conference activities.

7.2.2 What Arrived and How it was Translated

The spread of Euroregions can be characterized as both cross-national and within-national policy transfer, but it is clear that the dominating route has been transfer from North/West to South/East Europe (Dolowitz and Marsh 2000: 9). The actors referred to in the previous sub-section – the European Union and the Council of Europe, the regional Nordic Council, and to some extent the Central European Visegrad Four and CESCI – were all to varying degrees instrumental in transmitting a basic format for cross-border cooperation (the Euroregion institution), underpinned by certain policy goals (peace and prosperity) and policy ideas (that collaboration across borders and nations is an important way to reach those goals), to and within CEE. They did so through financial and legal policy instruments, which were possible due to the seismic geopolitical shift that took place in Europe in 1990. This sub-section explores, however, the argument that there was still significant leeway for local actors to translate and reinterpret those ideas, meaning that these new or more recent Euroregions have developed with a distinctive set of locally generated ideas and policy attitudes that have led to different operationalizations of these institutions. What we see are Euroregions founded with strong external origins that have gone through "processes of interpretation and implementation" (see Chapter 1, this volume) which have significantly transformed them. Two manifestations of this transformation stand out.

First, the goal of "prosperity," initially understood as prosperity through open markets, has been transformed to "a bit of prosperity" through access to external funding. Access to grants as a major motivation for the emergence of CEE Euroregions has already been catalogued (*inter alia*, Scott 1999; Clarke 2002; Perkmann 2002; Johnson 2009; Medve-Bálint 2013; Torzsok and Majoros 2015). For instance, Medve-Bálint (2013) compared how much funding for cross-border cooperation via the PHARE and INTERREG programs had gone to different border areas in Central Europe, namely borders between Germany and Austria on the one hand, and the four CEE countries Poland, the Czech Republic, Slovakia and Hungary on the other. He showed that the more established Euroregions there were along a border, the bigger was the size of the funding. The correlation was statistically significant, even though there was significant variation along the trend line (Medve-Bálint 2013: 158). Medve-Bálint and Svensson (2012) and Svensson (2013b) followed up this research with qualitative research at the Hungarian–Slovak border showing, in two out of three investigated Euroregions, ability to access funding to be one of the dominant motivation factors for local governments when deciding whether to join a Euroregion. Often this was expressed in vague terms, such as when a mayor of a small settlement in Slovakia explains that "I think it was because of development and such things, and the cooperation, EU funding calls, etc." (Mayor, Slovakia, Ister-Granum Euroregion) or indicates that the decision is based on cost–benefit analysis, with the financial and management costs for joining so low that joining can be justified even in the absence of concrete knowledge: "We thought that we had better not miss out on something" (Mayor, Hungary, Ister-Granum Euroregion).

Second, the goal of "peace," understood as "peace with your neighbors," has in many cases been transformed into "peace with your *ethnic* neighbors": the creation of Euroregions in borderlands with historical kinship minorities has been a prominent phenomenon. One example is the Hungarian–Slovak borderland, which has a significant Hungarian minority on the Slovak side. Hungarian borderlands are in general characterized by minorities, since there are Hungarians living in six out of its seven neighboring countries (varying in size and particular location in relation to the border). There are also small minorities of Slovaks, Romanians, Croats and so on within Hungary, and although these are largely assimilated this has been perceived or promoted as important in the creation of Euroregions.

Evidence for the importance of ethnic ties comes from the same studies that were cited above (Medve-Bálint and Svensson 2012; Svensson 2013b), where ethnic ties featured as an important theme in all three investigated Euroregions at the Hungarian–Slovak border. More than half of the over 80 interviewees referred to the idea of a common Hungarian identity/

polity in some form. The overwhelming attitude of these informants emphasized that the Slovak villages and towns in the cooperation were a part of Hungary before the Trianon peace treaty signed after World War I. As one interviewee implied, the Euroregion came as a chance to rectify the perceived wrong-doings against the Hungarian people through the border revisions contained in the treaty: "Here of course the Trianon story is a Hungarian specialty, and you can take care of this a little bit through the creation of the Euroregion" (Mayor, Hungary, Ister-Granum Euroregion). Even though Hungary and Slovakia were both part of the so-called Eastern Bloc during the Cold War, there had been few opportunities to create or nurture institutional cross-border links. "The political situation was such that there was almost enemy status between the two countries. We decided that we wanted to improve the situation" (Mayor, Slovakia, Hídverő Euroregion). In fact, there were no real opportunities for either institutional or civil/individual ties to be forged: "Perhaps we were allowed to go over [to other side of the border] twice a year. The young mayors don't even know how it was" (Mayor, Slovakia, Hídverő Euroregion). These local attitudes of historical wrong-doing and feelings of belonging together therefore did not have any outlets until the geopolitical changes that brought an opportunity to latch on to novel institutions such as the Euroregion which were brought in through the actors discussed in the previous sub-section.

That the language associated with Europe is picked up and used is also evidenced in how another interviewee states that "The goal is the Hungarian–Hungarian connection . . . the regional cohesion of the Hungarians" (Mayor, Slovakia, Ister-Granum Euroregion). The cherished "European" word of "cohesion" here becomes important as the "regional cohesion of Hungarians." For many of those who cherish this goal, economic gains become less important, since "what once was broken has to grow together" (Mayor, Slovakia, Hídverő Euroregion) and what matters is the (re)building of a community: "We want to build a spiritual bridge between Slovakia and Hungary. The two riverbanks that belong together should be bound together" (Mayor, Slovakia, Hídverő Euroregion). It should be noted that other parts of CEE also possess historical minorities in their borderlands, for instance the Polish minority in the Czech Cieszyn Silesia region. Whether these minorities have the opportunity to express kinship affinity via the set-up of Euroregions varies (there are no Russian-speaking cross-border cooperation structures at the Latvian–Russian and Estonian–Russian border for instance), but what can be safely claimed is that the phenomenon of Euroregions where ethnic kinship plays some sort of role is widespread.

The empirical data hence demonstrates how the Euroregion has to some degree served as a "policy shell" to be filled with content of choice. It has become a transferred institution with its original norms reinterpreted; the idea of "peace through cooperation," which originally implies an inclusive approach that will link different groups and thereby create or increase the available "bridging social capital," became something that can be used as an instrument of exclusion along the line of group-based "bonding social capital" (see Grix and Knowles 2003 and Malloy 2010 for a discussion on social capital in border regions). Thus the concept of the Euroregion, as a transferred policy institution, was not only a vehicle for EU aspirations but also "borrowed" (or hijacked) and adapted for an additional, or even contrary, set of policy objectives. Stone (2017) writes that "[t]he policy transfer literature also allows us to see the possibilities for convergence around broad policy objectives and principles but scope for divergence with regard to the instruments adopted, type of legislation or institutional modes of policy control/delivery." Here, what we have is the opposite, convergence around instruments and institutional modes, but divergence on the interpretation of policy objectives and ideals. In a way, what we see is *policy translation* in a more radical format (Prince 2010; Stone 2017).

7.3 POLICY SUCCESS AND/OR POLICY FAILURE?

This section discusses the assessment of policy success and failure of Euroregions, in sub-section 7.3.1 with regard to individual organizations, and in sub-section 7.3.2 concerning their aggregated presence in the region. As will be shown, these assessments often diverge depending on whether the criteria for assessment have been imported as a package along with the policy transfer or if they have been adjusted to take local motivations and expectations into account.

7.3.1 Are Euroregion Organizations a "Success" or a "Failure"?

Policy failure has been defined as a policy "that does not achieve the goals that proponents set out to achieve, and support is virtually non-existent" (McConnell 2010). Policy success is then the opposite: goals are achieved and there is substantial support. The aim of this sub-section is to see whether these two benchmarks for success always need to go together, and to do this we will discuss two events that took place in two different Euroregions at the Hungarian–Slovak border in 2011, the Ister-Granum EGTC and the Hídverő Association. In the first, on March 7 around 50 mayors were gathered in the ceremonial hall of the once-beautiful town hall of Esztergom, a Hungarian town of 30 000 with a long history as the

Catholic seat of the country. They had come from smaller and larger settlements in the surrounding area, where the Danube bends south after having served as an east–west border demarcation between Hungary and Slovakia for about 160 kilometers. The reason to be there was to attend a special general meeting; the task of the day was to dismiss and replace the director of the Euroregion. The atmosphere was tense, with heated discussions on procedural issues masking the larger problems underneath. Less than two years after Ister-Granum had reconstituted itself as an EGTC – with much publicity and as one of the first Euroregions in Europe to utilize this new legal form – the organization was in serious difficulties. There was widespread discontent among its members with the manager and there were members wanting to leave the organization or refusing to pay their dues. In the months to come it would also be clear that an EU-supported project that had already started was underfunded and at considerable cost would have to be terminated.

In the second event, two weeks later, on March 25, 30 kilometers west on the other side of the Danube, a smaller group of mayors had an amicable morning meeting. Radvan nad Dunajom (or Dunaradvány in the language of the Hungarian majority in this settlement located in Slovakia) hosted a monthly meeting of the Hídverő Association. As usual, most of the 18 local government members were present, and there was laughing and informal chatting over refreshments supplied by the host, the mayor of Radvan nad Dunajom/Dunaradvány. The agenda dealt mainly with administrative issues on the Slovakian side, but the participants who had come from Hungary seemingly enjoyed the time for talking despite the fact that there were few issues related to a cross-border dimension.

These two scenes are relevant for a discussion on policy success and failure, because the discrepancies between the members' own satisfaction with their Euroregions and actual policy output are in these cases remarkably sharp. If one considers the standard indicators for policy success, they are based primarily on the "prosperity" leg of the two ideas intertwined with the original Euroregion institution; that is, their success would ultimately be judged based on their ability to promote regional economic development. However, since that link is difficult to create directly, proxy indicators are used. These include organizational development (measured by for instance the legal basis), diversification of the resource base, the scope and depth of cooperation in multiple policy areas, and local visibility (Perkmann 2003: 159–60, 2007: 864; Szabó and Koncz 2006; Svensson 2013a; Törzsök and Majoros 2015).

Accordingly, we would expect Ister-Granum to do better. It had an advanced legal basis (the EGTC format), funding from different sources, and a track record of leading different projects. It also appeared to have relatively high name recognition among regular citizens in the area, since several of its initiatives had been advertised broadly, leading to it definitely being the "go to" actor when it came to cross-border cooperation in the area. Hídverő, on the other hand, after having had grander ambitions at its foundations in the early 2000s, in more recent years had had few funds of its own and had only pursued a narrow range of activities, mainly focused on cultural festivals and cultural exchange programs promoting Hungarian heritage and Hungarian-speaking activities. Ister-Granum had become the major vehicle for its members in terms of policy coordination and cooperation across the border, whereas the Hídverő members usually also sought out other strategies.

Thus the situation at the Hungarian–Slovak border reveals a paradox. While the organization where little was achieved received high support from its members, the members of the organization which actually achieved some results were generally dissatisfied. There was a marked difference between the satisfaction of members (internal evaluation) in relation to the actual outcome in terms of projects realized or policy aims achieved (external evaluation). In other words, McConnell's (2010) definition of policy failure and success is only partially useful in this context. This is likely to be typical for Euroregional development in CEE, since what happens here seems be a pattern of persistent support even in the absence of achieved expected goals and vice versa.

A clearer picture emerges if we acknowledge that what constitutes "goals" is fuzzy and, as mentioned above, not only tied to the idea of "prosperity." Officially stated organizational goals may influence the motivation of local governments to join Euroregions, but the motivations also influence the expectations of members and those that the general population have towards the organization, which in turn become goals to achieve. In the context of these particular institutions, it becomes important to consider the motivations of the local stakeholders in addition to the EU sponsored policy ideas behind the institutions. Interviews cited earlier reveal that members of the Hídverő Euroregion were more prone to be motivated by maintaining and nurturing the common Hungarian heritage and identity than by expectations of economic development. They expected that cooperation would help to reinforce Hungarian identity across the border and would facilitate cultural exchange between Hungarians living on both sides of the border. Expressing this sentiment, one mayor said: "We did this for the sake of the Hungarians in Slovakia. The Euroregion can help a lot to maintain and nurture the historical roots, to make sure that this connection continues to live and builds up, and does not break" (Mayor, Hungary, Hídverő Euroregion). Although this ethnically grounded motivation often appeared in interviews with mayors of

Ister-Granum too, in their case this view was nearly always accompanied by more materialistic expectations towards the cooperation. Most of the mayors were open about their expectations towards direct material gains for their settlements arising from their involvement in Ister-Granum. This sentiment was echoed by the management of Ister-Granum, emphasizing local economic development as the primary aim of the initiative (for elaboration see Medve-Bálint and Svensson 2013).

Euroregions can be seen as policy coordinators, that is, institutions that are formed to further policy development in a governance space that is extraordinarily complex due to the involvement of members coming from different jurisdictions operating with policy issues within which competencies are frequently asymmetrically allocated to different levels (local, regional, national) across the participating countries. The assessment of whether Euroregions are "successes" or "failures" needs to go beyond goal achievement and degree of support. Instead, the argument here is that organizational goals, initially defined by the founders of the cross-border initiatives, influence both their membership structure (such as number of members, regions and/or local governments as members, small or big settlements, closeness to the border) and the motivational background of the members. If for instance the membership is asymmetric in that it contains one or two bigger towns and many small settlements (for example Ister-Granum), that will mean a different power dynamic within the Euroregion than if the members are all small local governments immediately at the border (for example Hídverő). After the establishment of a Euroregion, the interaction between the three factors of organizational goals, expectations and membership structure determines future capacity for successful policy coordination. Later, members can observe how and to what extent the initially stated goals and their own expectations are fulfilled. If there are members who take up a dominating role, operations may become conflictual and the scope and type of projects carried out may not satisfy all the members, even if they are in line with the stated goals.

The perceived discrepancy between the original expectations of benefits of what Euroregion membership would bring and the membership experience fuels further internal conflict. As was the case with Ister-Granum, more generally, this may lead to the deterioration of the cooperation through the significantly decreased activity of the unsatisfied members. However, if the experience and initial expectations of the members meet each other over time, then that can lead to their sustained, active commitment to the initiative, for which Hídverő provides an example (see Medve-Bálint and Svensson 2013 for a full elaboration). The example of the two Euroregions in this sub-section also illustrates the difficulty in deciding whether more emphasis should be put on internal or external evaluation of a policy initiative that includes different levels of stakeholders. The picture might have been even more complex if a more nuanced view of citizens could have been assessed. Yet what is more important for the argument of the chapter is that "external evaluators" tend to be influenced by hegemonic ideas of (economic) development interlinked with the transfer process. These processes can be better understood if closer attention is paid to the motivation of members at the time of joining a Euroregion.

7.3.2 Assessing the Aggregate Impact of Euroregions

Euroregions, as an aggregated presence in CEE, can be assessed in multiple ways. The interest from policy-makers in the 2014–2020 funding cycle, on both the European and the national level, is to evaluate those that have adopted the legal framework of the EGTC. This is both because expectations are higher of EGTCs in terms of delivering regional economic development and because there are more opportunities to monitor them, since EGTCs are required to be registered with the Committee of the Regions, a European Union body.

Not surprisingly, given its geopolitical and historical situation, Hungary has been actively supporting stable legal opportunity frameworks for Euroregions. For instance, before the adoption of the 1082/2006 regulation on EGTCs, a Hungarian member of the European Parliament, István Pálfi, considered work on this instrument as one of his key priorities, and he was the first to advocate for its use in the Hungarian borderlands (CESCI 2016). Another telling sign of Hungarian activity is the large number of EGTCs with Hungarian participation: in 2015 they numbered 19 out of 53 registered organizations. Active entrepreneurship from organizations close to the government supporting the establishment of organizations such as the CESCI (see sub-section 7.2.1) have certainly helped, as has the establishment of a separate government fund for the operation of EGTCs.

Many of the same problems regarding assessment of organizational activity and policy output will also apply here, but there is strong pressure to increase efforts at evaluation, as shown for instance by increased requirements for evaluation of results and impact assessment of EU support for cross-border funding. CESCI has for instance developed an internal benchmarking tool for EGTC websites, assuming that the websites constitute crucial tools for national and European visibility, which is important for long-term development. The tool contains indicators such as availability of information in more than one language, number of postings, and frequency of updates, and is presented to the EGTCs regularly. CESCI is also working on a benchmarking tool that will be used for the assessment of cross-border cooperation policy output within the European 2014–2020

Regional Policy program, and the EGTC development will be an element of the tool. The Visegrad Fund has supported a research project on EGTCs at the Hungarian–Slovakian border, where a performance index was one of the project's outputs (Törzsök and Majoros 2015).

Rarely asked in these result-oriented evaluation exercises is the fundamental question of whether integration in borderlands can be successfully furthered without Euroregions. A study by the author compares the Hungarian–Slovak border, which has many Euroregions, with the Hungarian–Austrian border, which has none, and reaches the conclusion that there are some differences, but that these are only about administrative and political procedure. Policy output such as cross-border cooperation intensity and scope of activities, on the other hand, seem unaffected.

As discussed in earlier sections, grant access is one of the two key motivations driving the establishment of Euroregions. An online survey carried out in 2015 by the author with the managers and chairs of 12 of the EGTCs located at the Hungarian borders showed that the actors themselves are relatively satisfied with the extent to which they have been invited to take part in the planning of the 2014–2020 program for cross-border cooperation (the INTERREG program within the European Territorial Cooperation program; see sub-section 7.2.1). "In the preparatory work for the Hungary–Slovakia program, there were several occasions at which we could give opinions and suggestions. The preparatory group regularly submitted information, and there were quarterly information and consultation meetings arranged for the EGTCs" (Manager of an EGTC at the Hungarian–Slovak border). However, the extent to which this would translate into actual funding was unknown at the time of writing, since none of the cross-border cooperation programs had started to initiate calls for proposals yet. Also, some actors wanted direct funding to EGTCs rather than the funding open to different types of actors that can demonstrate a cross-border dimension. "We think that EGTCs should be drawn more into development, but that the EU doesn't support these institutions enough. We expect earmarked money for EGTCs" (Manager of an EGTC at the Hungarian–Romanian border). Since the overall amount of funding is relatively small in cross-border cooperation programs in comparison with the regular regional development operational programs, several managers also expressed their dissatisfaction at not having been able to access such resources for the borderland regions.

Given the importance assigned by many actors to cooperation based on ethnic affiliation, another aspect that is overlooked in conventional evaluations is whether Euroregions generally have the ability to create close and stable contact networks across borders within and outside their ethnic context. Empirical evidence indicates that there is still a massive difference between the cross-border and national contact networks at administrative levels (Svensson 2015), but the exact nature of these contact networks would need further research and is unlikely to be incorporated into formal externally induced evaluations or in self-evaluations of Euroregions. The ethnic aspect is generally downplayed on websites and it mostly features in personal communication.

7.4 CONCLUSION

Borderlands are often said to constitute important "laboratories" for testing what works and what does not when it comes to European integration (e.g., Schultz 2002; Knippenberg 2004; Committee of the Regions 2011; Medve-Bálint 2013). The expected role of Euroregions is to drive such experimentation in the borderlands with full normative commitment to European integration, but, as this chapter has argued, importing these institutions without their policy idea content (cross-cultural cooperation towards peace and prosperity) might even have counter-productive effects. The "counter-productivity" would be in relation to overall integration of people across lines that are nationality/ethnicity-based and in relation to the integration of markets. Instead other powerful policy ideas can be realized by local actors, such as the opportunity for kinship communities divided by (according to some) arbitrary borders to be, de facto, reunited through policy collaboration. In the language of a nationalist ideology, this would be successful national integration through non-conspicuous means. Aside from these counter-productive effects on norms, it can also be noted that grant-seeking behavior may create aid dependencies rather than strong economic regions in borderlands.

To summarize, the chapter has highlighted some complexities arising when assessing transfer of a policy institution from the "West" to the "East." It has further suggested that institutions can be transferred, but that ideas are translated and subject to continuous reinterpretation. The discussion has also revolved around the complexity of assessing the transfer of Euroregions in more traditional aspects of policy evaluation. It has shown how the analysis will shift depending on what is taken as the reference point for the analysis. From the perspective of local and regional governments joining Euroregions, the assessment of their achievements is highly dependent on initial motivations and expectations. Where these are geared towards accessing grants, disappointment and disillusionment are likely even when Euroregions can show some results in relation to their officially stated goals. For external and/or EU evaluators interested in sustainable economic development, the disappointment can be equally tangible.

Finally, a remark on the tightening of the European external borders and the reintroduction of internal border controls that took place in 2015 seems to be in order. It is clear that Euroregions cannot be blamed for the globally driven and geopolitically charged closure of previously open borders that took place in Europe in 2015 and early 2016. Nevertheless, the absence of representatives of Eastern Euroregions engaging in the public debate testifies to a failure to speak up for something that is of long-term vital interest for any Euroregion's opportunities for further integration, at either external or internal borders. It will be the task of future research to explore these dynamics further as the EU's own borders re-configure.

REFERENCES

Aguirre, Inaki (1999), 'Making sense of paradiplomacy? An intertextual enquiry about a concept in search of a definition', *Regional and Federal Studies*, 9 (1), 185–209.
Aldecoa, Francisco and Michael Keating (eds) (1999), 'Paradiplomacy in action: The foreign relations of subnational governments – introduction', *Regional and Federal Studies*, 9 (1), 4–8.
Anderson, Stanley V. (1967), *The Nordic Council: A Study of Scandinavian Regionalism*, Seattle: University of Washington Press.
Banat Triplex Confinium EGTC (2016), Archive of the news section of the institutional website, http://www.btc-Egtc.eu/ (accessed January 10, 2016).
Blij, H.J. de and Alexander B. Murphy (2003), *Human Geography: Culture, Society and Space*, 7th edn, Hoboken, NJ: Wiley.
Bufon, Milan (2011), 'Cross-border policies and spatial and social integration: Between challenges and problems', *European Spatial Research and Policy*, 18 (2), 29–45.
CESCI (Central European Service for Cross-Border Initiatives) (2016), CESCI-NET, organizational website, www.cesci-net.eu (accessed May 30, 2016).
Clarke, S.E. (2002), 'Spatial concepts and cross-border governance strategies: Comparing North American and Northern Europe experiences', EURA Conference on Urban and Spatial European Policies, Turin, April 18–20.
Committee of the Regions (2011), 'Opinion of the Committee of the Regions on "new perspectives for the revision of the EGTC Regulation (own-initiative opinion),"' *Official Journal of the European Union*, 2011/C 104/02.
Council of Europe ([1980] 2012), 'European Outline Convention on Transfrontier Co-operation between Territorial Communities or Authorities', Madrid, May 21, 1980, http://conventions.coe.int/Treaty/en/treaties/html/106.htm (accessed June 20, 2011).
Dolowitz, D. and David Marsh (2000), 'Learning from abroad: The role of policy transfer in contemporary policy-making', *Governance: An International Journal of Policy and Administration*, 13 (1), 5–24.
Engl, Alice and Carolin Zwilling (eds) (2014), *Functional and More? New Potential for the European Grouping of Territorial Cooperation – EGTC*, EURAC Book No. 63, Bozen: EURAC Research.
Euregio Egrensis (2016), Archive of the news section of the institutional website, http://www.euregio-Egrensis.org/ (accessed January 10, 2016).

European Commission (2015a), *Flash Eurobarometer 422: Cross-Border Cooperation in the EU*, http://data.europa.eu/euodp/en/data/dataset/S1565_422_ENG.

European Commission (2015b), *Flash Eurobarometer 423: Citizens' Awareness and Perceptions of EU Regional Policy*, http://data.europa.eu/euodp/en/data/dataset/S2055_423_ENG.

European Commission InfoRegio (2011), 'European territorial policy', http://ec.europa.eu/regional_policy/archive/cooperation/crossborder/index_en.htm (accessed November 12, 2013).

European Commission InfoRegio (2013), 'European cross-border cooperation', http://ec.europa.eu/regional_policy/cooperate/cooperation/crossborder/index_en.cfm (accessed November 12, 2013).

European Commission InfoRegio (2016), 'Interreg: European Territorial Coopera tion', http://ec.europa.eu/regional_policy/en/policy/cooperation/european-territo rial/ (accessed July 5, 2016).

European Union (2013), Regulation (EU) No. 1299/2013 of the European Parliament and of the Council of 17 December 2013 on specific provisions for the support from the European Regional Development Fund to the European territorial cooperation goal, *Official Journal of the European Union*, 347/259, http://eur-lex.europa.eu/legal-content/EN/TXT/?uri=celex%3A32013R1299.

Evrard, Estelle (2016), 'The European Grouping of Territorial Cooperation (EGTC): Towards a supraregional scale of governance in the Greater Region SaarLorLux?', *Geopolitics*, 21 (3), 513–37.

Grix, Jonathan and Vanda Knowles (2003), 'The Euroregion and the maximization of social capital: Pro Europa Viadrina', in James Anderson, Liam O'Dowd and Thomas M. Wilson (eds), *New Borders for a Changing Europe: Cross-Border Cooperation and Governance*, London: F. Cass, pp. 155–178.

Haselsberger, Beatrix and Paul Benneworth (2010), 'Do Euroregions have a future?', *disP – The Planning Review*, 46 (183), 80–94.

Janssen, Gerold (2009), 'European Groupings of Territorial Cooperation (EGTC) – experiences and prospects', in Heiderose Kiper (ed.), *German Annual of Spatial Research and Policy 2009: New Disparities in Spatial Development in Europe*, Berlin: Springer, 177–81.

Jaschitz, Mátyás, (2013), 'Key factors for successful territorial cohesion: Cross-border cooperation – how can some EU instruments create a new geography?', *European Journal of Geography*, 4 (4), 8–19.

Johnson, Corey M. (2009), 'Cross-border regions and territorial restructuring in Central Europe: Room for more transboundary space', *European Urban and Regional Studies*, 16 (2), 177–91.

Knippenberg, Hans (2004), 'The Maas–Rhine Euroregion: A laboratory for European integration?', *Geopolitics*, 9 (3), 608–26.

Malloy, Tove (2010), 'Creating new spaces for politics? The role of national minorities in building capacity of cross-border regions', *Regional and Federal Studies*, 20 (3), 335–51.

McConnell, Allan (2010), 'Policy success, policy failure and grey areas in-between', *Journal of Public Policy*, 30 (3), 345–62.

Medve-Bálint, Gergő (2013), 'The role of Euroregions in local development in Central Europe: Incentive structures and obstacles to cooperation', in Nicola Bellini and Ulrich Hilpert (eds), *Europe's Changing Geography*, London: Routledge, pp. 145–70.

Medve-Bálint, Gergő and Sara Svensson (2012), 'Why do local governments join (or not join) Euroregions?', in Martin Klatt, Dorte Andersen and Marie Sandberg (eds), *The Border Multiple: The Practicing of Borders between Public Policy and Everyday Life in Europe*, Farnham: Ashgate, pp. 219–43.

Medve-Bálint, Gergő and Sara Svensson (2013), 'Diversity and development: Policy entrepreneurship of Euroregional initiatives in Central and Eastern Europe', *Journal of Borderlands Studies*, 28 (1), 15–31.

Nordic Council (2012), Official website of the Nordic Council, http://www.norden. org (accessed July 5, 2016).

Patton, Michael Quinn (2002), *Qualitative Research and Evaluation Methods*, Thousand Oaks, CA: Sage.

Perkmann, Markus (2002), 'Institutional entrepreneurship in the European Union', in M. Perkmann and N.-L. Sum (eds), *Globalization, Regionalization and Cross-Border Regions*, New York: Palgrave Macmillan, pp. 103–24.

Perkmann, Markus (2003), 'Cross-border regions in Europe: Significance and drivers of regional cross-border cooperation', *European Urban and Regional Studies*, 10 (2), 153–71.

Perkmann, Markus (2007), 'Policy entrepreneurship and multilevel governance: A comparative study of European cross-border regions', *Environment and Planning C: Government and Policy*, 25 (6), 861–79.

Prince, Russell (2010), 'Policy transfer as policy assemblage: Making policy for the creative industries in New Zealand', *Environment and Planning A*, 42 (1), 169–86.

Richards, Lyn (2005), *Handling Qualitative Data: A Practical Guide*, 1st edn, Thousand Oaks, CA: Sage.

Robertson, David Brian (1991), 'Political conflict and lesson-drawing', *Journal of Public Policy*, 11 (1), 55–78.

Robertson, David Brian and J.L. Waltman (1992), 'The politics of policy borrowing', *Oxford Studies in Comparative Education*, 2 (2), 25–48.

Rose, Richard (1991), 'What is lesson-drawing?', *Journal of Public Policy*, 11 (1), 3–30.

Schultz, Helga (2002), *Twin Towns on the Border as Laboratories of European Integration*, Frankfurter Institut für Transformationsstudien Working Papers, Frankfurt (Oder): Viadrina.

Scott, James W. (1999), 'European and North American contexts for cross-border regionalism', *Regional Studies*, 33 (7), 605–17.

Spinaci, Gianluca and Gracia Vara-Arribas (2009), 'The European Grouping of Territorial Cooperation (EGTC): New spaces and contracts for European integration', *EIPAScope*, 2009 (2), 5–13.

Stone, Diane (2017), 'Understanding the transfer of policy failure: Bricolage, experimentalism and translation', *Policy and Politics*, 45 (1), 55–70.

Svensson, Sara (2013a), *Social Capital and Governance in European Borderlands: A Comparative Study of Euroregions as Policy Actors*, Thesis Collection, Budapest: Central European University.

Svensson, Sara (2013b), 'Forget the policy gap: Why local governments really decide to take part in cross-border cooperation initiatives in Europe', *Eurasian Geography and Economics*, 54 (4), 409–22.

Svensson, Sara (2015), 'The bordered world of cross-border cooperation: The determinants of local government contact networks within Euroregions', *Regional and Federal Studies*, 25 (3), 277–95.

Szabó, Gyula and Gábor Koncz (2006), 'Transboundary interaction in the Hungarian–Romanian border region: A local view', in James Wesley Scott (ed.),

EU Enlargement, Region Building and Shifting Borders of Inclusion and Exclusion, Aldershot: Ashgate, pp. 163–70.

Törzsök, Erika and András Majoros (2015), *A Comparative Analysis of the Evolution of EGTCs at the Hungarian Slovak Border*, Budapest: Civitas Europaica Centralis Foundation.

Zapletal, Jirka (2010), 'The European Grouping of Territorial Cooperation (EGTC): A new tool facilitating cross-border cooperation and governance', *Quaestiones Geographicae*, 29 (4), 15–26.

8. Hungarian international development policy: A case for conflicted success

András Tétényi

8.1 INTRODUCTION

The European Union (EU) has played a vital role in restarting the international development policies of the Central and Eastern European new member states. The re-creation of the international development policies (among other things) was a prerequisite for joining the European Union in 2004. Furthermore, Hungary as a member of the Visegrad group has agreed to the framework of the European Consensus on Development to provide 0.33 per cent of its ODA/GNI (official development assistance/ gross national income) for development assistance purposes. To date, none of the countries in the Visegrad group have come close to fulfilling these requirements and, in quantitative terms, levels are far below targets. Therefore, observing international standards for the delivery of development assistance is especially important for this group in achieving their maximum impact.

After the accession of 2004, the new member states were left to devise their own development policies (Horký 2010), with some external guidance from more established donors such as the United Nations Development Programme (UNDP), the Canadian International Development Agency and the European Commission (Szent-Iványi and Tétényi 2012). Hungary, similar to other countries of the region, had limited economic ties with developing countries, as it did not have sovereign foreign policies during the period of state socialism (Baginski 2002; Carbone 2004). Therefore the post-accession selection of partners from the immediate neighbourhood of the Western Balkans and former Soviet bloc countries, where there were economic and political ties, made practical and common sense. As Bucar and Mrak (2007: 11) argue, providing development assistance did not enjoy significant public support, although, once it was explained what development assistance was, the general public support for it increased (Bördős and Gregor 2013).

The European Union has been trying to increase both the quantity and the quality of the international development programmes of the Visegrad group of countries. However, to date, results remain mixed. One reason could be that, as has been observed by Lightfoot and Szent-Iványi (2014), the European Union's development *acquis* is not binding on member states but only takes shape as soft law. Some EU recommendations include budget support or joint programming. However, the four Visegrad countries have mainly resisted adopting these modalities, citing reasons such as the lower visibility of their programmes or lack of capacity for joint programming.

This chapter has two goals: first, to introduce Hungarian development policy since its re-creation and, second, in line with the general outline of the book, to focus on the internal and external factors that have influenced the local interpretation of Hungarian international development policy. In addition, the chapter seeks to explain why the eventual policy ended up the way it did.[1] The chapter builds on the literature of socialization, Europeanization, and policy success and failure in order to characterize Hungarian international development policy as a case of 'conflicted success'.

Section 8.2 details how policy success or failure can be understood in the case of Hungarian development policy. In this regard, McConnell's (2010) definition suffices: 'a policy is successful if it achieves the goals that proponents set out to achieve and attracts no criticism of any significance and/or support is virtually universal'. The chapter suggests broadening this definition to take into account processes of 'international socialization'. This concept is used to analyse how international organizations influence domestic politics (Checkel 2001, 2005; Kelley 2004) and Europeanization (Jacoby 2004; Schimmelfennig and Sedelmeier 2005; Vachudova 2005; Dimitrova 2010; Sedelmeier 2011), and has often been applied to assess the EU's influence on local actors.

Building on these insights, section 8.3 focuses on the recommendations of global and regional actors about what is considered to be the best practice for delivering aid. The chapter then investigates how these policies were placed into the local Hungarian context, and the present state of Hungarian international development policy. The contribution of the chapter to the literature is twofold. First, the socialization processes in post-accession countries are still somewhat under-researched. Second, utilizing the models of policy success and failure we will be able to better understand how to characterize Hungarian international development policy since joining the EU.

8.2 THE INFLUENCE OF INTERNATIONAL ACTORS

There has been much discussion in the literature on the question of why countries and their agents change their behaviour. Is it because of social rewards or sanctions (enhancing status, avoiding shaming) or material rewards (financial assistance, trade opportunities) (Checkel 2005: 808)? Schimmelfennig (2005) postulates that socialization is conceived as a process of reinforcement which has three aspects: first, high material and political rewards (such as EU membership), which can trigger sustained change; second, outcomes which depend on cost–benefit calculations of the governments; and, third, international socialization made sustainable by the government and opposition parties and their willingness to adapt to foreign norms. Schimmelfennig and Sedelmeier (2005) argue that Europeanization can be driven by the EU and/or by domestic actors. In addition, when it is being driven by a logic of consequences, it is driven by strategic logic to maximize profit and power. On the other hand, when it is driven by a logic of appropriateness, Europeanization takes shape through the adoption of new or reconfigured identities, values and norms. According to Hartlapp (2007) there are three schools which investigate why states comply with international rules. The first school analyses enforcement and looks at the penalties and pay-offs of compliance, arguing that international organizations are well situated to impose harsh penalties on their member states for non-compliance with international obligations. The second school of thought, the management approach, lists the reasons for non-compliance due to technical, financial or administrative problems, which can only be jointly solved once capacity building has been provided. The third school of thought, based on Checkel (2001), requires the changing of norms and values in the country in order to achieve compliance but also socio-political support.

Checkel (2005) differentiates between two types of socialization: in the case of Type 1, the agents, such as diplomats or ministry officials, learn to act appropriately in accordance with expectations, regardless of whether they personally identify with that role or not. This might occur when agents are placed in settings which have a long duration, when professional contact is deep and occurs on a daily level, or when the agent has significant previous experience in an international organization. In the case of Type 2 socialization, the agents accept the community or organizational roles imposed on them as the mutually accepted goals to follow. This might occur when the agent is new to the environment and therefore more motivated to analyse new information and has fewer ingrained beliefs which are alien to the new norms. In both cases of socialization conscious instrumental calculation of costs versus benefits is replaced, but, whereas in the case of Type 1 the actors play the role of agents who identify with the new norms, in the case of Type 2 socialization they actually believe in them as well, and thus their values and interests change. Thus Type 2 socialization is believed to be more sustainable, as the actors internalize the new values. Of course a challenge may be that the agents move on to other occupations, and the knowledge and know-how they have gained disappears from the institution – a phenomenon commonly experienced with development officials of Visegrad countries (Szent-Iványi and Tétényi 2012).

Jacoby (2004) understands the long-term success of EU supported reforms to be dependent on how detailed the *acquis* and the domestic legislation were in relationship to each other. In the case of international development assistance the local framework was weak; therefore the policy had to be built up from the very basics. The lingering question remained during and around the time of accession of whether firm structures would develop with time. Kelley (2004) expands on the socialization arguments above by pointing out that ownership of the new policies can significantly enhance the sustainability and embeddedness of the newly adopted norms. Kelley (2004) also points out that socialization methods rarely change state behaviour and, if they do, it is usually in cases where domestic opposition is low to the new norms. Thus membership conditionality can be quite an essential component, as this way the domestic opposition can be convinced, through the reward of their membership, that it is in their long-term interest to at least act in a manner expected by the international organization.

McConnell (2010: 351–2) defines five layers of political results, ranging from success to failure, which are particularly useful when analysing Hungarian international development policy. As noted earlier, he defines a policy as successful 'if it achieves the goals that proponents set out to achieve and attracts no criticism of any significance and/or support is virtually universal'. The next layer, 'resilient success' (tolerable failure) is the classic second best outcome. There is some opposition to the project the government has been trying to implement, but altogether the support outweighs the opposition. The third layer is 'conflicted success' (conflicted failure), in which some policy goals are achieved. However, the government has to backtrack or make significant changes to the proposed project or programme until it is codified. The success is not what was intended, and time delays, target shortfalls and considerable controversy are a part of the project cycle. The fourth layer, 'precarious success', borders on failure. Some measure of success has been achieved by the project, but the level of opposition makes it difficult to protect these achievements and they provide substantial liability for the government. And the last layer is 'policy failure', when the policy has not achieved the goals it set out to achieve and/or when opposition to the policy is nearly universal.

McConnell (2015: 227) expands on the explanation of policy failure by stating that failure can also include not meeting certain benchmarks (benchmarks can be questioned and may turn out to be inappropriate over time). Failure also entails: not benefiting target groups; costs outweighing benefits; not meeting legal, moral or ethical standards; failing to obtain support from key stakeholders; or failing to improve on the previous state of affairs. In addition, McConnell (2015) draws attention to the fact that the term of failure has to be augmented by the question: failure for whom? A policy which is considered a failure by certain population groups may be thought of as success or as neutral for other population groups. To summarize the forthcoming discussion, the initial low success rate of a policy, as was the case with Hungarian international development policy before 2014, should not make us believe that positive changes may not eventually occur notwithstanding the current situation of the policy being a case of conflicted success.

8.3   THE PAST AND PRESENT OF HUNGARIAN INTERNATIONAL DEVELOPMENT POLICY

CEE countries are often called new or emerging donors, which is not entirely accurate, since most of these countries did have quite extensive foreign assistance policies during communism. Until 1989, the international development efforts of the countries of the Eastern bloc were subject to the political and military goals of the Soviet Union. The modalities used were mainly the support of various equipment, the supply of expertise and know-how, provision of scholarships, and tied credits (Szent-Iványi and Tétényi 2008). The main recipients included socialist allies such as Cambodia, Cuba, Laos, Mongolia, North Korea and (North) Vietnam, as well as other developing countries which oriented themselves towards the Soviet bloc. ODA programs of the Soviet times did not differentiate between development and military aid, and development assistance also had a significant military component (HUN-IDA 2004).

After the transition process began in CEE, the countries all but ceased their international development activities and turned from being donors to recipients. International organizations like the World Bank and the European Commission (EC), as well as countries like the United States, Germany and the Netherlands, appeared as donors to support the transition process and provide expertise in building institutions. During the

1990s, the development cooperation activities of the CEE countries were limited to smaller *ad hoc* contributions to multilateral agencies, humanitarian aid and a limited number of scholarships to students from developing countries. After the turn of the millennium, however, the eight CEE countries which joined the EU in 2004 (the Czech Republic, Estonia, Hungary, Latvia, Lithuania, Poland, Slovakia and Slovenia) began re-creating their international development policies. The process began later in Romania and Bulgaria (Szent-Iványi and Tétényi 2013).

The main reason to (re-)establish the CEE countries' international development policies was external pressure: in order to gain accession to the EU, the *acquis communautaire* had to be re-created in the field of development policy. Whereas non-European international actors, such as the Organisation for Economic Co-operation and Development (OECD), played a major role in discovering and spreading best practice examples, the EU (primarily the Council Working Group on Development – CODEV) was the forum through which the practical aspects of delivering aid were discussed. The CODEV weekly sessions were a socializing context and enabled the representatives of the Visegrad countries to discover how the EU itself was running its development assistance programmes and thus improve the expertise of the Hungarian development officials (Lightfoot and Szent-Iványi 2014).

Development policy in the EU is considered to be a 'complementary' area, meaning the member states have full autonomy on how to pursue their international development objectives, even though the EU does have normative influence over the implementation of aid programmes, for instance through the work of CODEV (Horký 2010). In order to assist the accession states in 2004, a number of well-established donors such as the Canadian International Development Agency, the United Nations Development Programme and the European Commission stepped in to share their experience and best practices. These programmes were useful in addressing the management difficulties of delivering aid (Hartlapp 2007). Until 2012, the capacity building programmes provided by established donors mainly focused on increasing aid quantity, addressing dilemmas concerning aid allocation and issues related to the quality of CEE aid. The capacity building support has contributed to increasing ODA, the creation of institutional structures and operating procedures, and the training of personnel (Szent-Iványi and Tétényi 2013). In the case of Hungary, government willingness was still simply building momentum, as we will discuss later.

At the EU General Affairs and External Relations Council meeting in 2005, the Visegrad countries guaranteed to increase their aid spending to 0.17 per cent of their GNI until 2010 and to 0.33 per cent until 2015, in order to contribute to the EU's efforts to achieve the Millennium Development Goals (MDGs) (Drozd 2007: 3). Table 8.1 shows that neither deadline has been met. Since, the global economic downturn it does not appear likely that ODA/GNI figures will reach the 2015 or even the 2010 targets.

8.3.1   The Global and European Consensus on Delivering Aid

Szent-Iványi and Lightfoot (2015) have collected a pool of indicators which enable us to measure how Hungarian international development policy was shaped externally by international actors. One of the challenges of development assistance and development policy is that the 'recipe' for success, and documenting the modalities of it, has been constantly changing and therefore might be nearly impossible. Changing priorities are well exemplified in the field of development policy: during the 1950s the focus in development policy was on the physical accumulation of capital. However, at the turn of the millennium the focus changed to providing good governance and good institutions. The aid debate also reflected the mainstream of economic thinking. According to Burnell (2004), the terrorist attacks of 9/11 played a major role in drawing attention to the fact that global poverty may very easily affect the day-to-day lives of citizens in the developed countries. In the second half of the first decade of the 2000s a 'Global Consensus' emerged centred mainly around the OECD's Development Assistance Committee, in which the majority of the largest and most influential donors signed agreements on how best to deliver development assistance.

There are two major pillars of the Global Consensus: one is quantitative and the other one is qualitative improvement of development assistance. Quantitative improvement can be traced back to the acceptance of the UN Millennium Development Goals, which centred around eight targets, with the deadline of 2015 on how to decrease poverty. The novelty and importance of the MDGs lie in the fact that, on the one hand, they were unanimously accepted during the UN Millennium Summit and, on the other hand, they offered a set of guidelines for bilateral and multilateral agencies on how to spend their ODA if well-established donors wished to play a role in alleviating poverty. The Monterrey consensus of 2002 set a target for donors of providing 0.7 per cent of their GNI as ODA, and three years later in 2005 at the Gleneagles G8 meeting the participating countries pledged to provide 50 billion dollars in aid, of which half would go to Sub-Saharan African countries. Annual aid flows averaged until 2001 roughly around 50 billion dollars on an annual basis, and this had increased to over 100 billion dollars by 2005–2006 (OECD 2016). The 2005

Table 8.1   Net ODA disbursements in million dollars and as a percentage of gross national income in the Visegrad countries, 2005–2014

	2005	2006	2007	2008	2009	2010	2011	2012	2013	2014
Czech Republic	183.34	204.22	197.05	229.97	211.33	228.43	233.33	223.09	210.88	215.4
	0.11%	0.12%	0.11%	0.12%	0.12%	0.13%	0.12%	0.12%	0.11%	0.11%
Hungary	118.44	179.72	102.97	96.98	117.04	115.63	133.67	122.58	128.18	146.77
	0.11%	0.13%	0.08%	0.1%	0.09%	0.11%	0.1%	0.1%	0.1%	0.12%
Poland	259.16	357.34	371.17	325.05	400.43	384.55	404.65	438.28	487.12	447.31
	0.07%	0.09%	0.1%	0.08%	0.09%	0.08%	0.08%	0.09%	0.1%	0.09%
Slovak Republic	85.51	77	77.3	90.17	74.78	76.47	83.67	82.78	86.04	82.67
	0.12%	0.1%	0.09%	0.1%	0.09%	0.09%	0.09%	0.09%	0.09%	0.09%

Note: Absolute figures are in constant 2013 dollars.

Source: OECD (2016).

Paris Declaration on Aid Effectiveness sought mainly to address the qualitative issue of providing more effective aid and was centred around the five issues of ownership, alignment, harmonization of aid policies, managing for results and mutual accountability (OECD 2008). The challenge with the Paris Declaration was that it was not an international treaty but more a declaration of intent; therefore the enforcement mechanism was based on peer pressure and naming and shaming (Szent-Iványi and Lightfoot 2015). This may also account for the fact that out of 12 indicators only one was met by 2010 (OECD 2011), which calls into question the commitment of participating countries.

The European Union closely followed the development of the Global Consensus on delivering aid, and has created and accepted its own version of it, the aptly named European Consensus, in 2006. 'It reaffirmed EU commitment to poverty eradication, ownership, partnership, delivering more and better aid and promoting policy coherence for development' (European Consensus 2006: 2). 'Policy coherence for development' stands for the concept that non-development policies (such as trade, climate change and security issues) should also assist developing countries in achieving the MDGs. Thus the focus of the European Consensus can be considered broader than that of the Global Consensus, which deals mainly with a quantitative increase in addition to delivering effective aid. Five years later the European Consensus was updated, named Agenda for Change (European Commission 2011). The novelty of the document can be seen in the fact that it places considerable focus on facilitating private investment to developing countries as a tool to combat poverty.

Based on the frequency with which the targets are specified in the documents of the European Consensus and Agenda for Change, Szent-Iványi and Lightfoot (2015: 49) compiled a list of indicators which the Global Consensus and the European Union have both deemed to be 'best practice' in terms of aid. These are:

1. Increasing the quantity of aid, for CEE countries to 0.33% of their GNI by 2015.
2. Poverty reduction should be the goal of foreign aid policies.
3. A growing part of aid should be distributed to low income countries.
4. Aid should be untied.
5. Budget support should be increasing in volume to enable ownership, alignment and harmonization.
6. The creation of country strategy papers which have been created jointly with the partner country in order to reflect upon their needs.
7. Transparency of aid flows and multiannual programming.
8. Realistic number of partner countries.
9. Limiting activities to three sectors.
10. Joint programming with other donor countries.

In the following section, these ten points of best practice are addressed to Hungarian international development policy.

8.3.2 Hungarian International Development Policy in Light of the Global and European Consensus

Hungarian international development assistance can be characterized as organizationally fragmented, with weak central coordination (Paragi 2010). Responsibility for the implementation of development aid lies with several line ministries (such as the ministries responsible for education, healthcare, defence, the interior and justice) which disburse the majority of development contributions (79.3 per cent in 2014; Ministry of Foreign Affairs and Trade, Hungary 2015), while the Ministry of Foreign Affairs and Trade of Hungary coordinates the activities (Ministry of Foreign Affairs and Trade, Hungary 2014b). The Hungarian ODA legislation (Act XC of 2014) was ratified by the Hungarian Parliament in December 2014, and entered into force on 1 July 2015.

According to the Act, the goal of the policy is to combat poverty in addition to promoting humanitarian and minority rights, sustainable development and international security. Interestingly enough, the 2014 Hungarian international development strategy – less altruistically but with complete honesty – also points out that 'it [aid] can provide market access for certain segments of the Hungarian private and public sector (e.g. education, health), while promoting scientific and technological development' (Ministry of Foreign Affairs and Trade, Hungary 2014b: 7). According to the data in Table 8.1, Hungarian ODA has been increasing lately, in terms of both net spending and ODA/GNI, which is the highest among the Visegrad countries.

Hungarian foreign policy after 2010 can be characterized by the official idea of 'global opening', which entailed creating better foreign relations with countries of the South and the East (Ministry of Foreign Affairs 2011). Paragi (2010: 201) mentions that before 2010 no organizational questions (apart from the reconstruction commitment in Afghanistan and support for ethnic Hungarians) have ever been debated at any plenary session of the Parliament. Even though a 2011 policy brief on Hungarian foreign policy (Ministry of Foreign Affairs 2011) does not explicitly mention development assistance per se, we can safely say that building up relations with non-OECD countries is bound to entail some form of unilateral transfer of funds to developing countries to assist in building relations. In 2014, Hungary had 59 bilateral ODA partners, which indicates that Hungarian international development assistance was heavily fragmented. The International Development Strategy prepared by the Ministry of Foreign Affairs and Trade, Hungary (2014b) also pointed out that this fragmentation should be changed, as only 18 of these countries received contributions exceeding 100 000 dollars and only five countries exceeding 500 000 dollars. The lowest documented contribution in 2014 was 66 USD to Ukraine. Out of the 41 countries that received less than 100 000 dollars' worth of support, many were recipients of the recently launched Hungarian scholarship programme called Stipendium Hungaricum.

We can observe some positive developments in the sense that, whereas in 2011 5 per cent of ODA went to Africa and the Middle East, 43 per cent to the Western Balkans, 36 per cent to Asia and 16 per cent to Eastern Europe and Central Asia (Ministry of Foreign Affairs 2012), in 2014 the share of Africa had increased to 8 per cent and that of Asia to 54 per cent. Largest individual recipient countries in 2011 were Serbia (32 per cent), Afghanistan (30 per cent) and Ukraine (15 per cent), whereas in 2014 these were Jordan (17.65 per cent), Ukraine (14.66 per cent), Serbia (13.4 per cent), Vietnam (12.48 per cent) and Sri Lanka (9.34 per cent). Even though Hungary's Provincial Reconstruction Team commitments in Afghanistan had ended, the ministry managed to find three new development partners with which to cooperate, even though none of them are in Africa, and Jordan is classified as an upper-middle-income country. Nevertheless, it can be said that Hungary is increasingly focusing on low-income countries, thus fulfilling point 3 of the best practice recommendations. On the negative side, Sri Lanka and Vietnam were major recipients of 'tied aid' (Vietnam 770 000 dollars and Sri Lanka 1 028 000 dollars respectively), which is explicitly against the norms of both the European and the Global Consensus (point 4 above).

Tied aid programmes seem to have become an important modality for the Hungarian government. In 2016 two major projects were announced (25 million USD for the reconstruction of a biocombinat in Mongolia, as well as offering 30 million USD to Laos for the construction of a food-safety system and offering 36.5 million USD to Cambodia for the creation of a water treatment plant (*444.hu* 2016; *origo.hu* 2016). Budget support was not used in 2014 (point 5). Nor are country strategy papers used by the Ministry of Foreign Affairs (point 6). Aid flows are transparent (the Hungarian international development strategy notes that there are plans to apply International Aid Transparency Initiative (IATI) standards), and multiannual programming can be observed within the tied aid programmes and Stipendium Hungaricum (point 7).

Stipendium Hungaricum is slowly becoming one of the flagships of Hungarian development assistance, as its budget was set to reach 28.5 million USD in 2016 (approximately 8 billion HUF) and was planned to reach 71 million USD in the following years.[2] In the academic year

2016/2017 approximately 3500 new entrants, mainly from the developing world, were set to receive funding through this programme. The acknowledged goal of the programme is to assist the policy of 'global opening', improve human capacities in the Global South and assist Hungarian higher education in improving its English language programmes.

As has been mentioned earlier, Hungary had 59 partners in 2014, and 18 of them received more than 100 000 dollars. According to the Global and European Consensus these support modalities should be more focused on a selected few countries (point 8). Sectoral contributions can be mainly categorized in three areas: human development and educational support programmes through Stipendium Hungaricum and the United Nations' Food and Agricultural Organization; green growth programmes such as water treatment plants, sustainable water management and sanitation; and capacity building for public administration institutions (point 9). Joint programming is growing in importance, with an overall budget of 2.2 million euros to be implemented in Georgia and Egypt, as opposed to 2013 when only 142 000 dollars were spent on pursuing this form of support (point 10) (Ministry of Foreign Affairs and Trade, Hungary 2014a, 2015).

8.4   POLICY SUCCESS OR FAILURE?

At this point, it is worth considering what factors influenced Hungarian international development policy. There is a wide consensus in the literature that the international development policies of CEE countries and Hungary were initially adopted because of the looming EU accession of 2004 (Drozd 2007; Horký 2010; Szent-Iványi and Lightfoot 2015). Were socialization effects at play? According to Checkel (2005), in order to consider the socialization process 'successful', new policies should be sustainable and independent from external material incentives and sanctions. As shown in Table 8.1, Hungarian ODA has been steadily increasing in recent years, it has not been placed under an infringement procedure by the EC (thus discounting sanctions), and ODA expenditures are expected to increase (as outlined in the previous section), fulfilling in large degree the criteria of sustainability. This indicates that, even in the absence of accession conditionality, Hungarian development policy continued on a trajectory broadly in line with EU expectations.

Checkel (2005) has differentiated between two types of socialization, where Type 1 can be characterized by 'acting the way', whereas Type 2 is 'thinking and being the way'. In his observations of Hungarian ODA, Szent-Iványi (2012b) notes that Hungarian diplomats have learned to 'talk the talk', while Horký (2012) refers to the uptake and development of policy in this area as 'shallow Europeanization'. Accordingly, based on Checkel's (2005) characteristics, Type 1 socialization best approximates the case of Hungarian international development policy. Although it is difficult to substantiate empirically whether policy-makers' and officials' norms have changed, the case for Type 1 socialization can be made, for instance by the fact that, in CODEV, diplomats from new member states (including Hungary) almost never drive the agenda for discussion, in addition to their being more passive observers (Lightfoot and Szent-Iványi 2014). Hungary has only recently adopted an international development law and, in 2016, an international development strategy (the first since 2001). However, in order to become institutionalized, the informal rules (as outlined in the Global and European Consensus) have to be followed as well, and in this respect only moderate success has been achieved.

In terms of public support for international development, ODA policy is moderately popular with the citizenry. According to a survey by DemNet, a Hungarian non-governmental organization (NGO), 69 per cent of respondents said that Hungary was well enough developed to assist other, less fortunate countries. However, only 41 per cent of respondents were aware that Hungary engaged in international development assistance (Bördős and Gregor 2013). According to a Eurobarometer (2016) survey conducted in December 2015, 41 per cent of Hungarian respondents agreed to the statement that it should be one of the main priorities of the Hungarian government to tackle poverty in developing countries. Apart from Romania and Croatia, this was third highest positive response among the new member states. These results suggest that voters may be persuaded to support a higher involvement in development assistance, although policy-makers would need to make the case for a policy which is not well known at present.

Dimitrova (2010) posits that there were three possible outcomes to the adoption of EU rules and regulations post-accession: reversal, institutionalization and dead letters. If we take a look at Hungarian domestic politics during the post-accession period we can see that between 2004 and 2006 the policy area of international development was considered a low priority area, or as Sedelmeier (2011) would call it a low socialization area. Between 2006 and 2010, domestic Hungarian politics were in turmoil, in addition to suffering from the negative effects of the global financial crisis from 2008, limiting the build-up of aid policies. From 2010 onwards, with prime minister Viktor Orbán's Eastern and later on Southern Opening, the wish to focus on developing countries has gained traction. More generally, international development policy has been used as a foreign policy tool by other countries, utilized to gain influence in developing countries, to improve trade relations or to influence UN voting patterns (for instance,

Alesina and Dollar 2000; Collier and Dollar 2002; Szent-Iványi 2012a). Such tactics may have been one factor in Orbán's decision to focus on enabling ownership (the degree of domestic engagement in policy design, see Kelley 2004) in order for the policy area of development assistance to become more accepted and mainstream in Hungarian government affairs.

In any case, from 2013 onwards a form of institutionalization has taken place in Hungarian international development policy. The long-awaited law on international development assistance was adopted in December 2014, and a strategy for implementing it was also created. It should be noted that genuine consultation did take place, with several members of the NGO community and academia providing feedback on the draft law, of which some recommendations were implemented in the final documents. It is also clear that the Hungarian government has discovered in the field of development assistance an area where it can also obtain strategic gains while fulfilling international commitments. The two most popular modalities, as has been pointed out previously, are human development support programmes through Stipendium Hungaricum and green growth programmes with the use of tied aid. Stipendium Hungaricum has been very useful for Hungarian universities in building up their English language programmes and also gaining some extra revenue from the government. Tied aid, even though it is discouraged by the Global and European Consensus, has nevertheless been quite useful for Hungarian companies trying to gain a foothold in foreign markets.

8.5 CONCLUSIONS

This chapter has sought to address the question of whether the adoption of foreign rules and norms in the area of international development policy in Hungary can be considered to be policy success or failure. In order to answer the question, first the chapter introduced the literature of socialization, Europeanization and policy transfer. Building on this theoretical foundation, the chapter discussed the timeline of the (re-) creation of Hungarian aid policy and the consensus on the best practices which new EU donors are expected to achieve. In recent years, with the scope of Hungarian foreign policy changing and including countries of the Global South, international development assistance was (re)discovered as a tool of foreign policy with which Hungarian interest can be furthered. With the new international development law and implementation strategy, the Hungarian government has finally obtained a measure of ownership in this policy area. Even though the modalities used do not fully represent what is considered as best practices by the international aid community – as Hungarian aid is still very fragmented and the government uses tied aid extensively – at least some promising signs are present, that is, increased aid volumes, some form of multiannual financing through the human development and the green growth tied aid programmes, and greater institutionalization of the policy. Taken together, these signs mark out Hungarian development policy, in McConnell's (2010) terms, as a case of conflicted success.

NOTES

1. This chapter draws upon previous work commissioned by the World Bank Institute (Szent-Iványi and Tétényi 2012). As a methodological note, the author contacted the Ministry of Foreign Affairs and Trade (in May 2016) to seek information on the socialization process among ministry officials. However, the ministry decided not to comment. The author also attended an event organized by the Hungarian Association of NGOs for Development and Humanitarian Aid (HAND) on 24 September 2015, where all parliamentary parties were represented apart from the Democratic Alliance. Two party representatives (FIDESZ and MSZP) mentioned increasing development assistance as a crucial factor in providing opportunities for Hungarian companies, two party representatives (LMP and PM) argued that development assistance is needed to improve the livelihoods of the Global South, and the representative of Jobbik argued that development assistance should be reduced.
2. Interview by the author with a senior official at the Hungarian authority working on Stipendium Hungaricum (12 May 2016).

REFERENCES

444.hu (2016), '25 millió dolláros segélyhitelt adunk Mongóliának' [We will be providing 25 million USD of tied aid credit to Mongolia], *444.hu*, http://444.hu/2016/01/20/25-millio-dollaros-segelyhitelt-adunk-mongolianak (accessed 24 May 2016).

Alesina, Alberto and David Dollar (2000), 'Who gives foreign aid to whom and why?', *Journal of Economic Growth*, 5 (1), 33–63.

Baginski, Pawel (2002), 'Poland', in Michael Dauderstädt (ed.), *EU Eastern Enlargement and Development Cooperation*, Bonn: Friedrich-Ebert-Stiftung, pp. 12–20.

Bördős, Éva and Anikó Gregor (2013), 'Mennyire szolidáris a magyar? Kiket és hogyan támogatna Magyarország lakossága itthon és külföldön?' [To what extent do Hungarians practice solidarity? Who and in what ways would Hungarians support domestically and abroad?], *DemNet*, http://v4aid.eu/hu/kiadvanyok/hatteranyagok/263-mennyire-szolidaris-a-magyar (accessed 14 February 2016).

Bucar, Maja and Mojmir Mrak (2007), 'Challenges of development cooperation for EU new member states', Presented at the ABCDE World Bank Conference, Bled, 17–18 May 2007, http://siteresources.worldbank.org/INTABCDESLO2007/Resources/PAPERABCDEBucarMrak.pdf (accessed 23 May 2016).

Burnell, Peter (2004), *Foreign Aid Resurgent – New Spirit or Old Hangover?*, UNU-WIDER Research Paper No. 2004/44, Helsinki: UNU-WIDER.

Carbone, Maurizio (2004), 'Development policy', in Neill Nugent (ed.), *European Union Enlargement*, Basingstoke: Palgrave, pp. 242–53.

Checkel, Jeffrey (2001), 'Why comply? Social learning and European identity change', *International Organization*, 55 (3), 553–88.

Checkel, Jeffrey (2005), 'International institutions and socialization in Europe: Introduction and framework', *International Organization*, 59 (4), 801–26.

Collier, Paul and David Dollar (2002), 'Aid allocation and poverty reduction', *European Economic Review*, 46 (3), 1475–1500.

Dimitrova, Antoaneta (2010), 'The new member states of the EU in the aftermath of enlargement: Do new European rules remain empty shells?', *Journal of European Public Policy*, 17 (1), 137–48.

Drozd, Maciej (2007), 'The new face of solidarity: A brief survey of Polish aid', Manuscript, http://papers.ssrn.com/sol3/papers.cfm?abstract_id=1132246 (accessed 25 January 2016).

Eurobarometer (2016), *The European Year for Development – Citizens' Views on Development, Cooperation and Aid*, Special Eurobarometer No. 441, Brussels: European Commission.

European Commission (2011), Communication from the Commission to the European Parliament, the Council, the European Economic and Social Committee and the Committee of the Regions: Increasing the impact of EU development policy: An agenda for change, 13.10.2011 COM(2011) 637 final, Brussels.

European Consensus (2006), Joint statement by the Council and the representatives of the governments of the member states meeting within the Council, the European Parliament and the Commission on European Union development policy: 'The European Consensus', *Official Journal*, 2006/C 46/01, 24 February.

Hartlapp, Miriam (2007), 'On enforcement, management and persuasion: Different logics of implementation policy in the EU and the ILO', *Journal of Common Market Studies*, 45 (3), 653–74.

Horký, Ondrey (2010), *The Europeanisation of Development Policy: Acceptance, Accommodation and Resistance of the Czech Republic*, DIE Discussion Paper No. 18/2010, Bonn: Deutsches Institut für Entwicklungspolitik.

Horký, Ondrey (2012), 'The impact of the shallow Europeanisation of the "new" member states on the EU's actorness: What coherence between foreign and development policy?', in Stefan Grimm, Davina Makhan and Sven Gänzle (eds), *The European Union and Global Development: An 'Enlightened Superpower' in the Making?*, Basingstoke: Palgrave Macmillan, pp. 57–73.

HUN-IDA (2004), *A magyar műszaki-tudományos együttműködés és segítségnyújtás négy évtizedének rövid áttekintése napjainkig* [An overview of the four decades of Hungarian technical-scientific cooperation and assistance], Budapest: Hungarian International Development Agency.

Jacoby, Wade (2004), *The Enlargement of the European Union and NATO: Choosing from the Menu in Central Europe*, Cambridge: Cambridge University Press.

Kelley, Judith (2004), 'International actors on the domestic scene: Membership conditionality and socialization by international institutions', *International Organization*, 58 (3), 425–57.

Lightfoot, Simon and Balázs Szent-Iványi (2014), 'Reluctant donors? The Europeanization of international development policies in the new member states', *Journal of Common Market Studies*, 52 (6), 1257–72.

McConnell, Allan (2010), 'Policy success, policy failure and grey areas in-between', *Journal of Public Policy*, 30 (3), 345–62.

McConnell, Allan (2015), 'What is policy failure? A primer to help navigate the maze', *Public Policy and Administration*, 30 (3–4), 221–42.

Ministry of Foreign Affairs (2011), *Magyar külpolitikai az Uniós elnökség után* [Hungarian foreign policy after the EU presidency], Budapest: Ministry of Foreign Affairs.

Ministry of Foreign Affairs (2012), *Beszámoló Magyarország 2011. évi nemzetközi fejlesztési és humanitárius segítségnyújtási tevékenységéről* [Report on the Hungarian development and humanitarian assistance contributions in the year 2011], Budapest: Ministry of Foreign Affairs.

Ministry of Foreign Affairs and Trade, Hungary (2014a), *Beszámoló Magyarország 2013. évi nemzetközi fejlesztési és humanitárius segítségnyújtási tevékenységéről* [Report on the Hungarian development and humanitarian assistance contributions in the year 2013], http://nefe.kormany.hu/eves-beszamolok (accessed 15 February 2016).

Ministry of Foreign Affairs and Trade, Hungary (2014b), *International Development Cooperation Strategy and Strategic Concept for International Humanitarian Aid of Hungary 2014–2020*, http://nefe.kormany.hu/download/3/93/c0000/Internatio nal%20Development%20Cooperation%20and%20Humanitarian%20Aid%20Stra tegy%20of%20Hungary-v%C3%A9gleges.pdf (accessed 15 February 2016).

Ministry of Foreign Affairs and Trade, Hungary (2015), *Beszámoló Magyarország 2014. évi nemzetközi fejlesztési és humanitárius segítségnyújtási tevékenységéről* [Report on the Hungarian development and humanitarian assistance contributions in the year 2014], http://nefe.kormany.hu/eves-beszamolok (accessed 15 February 2016).

OECD (2008), *The Paris Declaration on Aid Effectiveness and the Accra Agenda for Action*, Paris: OECD.

OECD (2011), *Better Aid Effectiveness 2011*, Paris: OECD.

OECD (2016), OECD.stat, http://stats.oecd.org/Index.aspx?ThemeTreeId=3 (accessed 13 February 2016).

origo.hu (2016), 'A magyar exportbank segélyhitelt kínál Indonéziának és Laosznak' [The Hungarian export bank offers tied aid to Indonesia and Laos], *origo.hu*, http://www.origo.hu/gazdasag/20160521-19-3-milliard-forintnyi-kotott-segelyhite lt-ajanl-az-eximbank-indonezianak-es-laosznak.html (accessed 25 May 2016).

Paragi, Beáta (2010), 'Hungarian development policy', in Paul Hoebink (ed.), *European Development Cooperation: In between the Local and the Global*, Amsterdam: Amsterdam University Press, pp. 195–222.

Schimmelfennig, Frank (2005), 'Strategic calculation and international socialization: Membership incentives, party constellations, and sustained compliance in Central and Eastern Europe', *International Organization*, 59 (4), 827–60.

Schimmelfennig, Frank and Ulrich Sedelmeier (2005), 'Introduction: Conceptualising the Europeanization of Central and Eastern Europe', in Frank Schimmelfennig and Ulrich Sedelmeier (eds), *The Europeanization of Central and Eastern Europe*, Ithaca, NY: Cornell University Press, pp. 1–29.

Sedelmeier, Ulrich (2011), 'Europeanisation in new member and candidate states', *Living Reviews in European Governance*, 6 (1).

Szent-Iványi, Balázs (2012a), 'Aid allocation of the emerging Central and Eastern European donors', *Journal of International Relations and Development*, 15, 65–89.

Szent-Iványi, Balázs (2012b), 'Hungarian international development co-operation: Context, stakeholders and performance', *Perspectives on European Politics and Society*, 13 (1), 50–65.

Szent-Iványi, Balázs and Simon Lightfoot (2015), *New Europe's New Development Aid*, BASEES/Routledge Series on Russian and East European Studies, London: Routledge.

Szent-Iványi, Balázs and András Tétényi (2008), 'Transition and foreign aid policies in Visegrad countries: A path dependant approach', *Transition Studies Review*, 15 (3), 573–87.

Szent-Iványi, Balázs and András Tétényi (2012), *Assessing Existing Practices in Capacity Building and Experience Sharing for the Central European New Donors*, Final report of the mapping exercise commissioned by the World Bank Institute.

Szent-Iványi, Balázs and András Tétényi (2013), 'The East-Central European new donors: Mapping capacity building and remaining challenges', *Journal of International Development*, 25 (6), 819–31.

Vachudova, Milada Anna (2005), *Europe Undivided: Democracy, Leverage and Integration after Communism*, Oxford: Oxford University Press.

9. A resounding success or downright failure? Understanding policy transfer within the Bologna Process in Central and Eastern Europe

Liviu Matei, Daniela Craciun and Simona Torotcoi

9.1 INTRODUCTION

Has the Bologna Process been a success or failure in Central and Eastern Europe (CEE) in particular, and in Europe more generally? The question, asked time and again, is persistently misconstrued. This explains to a large extent both the inconsistent scholarly literature on the subject and the contradictory evaluations of the Bologna Process among politicians and policy makers, academics and higher education administrators, students and student organizations, other stakeholders and the general public. The chapter aims to reconsider the question and find a valid manner to address it. For this, it puts forward a comprehensive analysis of what is Bologna, a clear-cut approach to understanding policy transfer under this Process and a set of standards and benchmarks for gauging its success and failure in CEE.

In pursuit of reform models from the early days of transition, CEE countries made the choice to adopt 'European models' in higher education. Interestingly, they decided not to consider other possible models from other parts of the world. As soon as the Bologna Process was started, it largely become *the European model*. In the implementation of this model, CEE countries adopted a *wholesale, all-or-nothing, now-or-never approach*, with no room for testing, or trial-and-error tactics. The Bologna Process, however, was in reality not a defined, unitary model or policy, but a complex and evolving set of values, principles, priorities, objectives, tools and instruments. Success and failure in this case is a matter of degree and must also consider the defined aspects of the Process.

9.2   WHAT IS THE BOLOGNA PROCESS?

The Bologna Process is a complex phenomenon. Restricting it to only one of its components or facets, as is most often the case, makes it difficult to correctly understand and assess its evolution, outcomes and impact. The Bologna Process, for example, is not just a 'policy'. Studying it only as a 'policy' unintentionally misconstrues its nature and results in misleading assessments and interpretations. It is almost like taking a particular piece from an outsized, intricate mosaic and judging the whole based on this one piece alone. This section describes, in a succinct but comprehensive manner, the elaborate assemblage that is the Bologna Process.

The Bologna Process is one of the most remarkable and complex policy and political developments in Europe at the beginning of the twenty-first century. It started formally in 1999 when 29 European countries, from both East and West, signed the Bologna Declaration and committed themselves to building a common European Higher Education Area (EHEA). The Sorbonne Declaration, signed the year before by the ministers of education of France, Germany, Italy and the UK, not only anticipated the launch of the Process by 'encouraging a common frame of reference, aimed at improving external recognition and facilitating student mobility as well as employability' (Sorbonne Declaration 1998: 1), but is sometimes considered to be an integral part of Bologna. Since the initial launch in 1999, new objectives and policies have been added at various times. The Bologna Process has evolved in an extraordinary, although not uncontroversial, fashion until today, 'spanning half the globe, from Reykjavik to Vladivostok' (Scott 2012). It includes basically all European countries (48 as of April 2015), as well as the European Commission. Even non-European countries, like Israel and Kyrgyzstan, applied for membership in the common *European* Higher Education Area (although they were eventually rejected).

The magnitude of the developments triggered by the Bologna Process is unparalleled (Vögtle and Martens 2014). At times, bold metaphors such as 'planned movements of continental plaques' have been used to epitomize its nature and impact (Matei and Curaj 2014). Notwithstanding agreement that Bologna is a major historical development, at least in its intentions and the scope of work it has generated, there is no consensus on whether it represents a resounding success, as some say, a downright failure, as others argue, or anything in between (Rudder 2010; Szolár 2011). Certain scholars consider the Process to be completed by now, urging politicians and policy makers to '[c]elebrate Bologna's extraordinary achievements and bid it goodbye' (Lazerson 2015). Others argue that, while we can observe a degree of formal compliance with the overall commitments of the Bologna

Declaration, the main goals of convergence and harmonization of higher education systems are yet to be achieved. Some other voices argue that Bologna was harmful to students, teachers, national systems or the cause of higher education altogether (Pechar 2012). Its objectives either were wrong or, if they were positive, are yet to be achieved (Terry 2010).

This inconsistency in evaluating the Bologna Process is puzzling, and it is due to a large extent to a fragmentary understanding of the Process. In order to solve this conundrum, we put together a concise, comprehensive, multi-dimensional presentation of the defining components and characteristics of the Process. This takes the form of 'a conceptual scaffolding' of the 'Bologna mosaic', an inclusive framework of reference for understanding what is Bologna as a European agreed-upon model for reforms, what exactly is transferred from the broad Bologna 'model' or 'models', why and how this transfer takes place, and with what results. The framework is presented in Table 9.1, and it was developed, at first, in an inductive manner considering Bologna documents and activities. We then employed policy transfer theories of success and failure to test and consolidate the scaffolding and finalize it as a heuristic tool. Our understanding of policy transfer is derived from Chapter 1 in this volume, as well as the typologies of Dolowitz and Marsh (1996) and Maggetti and Gilardi (2015). Like other studies, we found quite rapidly that 'there is no generally accepted framework for judging policy success and indeed the academic literature in this field is very poor' (Marsh and Sharman 2009: 283). Nevertheless, following McConnell's (2010, 2015) framework for assessing policy success and failure, we identified distinct facets of the Bologna Process that help to better assess its achievements.

In this characterization of the Bologna Process we put forward in Table 9.1 we distinguish between two facets (political and policy) and different levels at which the Process unfolds (European, national, institutional). Considering these facets and levels (or scales) and their interaction, we can identify, organize and study a comprehensive list of distinct *objectives*. In the evaluation of the implementation of Bologna, many of these objectives are often ignored, conflated, or confused with each other. This 'conceptual scaffolding' also sheds light into the convoluted panoply of *means, tools and instruments* created within the Bologna framework. It helps to directly clarify *what is transferred* under Bologna, and to study *why* and *how* the transfer took place. Finally, as a heuristic device, it allows us to assess and explain success and failure (*what results* and *why these results*) with a good degree of clarity.

Table 9.1 reveals that the question of success or failure is not one single question, regarding one single particular aspect. We could proceed line by line or even cell by cell, and zoom in on particular aspects that need

Table 9.1 A characterization of the nature, scope, intended objectives and means of the Bologna Process

Facet of the Bologna Process	Scope/level	Main objectives (whether declared or not)	Means, tools and instruments
I. Political process	1. European level	a. Contribute to building an integrated Europe from a cultural, political and economic perspective. b. Contribute to building 'a European ethos and demos' (Matei 2012).	i. Creation of a multi-layered pan-European process and framework for higher education, with expected cultural, political and economic implications supportive of more integration in all these areas.
	2. National level	a. Use Bologna as a political justification or pretext ('international commitments oblige us') for promoting far-reaching and/or unpopular reforms at national level. b. Pursue European integration within and beyond higher education (that is, through labour mobility). c. Build and/or assert national identity by assuming or distancing from 'European identity'.	i. National legislation and higher education regulations/policies and tools inspired by Bologna completely, partially or only symbolically; new or transformed national institutions in higher education. ii. Particular positioning vis-à-vis Bologna (acceptance, partial embrace, rejection).

Table 9.1 (continued)

Facet of the Bologna Process	Scope/level	Main objectives (whether declared or not)	Means, tools and instruments
II. Policy process	1. European level	a. Create an EHEA. b. Promote reforms aiming at the modernization of higher education in Europe. c. Develop and put into practice European models in various areas of higher education.	i. Creation of a new type of space for policy dialogue in higher education, unique in its nature, transnational and trans-sectoral (this is also an objective, not only a tool). ii. Intergovernmental commitments for the implementation of the Bologna action lines. iii. Development of new concepts, policies, regulations, tools and instruments, including new institutions at national and European level.
	2. National level	a. Promote specific transformations in significant (although not all) parts of the domestic higher education systems.	i. National legislation and higher education regulations/policies and tools inspired by Bologna completely, partially or only apparently; new or transformed national institutions in higher education.
	3. Institutional level	a. Adopt or implement the Bologna models, policies and action lines, as promoted nationally or at the European level.	i. Institutional transformation supported, if not triggered or forced, by new national Bologna-inspired policies and regulations. ii. Institutional transformation supported by a direct participation in the European space for dialogue (and practice) in higher education.

Source: Authors' own compilation based on core policy documents of the Bologna Process.

to be taken into account. This will result in a good number of specific questions about success and failure. We can ask, for example, if Bologna is a success as a *political process*, thus looking at this particular facet, or if it is a success as a *policy process*, to take the other facet. These questions, however, would be still too broad to answer with any degree of accuracy. It is important, but still not sufficient, to add more precision by bringing into the discussion the various levels at which we can analyse the Process (European, national, institutional) and intersect them with a particular facet (policy or political process). The discussion appears to become really productive when we also take into account the objectives and means of the process individually, as detailed in the last two columns of Table 9.1.

To illustrate how this heuristic tool can help with our overall task here, we can ask for example if Bologna has indeed contributed to building a politically integrated Europe (set of objectives I.1.a in Table 9.1). The answer is probably yes, although it is difficult to indicate with precision the actual extent of success in this case. If we want to be more analytic, we can further distinguish between the objectives included in this set (cultural, political and economic integration) and assess them individually. For example, one particular European-wide objective of Bologna has been to bring about certain economic results, mainly in terms of employment and competitiveness. By analysing the extent to which these results have been achieved we can gauge the economic success or failure of the Process. Equally interesting, and only rarely if at all studied, we can ask what has been achieved with regard to the development of 'a European ethos and demos' (I.1.b) in the European Higher Education Area.

To sum up, each individual cell can support a separate, clean analysis applied to the key areas and characteristics of success and failure. It is the lack of awareness regarding the 'cells' in Table 9.1 that explains, at least in good part, the puzzling picture of its evaluation as a success and failure. Indeed, we need to talk about success, or degrees of success, for some elements of the Process, and failure, or degrees of failure, for others, rather than simply success or failure. The more general case in point here is that an indistinct discussion about success and failure can bring about only limited insight. We need to state each time what element or combinations of facets and levels we are talking about. The heuristic tool proposed in Table 9.1 also allows us to undertake such an exercise systematically and with lucidity, thus permitting important elucidations in both a practical and a scholarly order. Table 9.1 helps bring under the microscope aspects of the Bologna Process that are important for its understanding and evaluation, and which are otherwise understudied, ignored or just analytically confused. We will discuss the reasons why CEE countries have signed up for implementing Bologna reforms (relating to the political dimension), what is transferred in the process (relating to the policy dimension) and with what results (relating to the spectrum of political and policy success and failure).

9.3   THE BOLOGNA TRANSFER PROCESS IN CENTRAL AND EASTERN EUROPE

Since its start in 1999, the Bologna Process has played a particularly important role for the countries of CEE. For the last two decades the Process has been at the very core of systemic higher education transformations in the region. First, a particular justification for the special interest regarding Bologna in CEE has to do with the democratization and modernization of the higher education sector during the post-communist transition. Second, Bologna reforms represent a key segment of the overall efforts of these countries towards European integration, and are thus relevant beyond the area of higher education (Szolár 2011). The European Union's (EU) influence and its conditionality, accession and norms compliance requirements have been part of the implementation of the Bologna Process in the region, despite the fact that Bologna is not an EU policy or process *per se*. Third, the evaluations of the success or failure of Bologna in CEE alone are as puzzling as they are for the rest of Europe.

9.3.1   Why Have CEE Countries Signed Up for Bologna?

Having been engaged in a structural reform process, the new governments of the region looked for both general inspiration and specific policy models with regard to higher education. At this critical juncture, different pathways were possible. Theoretically, CEE countries could have opted for higher education models from other regions, such as the United States (then and now considered the most developed higher education system in the world) or even South-East Asia (in the early 1990s several countries in CEE did look with interest at the experiences of Singapore). Another option would have been to develop new home-grown models. However, none of these have happened. Instead, CEE countries have all joined the emerging European model or models put forward by the Bologna Process. As a 'European model', the Bologna Process contains some elements borrowed from non-European experiences (like the qualifications framework, which was inspired by Australia) and many new, original European elements (Matei 2012, 2014) assembled in a novel and unique type of *bricolage*, as understood in Chapter 1 of this volume. We can find a mixture of motivations for this choice ranging from political (European integration, new identity, etc.) to policy-instrumental (modernization of the whole higher education sector or specific areas of it).

In other words, CEE countries have opted not to experiment with, or borrow, models from outside Europe. Instead, and at least nominally, a 'wholesale political commitment' has been made to implement the emerging European model represented by Bologna. It is true that, for certain areas of higher education policy, transfer in CEE has taken place with reference to specific national models from other European countries, rather than the generic Bologna model (Kralikova 2016). Nevertheless, when we try to understand what exactly has been transferred from the generic Bologna model, how, and with what results, we find that all the cells in Table 9.1 are relevant in CEE, and that they are coloured by the tones of post-communist transition and Europeanization.

By signing the Bologna Declaration and through their ensuing membership in the EHEA, participating countries committed themselves to achieve commonly agreed-upon goals. In part, this reflects a political will for national gains under the greater umbrella of expected benefits from Europe. Owing to the embeddedness of the Process in the domestic level, the initiative has been described as a 'two-level game' (Putnam 1988; Racké 2006). On the one hand, participating countries can address problems that are transnational in their scope and cannot be dealt with by each country separately at the national level. On the other hand, a joint European initiative can help not only to overcome domestic resistance from universities, academics and students but also to provide legitimacy for the reforms. For example, newly promoted higher education laws in Lithuania were legitimized through the Bologna policy discourse by explicitly referring to specific action lines of the Process (Leisyte et al. 2015).

Another reason for policy transfer is the existence of supranational institutions and treaties that push individual states to implement certain policies. Because Bologna is a voluntary intergovernmental process, CEE countries put themselves willingly in a situation of experiencing external pressure by signing the Bologna Declaration and related documents (including the European Cultural Convention and the Lisbon Recognition Convention, signed before 1999, which were taken as the basis for defining the eligibility of a country for joining the Bologna Process later on). For the EU member states Bologna represented a step towards deeper integration, whereas for non-EU members it was a form of 'catch-up Europeanization' (Hörner 2014). For example, Miron (2014) argues that Romania's fast adaptation to the Bologna Process objectives was driven by the evolution of the European integration process and aspirations for EU membership. It represented a way for the country to move in this process from a logic of conformity to one of proactivity (Miron 2014).

The Bologna Process in CEE is not only part of the post-communist political transformation within the region, but also a window of opportunity for the Europeanization of the higher education sector (Szolár 2011). These related but still distinct objectives are reflected in cells I.1 (the European level of the political process), I.2 (the national level of the political process) and II.1 (the European policy process), depicted in Table 9.1.

Assessing the involvement of supranational institutions in European higher education, Barkholt (2005) claims that, even though higher education is not under the supervision of EU institutions, and Bologna is not an EU initiative or programme, the European Commission played a big role during this time in building external pressure. Specifically, the European Commission played an important normative role throughout these years in forming and shaping the higher education policy landscape through its memoranda and publications (that is, several 'communications' on the role of higher education between 2003 and 2014). Moreover, through programmes such as Erasmus (promoting student and staff mobility) it allowed for the promotion of 'European dimensions' in higher education, shaping at the same time the Bologna agenda. It is also important to note that, in the years preceding the Bologna Declaration, the TEMPUS/ PHARE programme of the EU, which ran between 1990 and 2000, played a particularly strong role in supporting the Europeanization of higher education in CEE by encouraging cooperation between higher education institutions from the EU and those from partner countries in CEE, and by supporting reforms and the improvement of the quality of higher education in these countries. The TEMPUS/PHARE programme, which was part of the pre-accession package made available by the EU, had a major, Marshall Plan type of impact on the higher education systems in the benefiting countries in CEE (Matei 2014).

9.3.2   What is Transferred through the Bologna Process?

Assessing the actual subject of policy transfer, Dolowitz and Marsh (1996) argue that what is transferred is policy goals and instruments, administrative techniques, institutions, ideas, attitudes, concepts and also negative lessons. This analytical perspective largely overlaps with our understanding of policy transfer. As a result, it was used while developing Table 9.1, taking into account facets, levels, objectives and means of the Bologna Process.

The original Bologna Declaration and ministerial communiqués adopted every two to three years represent the official documents of the Process, and outline its 'policy scripts'. A close look at these documents shows that Bologna encourages participating countries to implement tools, reforms, goals, objectives, principles, recommendations, European standards, priorities, guidelines, strategies, action lines and commitments. Broadly speaking, this is the array of possible transfers and a perplexing panoply of options.

In another attempt to systemize Bologna, Zgaga (2012) claims that principles (or core values) lead to general objectives, which are reflected in action lines, which in turn require setting up priorities for political action or specific policies (as we show in Table 9.1). This is a useful and parsimonious description that helps clarify the elements of Bologna which can be subject to policy transfer. We proceed to illustrate it in a particular policy area, which represents one of the most developed action lines of the Bologna Process: quality assurance (QA). We break down QA, referring back to the panoply of policy transfers by moving from general principles to specific policies at the institutional level, as follows:

- *Super-ordinate aim in QA under Bologna:* To create a European area of higher education where national identities and common interests can interact and strengthen each other for the benefit of Europe, its citizens and, more specifically, its students (adapted from the Bologna Declaration 1999).
- *Principle:* The need to address the interests of students, as well as employers and society more generally, through good quality higher education.
- *Priority:* The quality of higher education to be at the heart of setting up the EHEA.
- *Objective:* Higher education institutions to develop their own strategies for quality enhancement.
- *Standards and guidelines:* Standards and Guidelines for Quality Assurance in the EHEA (ESG) adopted by the ministers responsible for higher education in 2005 to contribute to a common understanding of quality assurance across borders and among stakeholders (Bergen Communiqué 2005); a revised version (ESG II) was adopted in 2015 (Yerevan Communiqué 2015).
- *Commitments:* For example, allow agencies on the European QA Register for Higher Education to perform their activities across borders within the EHEA, while complying with national requirements.
- *Strategy:* National strategies for QA (for example, in Romania the National Romanian Agency for QA in Higher Education is responsible for the development and monitoring of the strategy).
- *Tools:* For example, Diploma Supplement and European Credit Transfer System (ECTS) as tools for QA.

- *Policy:* Diversification of higher education institutions (for example, university classifications and programme ranking in Romania, linked to a new Bologna-inspired approach to QA at system and institutional level).

The various cells of Table 9.1 allow a detailed understanding of the developments promoted by Bologna in the QA area, as well as their precise evaluation, including in terms of success or failure of policy transfer. This approach inspired by Zgaga's (2012) analysis also helps in understanding the Bologna inventory of concepts used by both practitioners and academics. In this way, it contributes to a clarification regarding the 'success and failure of what' (that is, objectives, priorities, principles, commitments), which will be expanded upon in sub-section 9.3.3. For now, we note that such a breakdown of elements brings to light another important aspect to be considered when assessing success and failure. As becomes apparent, some of the transferred elements related to QA are more concrete, technical and specific (for example the introduction of the Diploma Supplement and ECTS), thus making it clear what should be transferred and how. Other elements are more ambiguous and undefined (for example the commitment to transnational QA), leaving greater flexibility to governments and higher education institutions to make decisions.

Most, if not all, transferred action lines of Bologna manifest such multiple dimensions. This conclusion is also found in the public policy literature, where it is stated that the complexity of a policy or a programme (multiple goals, issue salience, possible side effects, predictable outcomes) affects its transferability (Dolowitz and Marsh 1996). Having a clear understanding of the characteristics of 'what' is transferred makes for a more nuanced understanding of the results.

Policy transfer in QA was influenced by specific regional factors. When they joined Bologna, CEE countries found themselves in the middle of an overall transformation of higher education. In QA there was basically no previous experience in the region, unlike in Western Europe, where many countries had strong traditions and institutions. Starting from zero, CEE countries embraced completely the emerging 'Bologna model' in this area. They adopted (transferred) principles and priorities in quality assurance developed by Bologna and subscribed to the other commitments put forward as part of the Process. CEE countries committed to implementing the European Standards and Guidelines for Quality Assurance, introduced the concept and practice of accreditation (for the first time in this part of the world), and created new regulations and institutions to support these principles, policies and practices.

Policy transfer can be considered a success in this area, because useful new models, institutions and practices in quality assurance emerging within the context of the Bologna Process have been adopted and implemented in CEE. It can even be argued that the developments in CEE in this area are significantly more extensive than in Western Europe. Some commitments like transnational accreditation, however, have not been put into practice (the same is true for most of Europe), although there are recent signs of progress. If ever put into practice, the commitment to transnational accreditation would represent a major step in the direction of more European integration, even beyond the realm of higher education, as accreditation has been traditionally strongly linked with national sovereignty (Table 9.1, cell I.2.b).

It is possible to discuss similar examples for all other Bologna action lines presented in Table 9.1, although some (like QA) are more developed than others (like the social dimension of higher education). What these examples show is that we can analyse policy transfer, in particular *what is transferred*, within Bologna in a nuanced and realistic way using the framework proposed in Table 9.1, complemented with elements of the policy transfer literature. Only after the elements of transfer have been identified can the discussion move towards assessing the success and/or failure of this transfer.

9.3.3   Assessing Bologna's Results: A Spectrum of Achievement

With the rise of the 'evaluative state' (Hartmann 2008; Szolár 2011; Pasias and Roussakis 2012; Enders and Westerheijden 2014), concerns about policy success and failure have become central to public policy research and practice. The case of the Bologna Process is no different. We find that there is a growing interest in assessing the implementation of Bologna policies and their impact at the European, national and institutional level. There are several types of evaluations. A first category looks at the level of implementation. In this category we can place Bologna implementation reports published regularly by the EU through Eurydice (a coordinating unit based in the Education, Audiovisual and Culture Executive Agency in Brussels), by the European University Association (the *Trends* reports) and by governments (national implementation reports). A second category looks at the path taken by different countries or policies across time. This category also includes studies which deal with the supranational level and transnational policy dynamics towards policy convergence (Heckl 2001; Van Damme 2009; Vögtle 2014), policy coordination (Kauko 2012) or even the Europeanization of education (Kwiek and Maasen 2012). A third category looks at the required configurations needed for implementing Bologna policies. They assess the implantation of different action lines, like QA (Saarinen 2005), and country specific implementation aspects (Veiga and Amaral 2009), or follow all commitments systematically at the national (Matei and Curaj 2014) or institutional (Kettunen and Kantola 2006) implementation level.

In spite of the array of evaluations of the Bologna Process, there is no consensus on its achievements. This is because getting to the core of what policy success/failure is, how to measure it and how to determine its causes is not a simple matter. Reviewing the literature on policy evaluation, we find that

> there is some tendency to lump together policy failures arising from different sources and having different fundamental characteristics. This is a problem conceptually, as well as for building effective theory about policy failure, but it can also be a practical difficulty for policymakers if they fail to differentiate these various possible roots of failure. (Peters 2015: 261)

As noted in Chapter 1 of this volume, a nuanced understanding of policy success and failure is advanced by McConnell (2010, 2015). The idea he puts forward is that one should look at the different dimensions of a policy or set of policies and examine how success and failure are manifested within these dimensions. He argues that, since policies have different 'realms' (*process*, *programmes* and *politics*), they may fail or succeed in each of these 'along a spectrum' (McConnell 2010: 345). This perspective indicates that locating policies on a spectrum from success to failure 'involves judgment rather than scientific precision' (Wildawsky, in McConnell 2010). This approach is at the basis of the framework proposed in Table 9.1, and, as such, it helps to account for the inconsistency in the existing evaluations of Bologna in CEE, and in Europe in general.

As a *policy process*, Bologna has been hailed for opening up a dialogue space for higher education policy where different types and levels of actors cooperate towards a common goal (Table 9.1, cell II.1.i). Not only does the Bologna Process bring together governments from different European countries, but it also brings other types of actors and stakeholders into this new European space of policy dialogue and practices: national and supra-national organizations, and agencies and institutions from within and outside the higher education sector (Matei 2012, 2014). This continental space for policy dialogue in higher education is unprecedented in Europe, and also unique in the world.

However, as a *political process*, Bologna has been hijacked by national interests. In the context of low or limited awareness about Bologna policies and instruments (Veiga, in Harmsen 2015), governments have used the Process to control the policy agenda and legitimize policy choices (Table 9.1, cell I.2.a). Somewhat surprisingly, on the national level, higher education policy debates have been restricted under the banner of the Bologna Process, leading to what Harmsen (2015: 792) calls 'discursive closure'. Specifically, in CEE countries the formulation and implementation of Bologna policies were presented to national publics and higher education stakeholders either as part of EU accession conditions (Harmsen 2015) or as a way of 'embracing the "West", European integration and overcoming the eastern bloc systems' (Rudder 2010: 12). For example, Deca (2013) looks at the discursive uses of the Bologna Process in the Romanian higher education system and argues that actors in the field presented Bologna and its related concepts and policies as coming from the EU, inducing in this way a particular – and in reality skewed – perception of the whole Process. In the context of EU accession, the Bologna Process became an 'instrument of change, being framed as the reason why structural reforms had to be implemented without delay or much debate' (Deca 2013: 26). Presenting Bologna as the sole policy path and thus closing broader policy debates, the job of governing the higher education sector was made easier at the national level. Paradoxically, Bologna has opened a transnational space of discussion about higher education, but closed or foreshortened the national ones, which impeded effective policy design and implementation.

At the *national policy level*, the Bologna Process aimed to promote specific transformations in significant parts of the domestic higher education systems (Table 9.1, cell II.2.a) through national legislation, regulations and policies inspired by Bologna (Table 9.1, cell II.2.i or I.2.i). One can observe that, for many years, higher education reform programmes enjoyed the status of central, highly visible and highly valued policies in the countries of CEE. The Bologna Process, in its interconnection with EU policies, contributed to the centrality and perceived value of these reforms (corresponding to Table 9.1, cells II.1.c and II.1.iii). This in turn helps explain why the transfer of Bologna policies within CEE has taken place.

Not all countries position themselves in the same way vis-à-vis Bologna (acceptance, partial embrace, or rejection), and this is reflected in their policy implementation patterns (Table 9.1, cell I.2.ii). For instance, some countries have a rapid take-up and implementation of Bologna policies (for example Romania), while others have an incremental implementation trajectory (for example the Czech Republic). These political positions towards Bologna are also not fixed. At present, we are witnessing divergent evolutions in this context, with expected important consequences in terms of implementation (Matei 2015). Some countries remain committed to Bologna and to the centrality of higher education in their reforms and generic public policy endeavours. Other countries in the region are starting to downgrade the importance of the Bologna model or even of higher education altogether. This is happening for reasons that have to do with large-scale societal or political change – developments such as the stalled European integration process, or the corrosion of the knowledge society policy narrative, which previously helped generate broad political and general public support for higher education based on the idea that knowledge is the main factor of economic and social progress everywhere and higher education plays a key role in the production, transmission, dissemination and use of knowledge (Matei 2015). There are countries which after an initial full embrace of the Bologna Process stopped implementing some of its policies (for example Hungary).

At the *institutional policy level*, the picture of success/failure is not unambiguous either. Existing evaluation reports show that the 'hard' elements of the Bologna Process (that is, degree cycles, Diploma Supplement, ECTS) are successfully implemented in many countries, but the 'softer' issues (that is, learning outcomes, the recognition of prior studies, lifelong learning, the European dimension) have much less visible outcomes (Huisman et al. 2006). In more than half of the participating countries, 'there has been a 90% take-up of the two-cycle bachelor–master degree courses' in universities (Corbett 2012; see Table 9.1, cell II.3.a). On the other hand, not much has been done with regard to student mobility, mainly due to the lack of interest of governments in supporting university managers. Conversely, higher education institutions tried to compensate for the lack of government interest in student mobility. In the absence of a government strategy or programme to support mobility, Polish universities came together, adopted and then put into practice their own programme to promote international student mobility, sometimes partnering with local rather than national authorities (Matei and Iwinska 2015). In this case we witness partial success in Poland, in spite of the lack of governmental engagement, whereas in the case of Romania, where both government and university engagement are lacking in the area of mobility, we witness plain failure (Matei and Iwinska 2015).

9.4   CONCLUSION

Noting the highly inconsistent evaluations of the Bologna Process as either a success or a failure, the chapter sought to explain the sources of this perplexing lack of consensus through an analysis of the different features of success and failure in policy transfer and implementation. We aimed to show that the experience of CEE accession is prefigured by other related developments beyond the influence of the EU and its conditionality, accession and norms compliance requirements, like the Bologna Process.

Some of the most important conclusions are as follows. First, it is possible to understand the sources for the utterly contradictory evaluations of Bologna and move beyond the existing confusing assessments. For this, from a policy transfer perspective, it is important to clarify *what is transferred* or subject to transfer. To achieve this objective, we outline a heuristic instrument in Table 9.1 for understanding the 'conceptual scaffolding' of the 'Bologna mosaic'. Our heuristic framework allows us to zoom in and out of the different levels impacted by policy transfer in the case of Bologna (European, national, institutional). The aim of the chapter was 'less to develop "objective" measures of outcomes – the traditional aim of evaluation research – and more so to facilitate a dialogue among advocates of different criteria' (Majone 1989: 183) and to illustrate what such a conversation might look like.

Second, the policy transfer framework allows for a methodologically and theoretically precise investigation by looking not only at what is transferred, but also why and with what results. As such, it helps to clarify what success or failure is in this context. The illustrative examples cited in this chapter support the need to transcend the crude dichotomous distinction between success and failure and strive for a more refined understanding not only of what success/failure entails, but also of what it is exactly that succeeds or fails and at what level. The chapter has demonstrated that one cannot make sweeping statements about the success or failure of Bologna because of the complexity of the political and policy processes surrounding it. At the same time, it claimed that there is, indeed, both success and failure contained simultaneously in the architecture of Bologna, and that we can identify and study both in a relatively accurate manner.

Finally, a few important conclusions can be drawn for the case of assessing the success and failure of Bologna in CEE specifically. Bologna reforms and related policy transfers played a central role in the post-communist transition and Europeanization efforts of CEE countries, even beyond the higher education sector. These two processes explain to a large extent the specificity of the Bologna transfer in this part of the continent when compared to the rest of Europe. They also explain the differences within CEE, for example when we compare and contrast CEE countries that were given an EU accession path and those that were not.

CEE countries made a firm choice, at least nominally and at least for a certain period, to implement Bologna as a 'European model'. In the early days of transition, they decided to disregard or discard other possible models of reforming higher education from elsewhere. In the implementation of this model there has not been much room for testing or trial-and-error approaches. CEE countries adopted, or rather committed to implementing, Bologna 'wholesale'. What they committed to, however, was in reality not a defined model or policy, but a complex and evolving set of values, principles, priorities, objectives and tools. Both the complexity of the Process and its ever-evolving nature had an influence on the degree of success and failure of the various aspects of its implementation.

REFERENCES

Barkholt, K. (2005), 'The Bologna Process and integration theory: Convergence and autonomy', *Higher Education in Europe*, 30 (1), 23–9.

Bergen Communiqué (2005), *The European Higher Education Area – Achieving the Goals*, Communiqué of the Conference of European Ministers Responsible for Higher Education, http://www.ehea.info/Uploads/Declarations/Bergen_Com munique1.pdf (accessed 1 July 2016).

Bologna Declaration (1999), The Bologna Declaration of 19 June 1999: Joint Declaration of the European Ministers of Education, http://www.magna-charta. org/resources/files/text-of-the-bologna-declaration (accessed 1 July 2016).

Corbett, A. (2012), 'Growing respect for the Bologna Process', *University World News*, http://www.universityworldnews.com/article php?story=201211150900 20591 (accessed 1 July 2016).

Deca, Ligia (2013), 'The discursive uses of the Bologna Process in Romanian higher education reform', Paper prepared for the conference Bologna and Beyond, Strasbourg.

Dolowitz, David and David Marsh (1996), 'Who learns what from whom: A review of the policy transfer literature', *Political Studies*, 44 (2), 343–57.

Enders, Jürgen and Don F. Westerheijden (2014), 'Quality assurance in the European policy arena', *Policy and Society*, 33 (3), 167–76.

Frisch, J. (2009), 'Ten years of the Bologna Process: A more or less great failure', http://julienfrisch.blogspot.hu/2009/04/10-years-of-bologna-process-more-or.html (accessed 1 July 2016).

Harmsen, Robert (2015), 'Future scenarios for the European Higher Education Area: Exploring the possibilities of "experimentalist governance"', in Adrian Curaj, L. Matei, R. Pricopie, J. Salmi and P. Scott (eds), *The European Higher Education Area*, London: Springer, pp. 785–803.

Hartmann, E. (2008), 'Bologna goes global: A new imperialism in the making?', *Globalisation, Societies and Education*, 6 (3), 207–20.

Heckl, E. (2001), 'Towards a European Area of Higher Education: Change and convergence in European higher education', http://cadmus.eui.eu/bitstream/han dle/1814/1718/01_09.pdf?sequence=1 (accessed 1 July 2016).

Hörner, Wolfgang (2014), 'Introduction', in Tamás Kozma, M. Rébay, A. Óhidy and E. Szolár (eds), *The Bologna Process in Central and Eastern Europe: Studies in International Comparative Educational Science*, Dordrecht: Springer, pp. 7–13.

Huisman, J., J. Witte and J. File (2006), *The Extent and Impact of Higher Education Curricular Reform across Europe: Final Report to the Directorate-General for Education and Culture of the European Commission*, https://www.utwente.nl/bms/ cheps/publications/publications%202006/the%20extent.pdf (accessed 1 July 2016).

Kauko, J. (2012), 'The power of normative coordination in the Bologna Process: How universities learned to stop worrying and love quality assurance', *Journal of the European Higher Education Area*, 2012 (4), 23–40.

Kettunen, J. and M. Kantola (2006), 'The implementation of the Bologna Process', *Tertiary Education and Management*, 12 (3), 257–67.

Kralikova, R. (2016), *Transition Legacies, Rules of Appropriateness and 'Modernization Agenda' Translation in Higher Education Governance in Lithuania, Romania and Slovakia*, Budapest: Central European University.

Kwiek, Marek and Peter Maasen (eds) (2012), *National Higher Education Reforms in a European Context: Comparative Reflections on Poland and Norway*, Vienna: Peter Lang.

Lazerson, M. (2015), 'Beyond the Bologna Process', *Chronicle of Higher Education*, http://chronicle.com/article/Beyond-the-Bologna-Process/229093/ (accessed 1 July 2016).

Leisyte, L., R. Zelvys and L. Zenkine (2015), 'Recontextualization of the Bologna Process in Lithuania', *European Journal of Higher Education*, 5 (1), 49–67.

Maggetti, M. and F. Gilardi (2015), 'Problems (and solutions) in the measurement of policy diffusion mechanisms', *Journal of Public Policy*, 36 (1), 1–21.

Majone, Giandomenico (1989), *Evidence, Argument, and Persuasion in the Policy Process*, New Haven, CT: Yale University Press.

Marsh, D. and J.C. Sharman (2009), 'Policy diffusion and policy transfer', *Policy Studies*, 30 (3), 269–88.

Matei, Liviu (2012), 'A policy gap: Financing in the European Higher Education Area', in Lazăr Vlasceanu and Lesley Wilson (eds), *European Higher Education at the Crossroads: Between the Bologna Process and National Reforms*, New York: Springer, pp. 667–90.

Matei, L. (2014), 'Future of higher education', Bologna Process Researchers' Conference, http://fohe-bprc.forhe.ro/wp-content/uploads/2014/09/Final-Conference-report.pdf (accessed 1 July 2016).

Matei, Liviu (2015), 'The future of higher education and "the European level"', in Adrian Curaj, L. Matei, R. Pricopie, J. Salmi and P. Scott (eds), *The European Higher Education Area: Between Critical Reflections and Future Policies*, Heidelberg: Springer, pp. 1–9.

Matei, Liviu and Adrian Curaj (eds) (2014), *Building an Integrated Higher Education System in Europe: Romania's Commitments in the European Higher Education Area and Their Implementation at National Level*, New York: Central European University Press.

Matei, Liviu and Julia Iwinska (2015), 'National strategies and practices in internationalisation of higher education: Lessons from a cross-country comparison', in Adrian Curaj, L. Deca, E. Egron-Polak and J. Salmi (eds), *Higher Education Reforms in Romania*, London: Springer, pp. 205–26.

McConnell, A. (2010), 'Policy success, policy failure and grey areas in-between', *Journal of Public Policy*, 30 (3), 345–62.

McConnell, A. (2015), 'What is policy failure? A primer to help navigate the maze', *Public Policy and Administration*, 30 (3–4), 221–42.

Miron, Dumitru (2014), 'New and pressing challenges for Romanian higher education system after 10 years of Bologna values implementation', in Alina Mihaela Dima (ed.), *Handbook of Research on Trends in European Higher Education Convergence*, Hershey, PA: IGI Global, pp. 151–67.

Pasias, G. and Y. Roussakis (2012), 'Who marks the bench? A critical review of the neo-European "paradigm shift" through higher education policies and discourses', *Journal for Critical Education Policy Studies (JCEPS)*, 10 (1), 127–41.

Pechar, Hans (2012), 'The decline of the academic oligarchy: The Bologna Process and "Humboldt's last warriors"', in Adrian Curaj and L. Wilson (eds), *European Higher Education at the Crossroads: Between the Bologna Process and National Reforms*, Dordrecht: Springer, pp. 613–30.

Peters, B. Guy (2015), 'State failure, governance failure and policy failure: Exploring the linkages', *Public Policy and Administration*, 30 (3–4), 261–76.

Putnam, R. (1988), 'Diplomacy and domestic politics: The logic of two-level games', *International Organization*, 42, 427–60.

Racké, C. (2006), 'The Bologna Process and the EU: Neither within nor without', Third International EUREDOCS Conference, Kassel, http://euredocs.sciences-po.fr/en/conference/2006/euredocs06Rack%E9.pdf (accessed 1 July 2016).

Rudder, H. (2010), 'Mission accomplished? Which mission? The Bologna Process – a view from Germany', *Higher Education Review*, 43 (1), 3–20.

Saarinen, T. (2005), '"Quality" in the Bologna Process: From "competitive edge" to quality assurance techniques', *European Journal of Education*, 40 (2), 189–402.

Scott, P. (2012), 'The Bologna Process has been key to European universities' success', *Guardian*, http://www.theguardian.com/education/2012/apr/30/bologna-process-key-european-university-success (accessed 1 July 2016).

Sorbonne Declaration (1998), *Sorbonne Declaration: Joint Declaration on Harmonisation of the Architecture of the European Higher Education System*, http://www.ehea.info/Uploads/Declarations/SORBONNE_DECLARATION1.pdf (accessed 1 July 2016).

Szolár, É. (2011), 'The Bologna Process: The reform of the European higher education systems', *Romanian Journal of European Affairs*, 11 (1), 81–99.

Terry, S.L. (2010), 'The Bologna Process and its impact in Europe: It's so much more than degree changes', *Vanderbilt Journal of Transnational Law*, 41, 107–228.

Van Damme, Dirk (2009), 'The search for transparency: Convergence and diversity in the Bologna Process', in Frans van Vught (ed.), *Mapping the Higher Education Landscape: Towards a European Classification of Higher Education*, New York: Springer, pp. 39–55.

Veiga, A. and A. Amaral (2009), 'Survey on the implementation of the Bologna Process in Portugal', *Higher Education*, 57 (1), 57–69.

Vögtle, Eva Maria (2014), *Higher Education Policy Convergence and the Bologna Process: A Cross-National Study*, Basingstoke: Palgrave Macmillan.

Vögtle, E.M. and K. Martens (2014), 'The Bologna Process as a template for transnational policy coordination', *Policy Studies*, 35 (3), 246–63.

Yerevan Communiqué (2015), http://bolognayerevan2015.ehea.info/files/Yerevan CommuniqueFinal.pdf (accessed 1 July 2016).

Zgaga, Pavel (2012), 'Reconsidering EHEA principles: Is there a "Bologna philosophy"?,' in Adrian Curaj and L. Wilson (eds), *European Higher Education at the Crossroads: Between the Bologna Process and National Reforms*, Dordrecht: Springer, pp. 17–38.

10. Reforming through borrowing and learning: Easy, but so terribly difficult

B. Guy Peters

The policy reforms discussed in the preceding chapters in this volume represent important attempts to "get things right" in the countries of Central and Eastern Europe (CEE). Like so many other attempts to improve policy – whether through innovation or through learning and diffusion – the results may not fulfill the dreams of the advocates. This failure to achieve goals is hardly a new lesson on policy or administrative reform, but it is one that nonetheless is important as a potential source of continued improvement in public policies. If we, as scholars and practitioners, can understand more fully why reforms fail to live up to expectations, then we can with good fortune become better at this reform business.

The gap between expectations for success in policy reforms and the reality of the outcomes may be especially great when programs are being transferred from one setting to another. The political appeal of policy transfer is obvious (Radaelli 2000). There is a program that appears to work, so why not just borrow it and use it elsewhere? This seems simple, but at the same time it can be extremely difficult to make programs that depend upon certain social, economic and political parameters move into another setting that lacks those same characteristics.

The attempts to spread the ideas of the new public management (NPM) have offered a useful laboratory for learning about large-scale policy diffusion, but the lessons do not appear to have been learned as well as they might. Although the ideas of the NPM were embedded in particular political and economic settings, both international organizations, such as the World Bank, and national development organizations attempted to propagate the ideas more broadly. These ideas were tried in many Central and Eastern European countries, but with, at best, minimal success (Peters 2008).

10.1 COMPARATIVE POLITICS AND POLICY SUCCESS AND FAILURE

The chapters in this book provide us with the opportunity to look at the absence of success in reform through at least two lenses. The first is the lens of comparative politics. The case studies and comparative analyses presented here address reform in a limited number of countries, but that can provide some advantages for the would-be comparativist. We can think of these countries as "most similar systems" (Teune and Przeworski 1970) in which a number of factors – the communist era legacies, the new linkages to the European Union, and in some cases other common historical experiences (Becker et al. 2011) – are controlled so that more subtle differences among the cases become more relevant for the analysis. Using this approach the researcher has the task of finding such subtle differences among cases which may appear similar.

The similarities among these cases can be exaggerated, and for many scholars and citizens of these countries there are important differences. As the authors of the chapters in this volume point out, there are different legacies of the past and there have been very different mechanisms chosen to go forward. Thus, attempting to understand the influence of institutional and political differences among this "sample" of countries will provide insights into how politics connects to policy choices to produce different outcomes in different systems. Several of the chapters in this book, for example Chapter 2 by Kemmerling and Makszin and Chapter 3 by Adascalitei and Domonkos on pensions, point to the ways in which relatively common stimuli to the policymaking system produced somewhat different policy choices, as well as varying levels of success.

In the comparative politics perspective, the institutions of government are the most commonly discussed factors related to policy success and failure, and to the general quality of the policies selected. While the governments of the CEE countries have a number of similarities, they also have differences that appear to affect the ways in which policies are made and implemented (see Adascalitei and Domonkos, this volume, Chapter 3). Some of the successes and failures of contemporary governments in Central and Eastern Europe reflect the ways in which they have dealt with their Soviet influenced communist past.

The comparative politics lens also provides a means of looking at continuity and change in government, as well as in public policies. One danger in governance is that instability of institutions, of political parties or of individual leaders produces uncertainty and does not permit citizens to make reasonable predictions about their own futures – political or otherwise (see, among others, Tavits 2008). While this instability is often manifested in public policies (see below) the political instability itself can influence the capacity of systems to learn and to adjust to changing circumstances. Just like individuals, so too government institutions need memories if they are to perform well, and in some CEE countries the rapid changes in governments and parties reduce that chance to store information and ideas.

Another way to think about policy success and policy learning from the perspective of comparative politics is to think of the arguments about "institutional isomorphism" advanced by Dimaggio and Powell (1991). The argument of isomorphism is that over time institutions operating in the same fields will come to resemble one another. This may occur through simple mimesis, through learning or through coercion. So for the CEE countries considered here there is some copying, some attempt to learn from other countries, and some coercion coming from the European Union (EU) and from international donors that wanted these governments and their policies to resemble those in other European states. But there are also forces for divergence, as demonstrated by Hungary at the time of writing (April 2017) challenging EU norms of democratic rule, which could be interpreted as a dynamic leading to policy and political failures.

Institutional capacity is perhaps the most important element defining whether a government has the ability to make and implement policies, whether those policies are home-grown or borrowed (see Painter and Pierre 2005). Much of the policy transfer literature, as well as a good deal of literature on policy success and failure, focuses on the initial design of policies. If a policy is well designed then it is assumed that the policy should work. In this view if a government has the capacity to formulate policies effectively (see Jordan and Turnpenny 2015) then it will have the capacity to make good policy.

While the best designs may not work if they are put into a setting for which they are inappropriate, well-designed policies may also fail, and do fail regularly, because they are not well implemented. Therefore, building the capacity for success in policymaking involves not only building legislative institutions and think tanks that develop ideas and make policies but also building the bureaucracies at all levels within a country that implement those policies and investing in state capacity. And, in the CEE countries, there have been marked differences in the nurturing of effective and efficient public bureaucracies, as well as some significant back-sliding into patronage and corruption in some cases (Meyer-Sahling 2009). In the wake of the global financial crisis, the rise of austerity politics and policy, and the resurgence of populist sentiments, the "appeal" of international best practices and European membership has become somewhat tarnished.

10.2   POLICY ANALYSIS AS A LENS FOR UNDERSTANDING

The second lens, and the one which will be the principal focus of this chapter, is the public policy lens. In this assessment of policy failures the problem is not so much in the political system as in the design of public policies (McConnell 2010; Peters 2015). Although the nature of the political system may affect the policy designs adopted and affect the manner in which they are implemented (see Howlett et al. 2015), the particular aspects of the policy process that affect learning about, and adoption of, policies are especially important to understanding the contemporary design process. This concern with policy design is especially true for cases such as these that tend to be recipients of policy templates from other settings, albeit also producing some of their own innovations.

This emphasis with diffusion and policy learning as a source of design is one manifestation of the "evidence based policy" movement in government, and among academic students of public policy (Pawson 2006). The assumption is that policy can be best made when there is evidence from some other setting that can demonstrate that a particular policy design can be effective. As I will discuss below, and as the authors of many of the chapters in this book have pointed out very clearly, the assumptions of easy transmission of a policy from one setting to another are often excessively optimistic, and many attempts at policy transfer end in tears rather than in success.

Perhaps even more fundamentally the process has become, in a number of cases, what is known in reverse as "policy based evidence making." That is, as well as using evidence to advocate policies, individuals who have commitments to policy may attempt to develop evidence that can support their own policy and ideological preferences. At the same time that the available evidence for making good policies has been proliferating, the openness to new ideas appears to be waning. Therefore, the task of those attempting to promote high quality policymaking remains keeping the policy process open to new ideas, and the possibility for the real use of evidence and advice.

Policy analysis as a lens for understanding leads to several other questions that can illuminate why and how the policies are able to prosper, or not. The most important of these are how we can understand what is success, and what can explain that success. These are not simple questions, but failure to address them can lead to significant misunderstandings of the policy dynamics. In addition, policy analysis should not assume that all policies are the same. Although we commonly speak about policies rather blithely, we need to understand the wide variations in their characteristics.

10.2.1   Defining Failure and Success

The authors in this book have struggled with the fundamental question of defining success and failure of policy transfers. This question is, however, merely a subset of the larger question of defining policy success and failure more generally (Bovens et al. 2000; McConnell 2010). A policy failure that occurs after the transfer may simply have been transferred into a setting for which it was unsuited or it may not have been well designed in the first instance. Moving the policy into a new setting may simply have made the deficiencies of the policy more evident.

But observing manifest failures may not answer the more basic question of what is success and failure for a public policy? The extreme cases may be clear. A policy that produces the type and level of services intended and does so at a reasonable cost can plausibly be called a success on policy grounds. But few if any policies have outcomes that are this clearly positive, just as there are few policies that are abject failures. Most fall into the category of "residual" success or failure, with the degree of success or failure to some extent being a function of the framing of the outcomes (see Zentai, this volume, Chapter 5).

One dimension of failure distinguishes between objective and subjective issues in the performance of the policy. A program may appear to be a success, and may be discussed as such in objective terms. But, if the public does not like the program, and perceives it to be inadequate or excessively costly, then politically we may have a failure (see examples in Bovens et al. 2000). The perceived failings of public programs are often the product of excessive ambitions and unreasonable expectations, factors that may have special relevance for the relatively new democracies of Central and Eastern Europe. Governments may be under pressure to produce rapid improvements in the lives of their citizens, and any failure to make those improvements may be perceived as failures.

On the other hand, however, some programs appear to be failures objectively but continue to receive support from both political elites and the public. Chapter 7 in this volume, by Sara Svensson, on Euroregions is a good example of this phenomenon, with significant levels of political support for a program that appears ill suited, to external audiences at least, to the needs of the cross-border regions of CEE countries into which it is being implemented. This continued support may be a result of the absence of alternative programs to achieve the same end. Or in the case of the Euroregions it may have been perceived as simply the price to be paid for being part of the Council of Europe. Whatever the cause, it is crucial to remember that political and objective success may diverge, and the astute policy analysis must be attentive to both dimensions.

We can complicate the above assessment of the success and failure of policies if we consider the unintended consequences of programs. In the extreme case of failure, programs may produce outcomes which are exactly the opposite of those intended (Sieber 1980), but most programs have effects that extend beyond their primary target area. These unintended consequences can be positive, but most of those that attract the attention of policymakers or the public are negative. Therefore, we must assess the extent to which negative side-effects of a program negate the general utility of an intervention. Also, we may expect that the unintended consequences of programs may be more likely when programs are copied from external sources than when they are designed within a particular social and political setting.

For new democracies with high aspirations, time presents an additional problem for assessing success and failure. All governments have difficulties producing and maintaining policies that may produce long-term benefits but which impose short-term costs (taxes if nothing else). Therefore, a significant proportion of policymaking tends to err toward short-term patches for major problems (Jacobs 2011), rather than generating more comprehensive solutions. And when a government is attempting to build legitimacy and to institutionalize itself and patterns of democratic governance – as is the case of the CEE governments – the need to produce short-term benefits, or at least to avoid costs, is stronger.

The potential failings of short-termism in making policies lead to consideration of an additional impact of time on policy success and failure. A good deal of policymaking in contemporary governments reflects "fads and fashions," most spread by a range of diffusion mechanisms that have been discussed throughout this volume. But sometimes the tortoise has the advantage over the hare (see Olsen 1996) and adopting innovations more slowly may provide time to learn more fully about the policies and avoid the perils encountered by early adopters. This is something that can clearly be seen in the recent history of pension reforms in the region.

10.2.2   Not All Policies Are the Same

While we can assess the learning and reform capacities of governments, and the impact of diffusion on policy, there can be some tendency to assume that all policies are the same. But that is not the case and there are several important dimensions of policy that can affect the manner in which they can be transplanted, and their likelihood of success. These differences may be ignored in the rush to adopt a workable policy, or an excessively narrow focus on one or another type of policy may not produce sufficient insight into real policy differences.

As already discussed above, policies involving ideas and values may be easier to transplant than are others involving a range of inter-connected instruments. While this may appear counterintuitive, transferring ideas that involve primarily normative commitments to goals require relatively few resources, and are unlikely to produce major negative unintended consequences. While the normative commitments may not produce any significant changes in actual behavior, they may provide a government with the opportunity to do something (blame avoidance if nothing else) while risking relatively little in terms of more tangible resources.

In addition to the degree of ideas versus instruments that may be involved, policies differ in the extent to which they depend upon stability and persistence. In a setting with relatively new governments attempting to create an effective array of policies it may be natural to assume that there will be substantial volatility in policies (see Kemmerling and Makszin, this volume, Chapter 2). But, while that volatility and continued reform in many ways could be applauded for some reasons, it can create problems for some policies. Citizens and businesses need some predictability when they make decisions about how to organize their lives and how to invest their resources, so that the uncertainty created by policy volatility imposes costs on the society.

One of the most important differences among policies is between programs that depend upon accumulating stocks of resources and those that depend on shorter-term flows of resources. Policy adaptations that can be successful for one type of program may not be successful for another. Pensions are the most important stock based policy area in government. Citizens must make decisions during their working years that enable them to retire with an adequate income. If governments cannot provide some level of stability for these individual choices then the probabilities of policy failure are intensified. And for governments under-funding pensions during the working lives of individuals will mean that the funds will not be available to pay pensions when they are due. For example, in a different context, this is a major problem for many cities and states in the United States which have pension obligations far beyond their available resources.

This need to maintain predictability for pensions and analogous programs is similar to the argument about "credible commitment" for public sector programs (Majone 2001). The logic here is that governments need to ensure that businesses and individual citizens can rely on their programs to make long-term decisions. The absence of such commitment is a potential source of failure in the public sector, especially in economic and regulatory policy. This commitment to a particular policy may appear rather conservative, when there are so many innovations and possibilities for diffusion available, but it can be important for maintaining confidence.

The policy lens provides an additional array of insights into the process of borrowing or designing new policies. Although distinct from the comparative politics lens above, it still identifies a number of ways in which politics do matter for policy, and in which policy does matter for politics. By understanding policy *per se*, scholars and practitioners can consider the internal effects of selecting types of policies as well as the alternative means of understanding what is success and what is not.

Both the comparative politics perspective and the policy studies perspective provide numerous, if different, insights into the success and failure of policies. The chapters in this volume make a very strong case for an explicitly comparative perspective in policy analysis. By bringing in the political and cultural dimensions from comparative studies we can understand better the ways in which policies, as interventions into the social systems, produce intended and unintended consequences. And by understanding the policies themselves more fully we can perhaps choose more wisely the nature of the interventions.

10.3   INNOVATION AND BORROWING: HOW TO MAKE AND IMPLEMENT POLICIES

The several chapters in this book make a number of points about how to learn from the experiences of other countries, how to borrow and how to change or alter what is borrowed. Many of these lessons about policy transfer and borrowing have been learned at some substantial cost to the governments involved, and perhaps especially to the citizens, but these lessons can provide some source of appropriate caution to temper any future enthusiasm about the capacity or desirability to "simply" borrow and implement programs. The process is far from easy and can lead to significant policy failure and significant opportunity costs.

Yet neither is policy innovation an enterprise without significant perils. Like "evidence based policymaking," innovation in the public sector has strong normative support (bordering on being a fad or becoming a tolerated consensus), being seen as the means to bring new ideas and new technologies to bear on difficult public problems. But which new ideas are really appropriate, and how can they be translated into effective action? Furthermore, not only is any apparent innovation being inserted into a policy space that is already extremely crowded with previous innovations, but understanding how the new program would work cannot be done in isolation from the interactions with existing programs (see Carter 2012).

10.3.1 Experimentation

The authors in this volume make an important case about the importance of experimentation in policymaking and in policy analysis. Although most policymaking is not amenable to laboratory-style controlled experiments,[1] natural experiments are still available and very useful for learning. Indeed, at one level almost all policymaking is experimentation (see Campbell 1997). Neither academic students of public policy nor practitioners of the dark arts of governing really have sufficient and precise knowledge about the dynamics of social and economic systems to be able to say *ex ante* that some intervention X will produce some desired outcome Y. Therefore, any policy intervention, even when based on evidence, should be considered in essence trial and error. That style may be difficult to sell politically to the public, but it is an important reality that is understood by policymakers.

In the policy cases discussed in this volume there was perhaps more opportunity for experimental interventions than would be true for most other governments (Sabel and Zeitlin 2010). For a group of governments beginning, at least to some extent, with a *tabula rasa* the opportunities for experimentation were greater than would be the case in the established countries of Europe. If nothing else, there may be fewer contamination effects resulting from the interaction of new policies with those already in place. (Those effects cannot be eliminated entirely, and all these countries do have histories and patterns of governing, and older citizens may have unpleasant memories of other policy interventions in the not too distant past.) Further, in a less crowded policy space with fewer interactions the probabilities that an innovative program might be successful could be greater.

The above having been said, experimentation may be more politically risky in transitional governments still attempting to legitimate themselves fully (see Suurna and Kattel 2010). Experimentation inherently involves error and the potential use of scarce resources in less than efficient ways. When resources are scarce and the political systems are still relatively young and perhaps less than fully legitimated, then engaging in innovative and experimental policies can entail significant political risks.

10.3.2 Indigenization

If we accept and assume that direct borrowing of policies and programs is not a simple task we must begin to consider ways of making that process more viable, given the wide array of policy innovations and experiments that have been undertaken. Even removing the bloated political rhetoric that surrounds many presumed successes by policymakers and their advocates, there are policies that have produced demonstrable benefits for their societies, and policymakers and analysts alike need to understand why they have been successful, and the extent to which they can be transplanted into new settings.

Perhaps the most important lesson learned from these cases is that it is more appropriate to transfer ideas and norms about policy than it is to transfer the whole working programs. For these countries having emerged relatively recently from the long period of communist control, adopting international norms about policy was an important first stage of creating a policy regime not unlike those found in their European neighbors (see Krizsan, this volume, Chapter 4). The European Union as an institution, as well as the member countries, had both political and policy values that needed to be accepted as the CEE countries moved into the Union and continued their political development. But the spread of norms also comes from other transnational sources such as the United Nations and social movements, sometimes complementing and bolstering EU dispersions.

The norms were not so far removed from the values of the new demo-cratic regimes, but still had to be accepted formally and then implemented. That acceptance meant that the international values had to be translated into, and made compatible with, the political language and norms of the new host country. The concept of "indigenization" of policies that is discussed in these chapters represents a significant contribution to the discussion of policy transfer and learning. There is some tendency in that transfer literature to assume that policies can be transferred directly, or at least that there perhaps should be attempts to transfer those policies directly (see Gilardi 2012). But policy ideas, and especially programs, are rarely so simple that they can be picked up and moved into a new setting. The important aspect of policy transfer therefore becomes how to take those policy ideas and make them compatible with the political, legal and social systems into which they are being inserted.

The process of "indigenization" therefore involves some blending and integration of ideas, and perhaps also the need to understand more about one's own social and economic system than might normally be taken into account when making policy. While this concept is discussed in terms of transfers across countries, the process of policy integration can be seen as analogous (see Jordan and Lenschow 2010). That is, whenever a new policy is adopted, whether by transplantation or by innovation, it must be fit into an existing array of policies. In some cases, the new policy will replace an old one, but in most instances there is an attempt to modify the existing policies. And even if there is an entirely new policy intervention it still must be fit into a range of other policies which it affects and which affect it.

The process of "indigenization" of policies should be understood both from the perspective of the national government, which must adopt the policy and make it work within a particular setting, and from the perspective of the policy, which has its own internal logic that may be incompatible in a different setting. The national government policymakers must attempt to understand why and how a policy was successful in its original setting, and then attempt to replicate, in so far as is possible, those conditions in the destination country. From the perspective of the policy and its advocates (especially when those advocates may be outside the country, based in international organizations, neighboring governments or bodies like think tanks), the policy framework requires not only competent bureaucratic capacities within the adopting state but also political will and commitment to effectively implement the adopted policy.

10.3.3 How to Learn?

Even more basic than the question of how to fit borrowed policies into a political system is the fundamental question that this book raises, which is how we learn about policies and how to make policy. In Donald Schon's terminology this is then a question of "deutero-learning," or learning about learning (see Visser 2007). Over time we would expect countries that are borrowing policies from one another to get better at this process, and to develop methodologies for improving their performance in copying and implementing programs from other settings (see Rose 1993). This type of copying of programs has been occurring at least since the time of the formation of the Welfare State, and with the proliferation of international organizations and international regimes has become all the more prevalent. For example, Woodrow Wilson was criticized for his praise of the Imperial German bureaucracy, but argued that he could still learn from "a murderous fellow sharpening a knife cleverly."

The examples of the CEE countries provide a number of insights about policy learning. These countries were in a particularly advantageous position to learn, and to develop mechanisms for effective learning. They were engaged in modernizing their policy portfolios in a period in which technology was making information more readily available for those who wished to learn. Also, their membership in the European Union, and the presence of other international organizations concerned with policy, such as the Organisation for Economic Co-operation and Development, provided a range of options for learning. And membership in the EU during the accession process provided a certain urgency to the need for learning and adopting policies.

Even with those advantages, effective learning appears to have been difficult for at least some of these countries. Some lagged far behind others in adopting policy innovations, and others appeared not to translate policy messages and norms from the EU. While most of the analysis in this volume has focused on the policies *per se* that were being borrowed, the studies do raise important questions about how to structure governments in order to learn effectively, including learning from one's own failures. Perhaps most importantly, the rapid turnover in governments and rapid changes in party systems appear to make learning more difficult, with potential negative consequences for governance. The effects on learning may be especially pronounced given tendencies to replace government officials and alter structures with each change in government.

And learning from failure also means finding some means of modulating the natural desire to "repeal and replace" quickly those policies that do not appear to be working. But policies also have sleeper effects that may not manifest themselves for years, meaning that replacing them too quickly may undermine future benefits. These sleeper effects, and the decay in beneficial effects that may be experienced by seemingly successful programs, are indications of the need to learn effectively, and to extract lessons from prior policy experiences when thinking about new borrowing or new designs.

10.4   SUMMARY

Policymaking can be difficult in any setting, and policy failures occur at what may appear an alarming rate. Those failures are generally not the product of stupidity or venality on the part of the policymakers, but rather reflect the numerous barriers to making and implementing policies. One of the ways of avoiding some of the pitfalls of policymaking is to borrow successful policies from other countries, or perhaps from lower level governments within a country. But that strategy has its own potential for error and failure, so must be considered very carefully and also implemented with close attention to the numerous contextual factors that can shape policy success and failure.

This volume has, we believe, demonstrated the possibilities of transferring policies from one setting to another, and also the ways in which those transfers can be associated with success and failure in those policies. The countries of Central and Eastern Europe represent an important laboratory within which to understand transfers and learning. They have undergone major political and economic transformations, first at independence and second through accession, and have attempted to alter their policy regimens during those processes. But at the same time they have significant legacies from the past that color their adoption of, and "indigenization" of, those policies.

NOTE

1. With the increased emphasis on behavioral policy analysis there may be more opportunities for using laboratory style experimentation, but then the external validity problem of experimental research becomes acute. If governments want to launch a major policy intervention based on laboratory research they may encounter some rude surprises in the real world of policy.

REFERENCES

Becker, S.O., K. Boeckh, C. Hainz and L. Woessman (2011), *The Empire Is Dead! Long Live the Empire! Long-Run Persistence of Trust and Corruption in the Bureaucracy*, Discussion Paper, Bonn: IZA.

Bovens, M.A.P., P. 't Hart and B.G. Peters (2000), *Success and Failure in Public Governance*, Cheltenham, UK and Northampton, MA, USA: Edward Elgar Publishing.

Campbell, D.T. (1997), 'The experimenting society', in W.N. Dunn (ed.), *The Experimenting Society: Essays in Honor of Donald T. Campbell*, New Brunswick, NJ: Transaction, pp. 11–35.

Carter, P. (2012) 'Policy as palimpsest', *Policy and Politics*, 40, 423–43.

Dimaggio, P. and W. Powell (1991), 'The iron cage revisited: Institutional isomorphism and collective rationality in organizational fields', *American Sociological Review*, 48, 147–60.

Gilardi, F. (2012), 'Policy interdependence: Transfer, diffusion, convergence', in I. Engeli and C. Rothmayr (eds), *Comparative Policy Studies: Conceptual and Methodological Challenges*, Basingstoke: Palgrave Macmillan, pp. 185–204.

Howlett, M., I. Mukherjee and J.J. Woo (2015), 'From tools to toolkits in policy design studies: The new policy design orientation toward policy formulation research', *Policy and Politics*, 43, 291–311.

Jacobs, A.M. (2011), *Governing in the Long Term: Democracy and the Politics of Investment*, Cambridge: Cambridge University Press.

Jordan, A. and A. Lenschow (2010), 'Environmental policy integration: A state of the art review', *Environmental Policy and Governance*, 20, 147–58.

Jordan, A. and J.R. Turnpenny (2015), *The Tools of Policy Formulation*, Cheltenham, UK and Northampton, MA, USA: Edward Elgar Publishing.

Majone, G. (2001), 'Two logics of delegation: Fiduciary and agency relationships in EU governance', *European Union Politics*, 2, 103–22.

McConnell, A. (2010), *Understanding Policy Success: Rethinking Public Policy*, Basingstoke: Macmillan.

Meyer-Sahling, J.-H. (2009), *Sustainability of Civil Service Reforms in Central and Eastern Europe Five Years after Accession*, Sigma Papers, Paris: OECD.

Olsen, J.P. (1996), 'Reluctant reformer, slow learner – or another triumph for the tortoise?', in J.P. Olsen and B.G. Peters (eds), *Lessons from Experience: Experiential Learning about Administrative Reform in Eight Democracies*, Oslo: Universitetsforlaget, pp. 180–213.

Painter, M. and J. Pierre (2005), *Challenges to State Policy Capacity: Global Trends and Comparative Perspectives*, Basingstoke: Macmillan.

Pawson, R. (2006), *Evidence-Based Policy: A Realist Perspective*, London: Sage.

Peters, B.G. (2008), *Mixes, Matches and Mistakes: New Public Management in Russia and Former Soviet Republics*, Budapest: Open Society Institute.

Peters, B.G. (2015), 'State failure, governance failure and policy failure: Exploring the linkages', *Public Policy and Administration*, 30 (3–4), 261–76.

Radaelli, C.M. (2000), 'Policy transfer in the European Union: Institutional isomorphism as a source of legitimacy', *Governance*, 13, 25–43.

Rose, R. (1993), *Lesson-Drawing in Public Policy: A Guide to Learning across Time and Space*, Chatham, NJ: Chatham House.

Sabel, C.F. and J. Zeitlin (eds) (2010), *Experimentalist Governance in the European Union: Towards a New Architecture*, Oxford: Oxford University Press.

Sieber, S.D. (1980), *Fatal Remedies: The Ironies of Social Intervention*, New York: Plenum.

Suurna, M. and R. Kattel (2010), 'Europeanization of innovation policy in Central and Eastern Europe', *Science and Public Policy*, 37, 3–19.

Tavits, M. (2008), 'Party systems in the making: The emergence and success of new parties in new democracies', *British Journal of Political Science*, 38, 113–33.

Teune, H. and A. Przeworski (1970), *The Logic of Comparative Social Inquiry*, New York: Wiley-Interscience, pp. 32–4.

Visser, M. (2007), 'Deutero-learning in organizations: A review and a reformulation', *Academy of Management Review*, 32, 659–87.

Index